ANDROIDS

ALSO BY CHET HAASE

Round & Holy: An Homage to Donuts

When I Am King...

When I Am King... II

Filthy Rich Clients:
Developing Animated and Graphical Effects
for Desktop Java Applications
(with Romain Guy)

Flex 4 Fun

ANDROIDS

THE TEAM THAT BUILT THE ANDROID OPERATING SYSTEM

BY CHET HAASE

no starch press

San Francisco

Printed in the United States of America
First printing

25 24 23 22   1 2 3 4 5

ISBN-13: 978-1-7185-0268-0 (print)
ISBN-13: 978-1-7185-0269-7 (ebook)

Publisher: William Pollock
Managing Editor: Jill Franklin
Developmental Editors: Laureen Hudson and Jill Franklin
Production Manager and Editor: Rachel Monaghan
Cover and Interior Illustration: Dan Sandler
Cover and Interior Design: Gretchen Achilles
Interior Design and Composition: Maureen Forys, Happenstance Type-O-Rama
Proofreader: James M. Fraleigh

All author profits from this book will be donated to charity.

For information on distribution, bulk sales, corporate sales, or translations, please contact No Starch Press, Inc. directly at *info@nostarch.com* or:

No Starch Press, Inc.
245 8th Street, San Francisco, CA 94103
phone: 1-415-863-9900
www.nostarch.com

Library of Congress Cataloging-in-Publication Data
Names: Haase, Chet, author.
Title: Androids : the team that built the Android operating system / Chet
    Haase.
Description: First edition. | San Francisco, California : No Starch Press,
    [2022] | Includes bibliographical references and index.
Identifiers: LCCN 2021060926 (print) | LCCN 2021060927 (ebook) | ISBN
    9781718502680 (paperback) | ISBN 9781718502697 (ebook)
Subjects: LCSH: Google (Firm)—History. | Android (Electronic resource) |
    Operating systems (Computers) | Computer software—Development—History.
    | Mobile computing—History.
Classification: LCC QA76.774.A53 H33 2022 (print) | LCC QA76.774.A53
    (ebook) | DDC 005.4/45—dc23/eng/20220111
LC record available at https://lccn.loc.gov/2021060926
LC ebook record available at https://lccn.loc.gov/2021060927

[S]

To Kris:
First reader, last reviewer,
toughest critic, best friend

ABOUT THE AUTHOR

Chet has spent many years working in high-tech companies across Silicon Valley, usually on graphics software. He joined the Android team at Google in 2010, where he has written animation and UI software, led the UI toolkit team, served as Android's Chief Advocate in developer relations, and is now an engineer in the graphics team. He writes books and articles, creates videos, and gives presentations, either humorous or technical (often both). This is Chet's sixth book. His other books include two programming books, two humor books, and one slim volume of poetry about donuts.

CONTENTS

Part III: The Android Team

Part IV: Launches

Part V: Why It Worked

Appendices

CAST[1]

(Listed in order of appearance on the Android team)

Note: This list is not complete; it is mostly limited to the people I interacted with directly about this book. There were many other people on the Android team at that time who contributed substantially to the product.

CAST MEMBER	ROLE
Andy Rubin	*Founder, robot maker*
Chris White	*Founder, designer, engineer, electric skateboarder*
Tracey Cole	*Administrative business partner, manager of managers*
Brian Swetland	*Engineer, kernel hacker, systems team lead*
Rich Miner	*Founder, mobile entrepreneur*
Nick Sears	*Founder, carrier deal-maker*
Andy McFadden	*Engineer, demo/calendar/simulator/runtime developer*
Ficus Kirkpatrick	*Engineer, kernel driver driver, "Crazy" ringtoner*
Wei Huang	*Engineer, browser, communicator*
Dan Bornstein	*Engineer, Dalvik creator*
Mathias Agopian	*Engineer, graphics flinger*
Joe Onorato	*Engineer, build, UI, framework, and more*
Eric Fischer	*Engineer, Mr. TextView*
Mike Fleming	*Engineer, telephony and runtimes*
Jeff Yaksick	*Designer, toys and UIs*
Cary Clark	*Engineer, browser graphics*
Mike Reed	*Skia lead, serial graphics entrepreneur*
Dianne Hackborn	*Engineer, framework. Most of it.*

CAST MEMBER	ROLE
Jeff Hamilton	Engineer, Binder, database, and contacts
Steve Horowitz	Engineering manager, compromiser
Mike Cleron	Engineer, UI toolkit rewriter and framework manager
Grace Kloba	Engineer, Android browser
Arve Hjønnevåg	Engineer, drivers and debugging: few words, much code
Hiroshi Lockheimer	TPM, manager of partners
Jason Parks	Engineer, jparks broke it
Iliyan Malchev	Engineer, Bluetooth, camera, and other drivers
Cédric Beust	Engineer, Gmailer
David Turner	Engineer, Android emulator
Debajit Ghosh	Engineer, in service of Calendar
Marco Nelissen	Engineer, sound code
Ryan PC Gibson	TPM, release namer and shipper
Evan Millar	Engineer, testing, testing
Xavier Ducrohet	Engineer, tool tech, totally
Michael Morrissey	Engineering lead, servicing server services
Bob Lee	Engineer, core libraries
Romain Guy	Engineer, UI toolkit intern extraordinaire
Tom Moss	Lawyer, business development, deal maker
Brian Jones	Receptionist, admin, device hook-up guy
Dan Egnor	Engineer, over-the-air updater
Dave Sparks	Engineer, media manager
Peisun Wu	TPM, media, messaging, and donut burgers
Ed Heyl	Engineer, build. test. release. repeat.
Dirk Dougherty	Tech writer, RTFM
Charles Mendis	Engineer, location navigator

CAST MEMBER	ROLE
Dave Burke	*Engineering lead, London mobile team*
Andrei Popescu	*Engineering lead, London browser team*
Nicolas Roard	*Engineer, gearing up for Android browser*
San Mehat	*Engineer, kernel drivers and SD card debugging*
Nick Pelly	*Engineer, Bluetooth wrangler*
Rebecca Zavin	*Engineer, device bringup, Droid driver*
Chiu-Ki Chan	*Engineer, checking in*
Mike Chan	*Engineer, kernel security*
Bruce Gay	*Engineer, monkey keeper*
Jeff Sharkey	*Engineer, contest winner*
Jesse Wilson	*Engineer, terrible API mitigator*
Dan Sandler	*Engineer, System UI, illustrator, Easter egger*

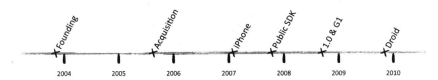

[1] A casual glance at this list reveals a large gender gap on that early team. That was certainly true on Android, as it was true in tech in general, and it is still unfortunately true today. Android, Google, and other tech companies are making efforts to improve diversity, but it's a long journey that is just beginning.

We can't fix history, but we can try to fix the future.

ACKS[1]

Thanks to Romain Guy, without whom this book would never have happened. Not only did he bring me onto the team (even having to try twice before it actually worked), but he was instrumental in helping me develop the ideas of the book (some of which came from presentations we've given together at tech conferences). He also assisted in many of the interviews I conducted for the book. Oh, and he wrote a lot of the code that many of us still work on and billions of people use today.

Thanks to my wife Kris, for her thoughtful insights and assistance in the very-early and very-late stages of this project, along with her expert editorial feedback many times along the way. Also, thanks for not killing me for allowing the project to dominate our home lives for so very, very long. It's done now. I think.

Thanks to Tor Norbye, my long-time co-host (along with Romain) for *Android Developers Backstage*,[2] a podcast where we talk to other Android developers about how Android works. Some of the interviews we've done (including those with Ficus Kirkpatrick, Mathias Agopian, and Dave Burke) contributed directly to this story, since they were about Android history. But all of them contributed to my love of talking to people about what they do that became the genesis, heart, and soul of this project.

Thanks to Dan Sandler for his excellent, fun artwork adorning the cover and pages of this book. I always enjoyed seeing his cartoons left like fingerprints on whiteboards when he would visit the Mt. View offices and I love seeing his drawings here, capturing the playfulness in the team and the product.

Thanks to Gretchen Achilles, friend and book designer extraordinaire, for helping to craft the book into shape for publication.

---

[1] ACK, or "acknowledge," is a signal used in computer communications, where data can be lost in transmission. When one system sends a message to another, the second needs to respond with an ACK, meaning "Yep, got it," so that the sender knows it doesn't have to send it again.

[2] *https://adbackstage.libsyn.com*, or look for it in your favorite podcast app. It's there.

Thanks to Jonathan Littman, author of several successful books, who patiently answered my questions about how things work in the real world of books, authors, and publishers.

Thanks to my editor Laureen Hudson, without whom this book would be a lot less polished, pulled together, cleaned up, and generally readable. I first worked with Laureen on technical articles I wrote (and she edited) while we were at Sun Microsystems many years ago. It was a pleasure to renew that relationship and have her return to clean up my messes once again.

And a special callout to Dave Burke, VP of Android engineering at Google. Dave agreed that this was a story worth telling and helped me cross the hurdles that tend to crop up when telling a story from the inside about a company, its people, and its products.

Apologies to all of those people who also helped out building Android in those early days whom I didn't get a chance to talk to. I would happily have carried on doing interview after interview (by far the most fun part of the entire project), learning about the people, what they worked on, where they came from, and how they helped create this thing. But at some point, I needed to actually finish the book.

And thanks to all of the Android employees, past and present, who selflessly gave of their time, opinions, and stories, so that I could better tell the story of what actually happened way back then. I'd particularly like to thank everyone that helped out with interviews, both conversational and through email. Nearly everyone I asked was not only willing to put up with my questions, but was enthusiastic about the project and our conversations.

Though the story of Android goes beyond the people I directly interviewed, talked to, emailed, or otherwise bothered, I wanted to explicitly thank the people who spent time helping me get the facts and possibly completely fabricated stories correct: Mathias Agopian, Dan Bornstein, Cédric Beust, Irina Blok, Bob Borchers, Dave Bort, Dave Burke, Chiu-Ki Chan, Mike Chan, Cary Clark, Mike Cleron, Tracey Cole, Chris DiBona, Dirk Dougherty, Xavier Ducrohet, Dan Egnor, Eric Fischer, Mike Fleming, Bruce Gay, Debajit Ghosh, Ryan PC Gibson, Romain Guy, Dianne Hackborn, Jeff Hamilton, Ed Heyl, Arve Hjønnevåg, Steve Horowitz, Wei Huang, Brian Jones, Ficus Kirkpatrick, Grace Kloba, Bob Lee, Dan Lew, Hiroshi Lockheimer, Iliyan Malchev, Andy McFadden, San Mehat, Charles Mendis, Evan Millar, Rich Miner, Dan

Morrill, Michael Morrissey, Tom Moss, Marco Nelissen, Joe Onorato, Jason Parks, Nick Pelly, Andrei Popescu, Jean-Baptiste Quéru, Mike Reed, Nicolas Roard, Andy Rubin, Dan Sandler, Nick Sears, Jeff Sharkey, Dave Sparks, Brian Swetland, David Turner, Paul Whitton, Jesse Wilson, Peisun Wu, Jeff Yaksick, and Rebecca Zavin.

I'd also like to thank the many people who took the time to read the draft and offer feedback. Code is always better for being reviewed, and so is this book. I would particularly like to call out the significant efforts of a few of the people who carefully went through the entire thing, identified gaps, caught redundancies, corrected mistakes, provided additional information, and generally added hugely to the final product by their careful review of the manuscript. I'm pretty sure that there was another entire book written in the feedback comment threads of this book. In particular, Dianne Hackborn, Brian Swetland, and Andy McFadden were all incredibly responsive, thoughtful, and complete in their reviews, which helped with the technical accuracy of the result. Also, thanks to my friend Alan Walendowski for an eleventh-hour read and review that helped catch lingering issues that are so difficult to see after re-reading and re-editing the same text so very, very many times.

Thank you all. Thank you, thank you, thank you, and apologies for all of the details that I got just slightly, maddeningly wrong. Please file a bug.

INTRODUCTION

In mid-May of 2010, I walked into building 44 on the Google campus for my first day on the Android team. Not far from my desk were at least a half-dozen machines for brewing a wide variety of great, strong coffee. I was surprised at the focus on caffeine, but not for long.

The team was finishing up one release[1] while starting work on the next one[2] in parallel. Both were difficult, time-consuming, and critical as we tried to make Android relevant in the crowded smartphone market at that time. There was a constant feeling of racing furiously toward a goal, doing whatever we could to reach it and not knowing if we would. The pace was frantic, but the work was exhilarating—and not just because of the caffeine. The excitement came from being on a team singularly dedicated to its purpose, no matter how much effort it took.

Working on Android was a stark difference from where my career began.

I started my work life with a nine-to-five job at a conservative old firm in Minnesota. The company relied on people sticking around for their entire careers and beyond, offering retirees a free turkey every Thanksgiving. I was all set; I just needed to clock in my forty hours a week and rise slowly through the ranks until I was ready for my retirement and my turkey.

Within a year, I was bored out of my mind, and within two I'd left for graduate school, to reboot my skills into something I actually enjoyed: computer

---

[1.] Android 2.3 Gingerbread

[2.] Android 3.0 Honeycomb

graphics programming. After grad school, I headed to Silicon Valley, the land of tech opportunity.[3] I joined Sun Microsystems, where I thrived for the next couple of years . . . until another interesting job beckoned.

I spent the next several years moving from company to company as other jobs, technologies, and people offered a continually shifting variety in my tech life. I worked at Sun (a few different times), Anyware Fast (a contracting company started by a couple of friends), DimensionX (an early web startup acquired by Microsoft), Intel, Rendition (a 3D chip startup acquired by Micron), and Adobe.

My father, who retired from the US Navy after 21 years, was never comfortable with my frequent job changes. What about a pension? What about job security? What about stability for my family?

What he didn't see was that this was the way things were, and are, in Silicon Valley, and increasingly in high tech everywhere. For every job I started, I built a new set of skills that contributed to future prospects and products. That same attitude, and reality, applies to all of the engineers shifting between tech firms; we're building skills that we'll continue to draw from as we move around creating all kinds of products. It's exactly these diverse backgrounds that contribute much-needed skills to new projects, to tackle unknown problems and deliver innovative solutions.

In 2010, another opportunity presented itself. Romain Guy, a friend whom I'd worked with (and authored a book with[4]) when he was an intern at Sun in 2005, had a problem. He had joined the Android team in 2007 and was too busy to write the animation system that he knew was needed. But he knew me, and he knew that that's the kind of project I love. Several interviews and five months later, I joined Android's UI toolkit team in building 44 on the Google campus in Mountain View and started working harder than I ever had before.

I began by creating the new animation system, then worked on low-level performance and graphics software as we labored to finish the upcoming

---

[3.] Or at least the land of tech companies, which is helpful when you need a job in the field.

[4.] *Filthy Rich Clients: Developing Graphical and Animated Effects for Desktop Java Applications.* So yes, if you like this book, there are others I wrote that you could also pick up. But *Filthy Rich Clients* probably isn't one I'd suggest. I mean, I really like the book, but the content dates from 2007, which is at least several decades ago in technology-years.

release. I continued working on that same team for many years, writing graphics, performance, and user-interface code, and wound up leading the team for several years.

Most of my projects prior to Android were really enjoyable . . . but not very visible. If my family asked what I did, I'd tell them about the software I wrote. And then I'd describe in a hand-wavy way the kinds of applications that might use my software, because the reality was that they'd never see the results of my code. It just wasn't stuff that real people (consumers) encountered in the real world.

Then I joined the Android team and I was writing software[5] that people across the world would use every single day. Or at least they would if Android managed to survive.

CHALLENGES

We didn't know if it was going to totally flop or if it was going to work. When it worked, I think people were as surprised as they were excited.

—EVAN MILLAR

The early team at Android consisted of people with lots of experience and very strong opinions. They were confident in what they were trying to build, but they faced an uphill battle to get it to its initial 1.0 release.

The team's goal was to create the Android operating system (OS). This included everything from the low-level kernel and hardware drivers to the overall platform software. It also entailed creating APIs for applications, tools to help build those applications, several applications to bundle with the platform, and services on the backend for those applications to communicate with. Oh, and they wanted to ship all of this with a new phone as well.

The software would be provided to manufacturers for free to build their own phones. These partners would build the hardware and Android would provide the software. The OS would help phone manufacturers by allowing

---

[5.] And bugs. The only code that doesn't have bugs is code that is not yet written. We test as much as we can, but the complexity of modern software systems means that there will always be bugs. The trick is to make sure the bugs are not critical, and that we fix them when they are found. Then we can get back to writing more code (and more bugs).

them to focus on their hardware products, leaving the increasingly complex software problem up to Android. At the same time, Android would help application developers by creating a uniform platform across a variety of phones. Developers would be able to write a single version of their app for all of these devices, instead of requiring different versions for different devices.

The Android team had financial backing from Google, access to an internal pool of engineers experienced at writing software at a very large scale, a rapidly growing smartphone market, and a dedicated team working on the product until it was ready. How could it fail? It might seem, in hindsight, like Android's success was a given.

But in the early days, the team was living in a very different reality, and Android's continued existence was far more tenuous.

For one thing, the team might have had Google's economic backing, but Android was just one of many projects that Google invested in. Google's bet on Android wasn't about Google putting its full weight behind it, but about the company sponsoring a team to see what was possible.[6]

Also, Android was entering an industry with many entrenched competitors and no clear opening for new players. On the lower end of the market, there were numerous Nokia phones available worldwide. Danger, Black-Berry and Palm all offered interesting smartphone[7] options to their passionate and loyal users. And there were various Microsoft phones available. And anyone who's worked in the software industry knows that you should always be wary of competing against Microsoft.[8]

---

[6] Google was taking similar strategic bets around the same time in web technologies, as it started building its own browser (Chrome), knowing that it needed to at least explore these spaces as a hedge against other companies potentially owning them in the future.

[7] Here I am using a very broad definition of the term "smartphone." When the term was first used, it meant, essentially, a phone plus data, which allowed for more communication through things like email and instant messaging; basically a richer communication device. Today, a smartphone encompasses much more than these fundamental pieces, including things like apps, games, touchscreens, and the plethora of technologies that have come online since a phone was first married to a data plan.

[8] Bob Borchers, the director of product marketing for the original iPhone, observed: "You never count out Microsoft. They will continue to spend money and work things until they actually get a real product out." As a colleague of mine put it many years ago, "When Microsoft gets into your market, get out."

Then Apple entered the market in 2007, unveiling yet another competitor in an already crowded field. Apple might have been new to mobile phones, but they already had a proven track record with operating systems, consumer computing devices, and their popular iPods.

All of these players were well-established before Android launched even a press release, much less a product.

To attempt to compete in this tough market, the early team focused with a singular drive on reaching 1.0. Everyone fixated on that goal, with most of them working non-stop during insane crunch periods.

But knowing they wanted to build this OS didn't mean everyone agreed on *how* to build it, or that it would succeed, or even exactly what they were trying to build. Andy McFadden, an engineer on the team, said, "We had a lot of people with strong feelings about the right and wrong ways of doing things. Sometimes they disagreed, which got colorful at times."

Even when Android reached 1.0 and the first Android phone shipped, it wasn't obvious to people on the team that the project would succeed or even continue. Ryan Gibson, a technical program manager (TPM) on the team, said, "In those early years, the atmosphere within Android was that of an underdog, constantly on the brink of failure and having to work incredibly hard to eke out every inch of progress. Success was far from a foregone conclusion. We were a year behind. Had we slipped into the next year, we might have been a historic footnote rather than a viable alternative."

Over the years since I joined the team, I heard about Android's early development and difficulties, as everyone struggled to get the platform where it needed to be to compete. And then, during my time on the team, I saw Android achieve some measure of success, which begged the question: how? That is, what were the elements in Android's development that led to its phenomenal growth since those early, tenuous years?

The idea to write this book began when I realized the story of Android's development would eventually be lost as the people who built it moved on to other projects[9] and forgot what had happened. In 2017, I started to record conversations with people from the early team, to capture that story.

---

9. See my story earlier in this chapter about people moving on to other projects and companies. It's just as true at Google, and on Android, as it is at every other company in tech. Engineers move around.

IMPLEMENTATION DETAILS[10]

This is a long book (much longer than I thought it would be when I started writing it, though much, *much* shorter than my first draft. You're welcome). Here are a couple tips for reading it, to make the organization of this large topic a bit clearer.

First, a note on the word *Android*. One of the things that had my editor tearing her hair out was my frequent use of the word *Android* to mean anything from the startup company, to the team after it was acquired by Google, to the software platform being built, to the phone product, to the open source code, to someone's nickname.

The underlying problem here is . . . that's the way the Android team used the word: It meant the company, it meant the department inside of Google, it meant the software, it meant the phones, it meant the ecosystem, it meant the team.

There's an episode of *Rick and Morty*[11] where inhabitants of a different planet use the word *squanch* in various seemingly unrelated ways. Eventually Rick explains, "Squanchy culture is more . . . contextual than literal. You just say what's in your squanch and people understand."

Android is like that. You just say what's in your Android and people understand.

Second, the story is told in chronological order . . . ish. That is, I describe the things that happened and the people who did those things in a time-flows-forward fashion, because time is a helpful way to organize complex, interrelated things. However, it is impossible to actually tell the story in a strictly chronological way because so many things happened in parallel. So you'll notice that the story may follow what someone worked on through 1.0 or beyond, and then the timeline might rewind to tell the story of someone else on the team.

[10.] "Implementation details" is a phrase heard often in engineering discussions, when someone wants to focus on the larger ideas without getting bogged down in the tedious details of how the thing will actually be written. Of course, the implementation and completion of a software project is actually the difficult and time-consuming part, so it's like pretending that the tip of the iceberg would be floating just fine on its own without the rest of that thing below the surface.

[11.] Season 2, episode 10: "The Wedding Squanchers"

Speaking of time, the book's story begins with the founding of Android and continues until late 2009. Most of it takes place in the time leading up to the 1.0 launch,[12] in late 2008. By 1.0, most of the pieces that enabled Android's future were already in place. The timeline stretches out another year, to the end of 2009, which is when the first glimpse of Android's future success was visible, after the launch of the Motorola Droid in the US.

Finally, I want this book to be readable by everyone, not just software and hardware engineers who know (and, let's face it, might actually care) about the technical details. I try hard to avoid the too-technical weeds, in the interest of not losing people along the way. But it's impossible to describe how an OS was built without using terms like "OS" that may be unfamiliar to people who don't happen to write code for a living. I try to define the terms as I go,[13] but if you get stuck on a passage wondering what *APIs* are again, or what I mean by *CL*, check out the "Jargon" section in the appendix.

AND SO IT BEGAN

In August of 2017,[14] I started having conversations with that early team, starting with a recorded lunchtime chat[15] with Dianne Hackborn and Romain Guy. I continued from there, interviewing (mostly in person, though sometimes over email) most of the people on the early team over the course of the next few years.

For in-person interviews (live or over video chat), I brought a recording microphone,[16] realizing quickly that handwritten notes would not suffice. For one thing, people like Dan Sandler and Dianne Hackborn speak faster than

---

[12] 1.0 was the first release that was commercially available to consumers, as well as the first release that other companies could use to build their own Android-based devices. 1.0 was initially available only on the G1 phone.

[13] I make generous use of footnotes. You should, too.

[14] As I read through this section again, in February of 2021, nearing the end of another (but not the last) long editing phase, I realized that I have spent longer writing the story of Android than the team spent building the entire operating system and shipping the 1.0 product.

[15] Interviewing pro tip: When recording conversations, don't do it over lunch or you will end up spending too much time later re-listening to everyone chewing.

[16] I also often brought my friend and colleague Romain Guy, who was one of those early team members and who helped me organize and conduct many of the interviews.

I can think, much less write. But also, recording the conversations allowed me to participate more than I could have if I were furiously scribbling notes.

I spent many hours having these conversations. Then, because written text is easier to refer back to and search than audio recordings, I spent many *more* hours transcribing the conversations into text documents.[17] As I did this, spending a lot of quality time listening to, transcribing, and reading these conversations, I realized a beautiful thing: the conversations weren't just research for the book; they *were* the book. I had intended to use the interviews as background to help me understand the big picture, the chronology, and some of the details that I wouldn't have discovered otherwise. But what I didn't anticipate was how well everyone was going to tell the story, in their own words.

I use a lot of quotes from these interviews in this book. In fact, I use quotes instead of my description wherever I can, because the story is best told from the point of view of people who were there, each in their own voice and with their own unique take on the events.

Please join me for this journey into the heart of Android for the story of how the team and the OS came to be, through the voices of the people who made it all happen.

[17.] Another interviewing pro tip: If you ever have to do this, get software that lets you play back audio at a speed that's closer to your typing speed. For me, it was about 40 percent of the real-time speed, depending on the person I was interviewing. The only downside with this approach was that, at that much slower speed, everyone in the conversation sounds drunk. Even better: always wait for technology to catch up. In 2020, when I was recording a final handful of conversations, Google launched an Android app that records audio and creates a transcription automatically. You have to love the pace of technology, except when it's almost too late to be useful.

PART I

IN THE BEGINNING

There definitely wasn't a sense of inevitability in the beginning. There were a lot of reasons why Android shouldn't have been as successful as it was. It's the sort of thing that I think if you wanted to make happen again, you wouldn't be able to. There's some magic there.

—EVAN MILLAR

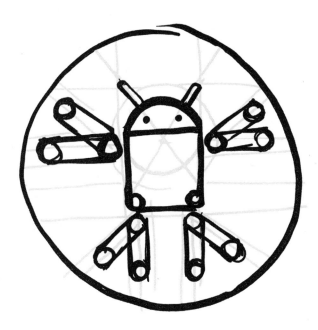

1

ANDROID THE . . . CAMERA OS?

Wi-Fi interfaces for digital cameras were starting to be a thing in the nicer DSLRs. These things were getting more powerful, but the UIs were terrible.

—BRIAN SWETLAND

In the beginning, Android was building a digital camera platform called FotoFarm.

Digital camera technology in 2003 was becoming interesting; digital single-lens reflex cameras (DSLRs) combined high-quality lenses with increasingly large sensors to capture more and more detail in digital image files. But the software for these cameras was . . . not great.

Andy Rubin, who had founded and recently left the mobile phone manufacturer Danger, was looking for a new project. Along with Chris White, a former colleague at WebTV, he started a new company to make better camera software. With Andy as CEO and Chris as CTO, they founded FotoFarm in late 2003 to provide an operating system for digital cameras. The software they envisioned would enable better UIs and networking, along with the ability to run apps. Combined with superior camera hardware, they would push the boundaries of photographic and imaging functionality and experience.

Chris told Andy he thought they could come up with a better name than "FotoFarm." Andy already had the URL android.com, so they changed the name to Android and hired the design firm Character to help create their corporate identity, including their logo and business cards.

All they needed was for investors to buy into their vision of an Android camera platform. But nobody else cared about cameras; everyone wanted to talk about phones.

Andy invited Nick Sears to meet with him at Android's offices in Palo Alto to pitch the camera OS. The two had worked closely together on Danger's phone, the T-Mobile Sidekick. Nick had decided to leave T-Mobile, but to continue working on mobile phones. He wanted to build a consumer smartphone that went beyond what they had been able to build at Danger. Nick felt that one of the reasons Danger hadn't succeeded as much as they'd hoped was the interface and form factor of the device itself. "Everybody looked at it as this iconic device, but we knew that the form factor wasn't small enough yet that people wanted to carry it in their hands. It was still a thick device and had to have the screen as a separate thing."

Android's vision didn't appeal to Nick; he wasn't interested in cameras. Phones were where his experience and his interests were. He told Andy, "If you change your mind and end up doing phones, give me a call."

Soon after that conversation, Andy spoke with another colleague from the Danger days: Rich Miner. Rich, on behalf of his employer, the mobile carrier Orange, was an early investor in Danger. After getting to know Andy through that experience, Rich kept in touch to see what else he'd do in the future.

Rich, like Nick, suggested that Andy's startup should consider building mobile phones instead of cameras. Rich had a long history with the mobile phone market and saw an opportunity for Android to make a difference there. Chris was also talking to Andy about that possibility. But Andy was still resistant.

Andy didn't *want* to do phones again. He was ultimately frustrated by his experiences at Danger, which hadn't turned out as well as he had hoped. But at the same time, he was pitching the camera idea to venture capitalists (VCs) and not getting any interest. Also, he was looking at the realities of the camera market and saw that sales at the time were going down, as manufacturers started to put cameras in mobile phones.

In November of 2004, Andy was at another meeting with VCs. His pitch for the camera OS met with the same lack of interest. So he mentioned phones as a possibility and saw ears in the room perk up.

Andy gave up. He got back in touch with both Nick and Rich and told them that he was now ready to do a phone OS.

That was all that Rich and Nick needed. They both started working with Andy to pull together a business plan and a pitch deck around a phone OS. And in early 2005, they joined Android as co-founders.

Andy didn't get to build his camera OS. But given how critical the camera is on phones today, you could argue that he created the most widely used camera OS ever; he just did it in a roundabout way.

2

THE FARM TEAM

This was one of the cool parts of Android: Out of the first hundred
people, almost everybody had done this before. I was working on things
that I had already made mistakes on and learned from. Everybody was.

—JOE ONORATO

Android, like basically every other piece of technology, is not so much the product and releases that ship as it is the people who built it and the collective experience that they brought to bear in shaping it. So the story of how Android (the phone OS) came to be starts much earlier than the startup, in the collective histories of the people on the team.

Android happened because so many other efforts happened first. Or, more precisely, Android exists because the people who built it worked together previously at various other companies, in an ever-shifting Venn diagram of mobile and desktop platform companies. It was at these other companies that the early Android pioneers built up their knowledge, skills, and collaboration with their peers. When they arrived on the Android team, they were able to hit the ground running and build a new operating system from scratch in a relatively short amount of time.

The companies that had the biggest impact on the early Android team were Be/PalmSource,[1] WebTV/Microsoft, and Danger. None of them fed directly into Android, and most of them failed to make a large dent in the marketplace. But all of them provided a fertile proving ground where engineers learned critical skills that they would capitalize on when they later built the Android OS.

BE, INC.

The Be Operating System (BeOS) is now just a footnote[2] in computer history. In fact, you may not have even heard of Be or BeOS before, much less used the company's software or hardware. But Be's impact on computing platforms is huge, if for no other reason than that it collected, either as employees or as avid users and developers, so many of the people who later went on to form Android.[3]

Be was a late entrant to the desktop computing wars, coming along in the early 1990s with a new OS that attempted to compete with the entrenched Microsoft and Apple desktop systems. It didn't fare well.

Be tried various things along the way. They sold their own computer hardware (the BeBox). They ported BeOS to PC and Mac hardware and attempted selling the OS. They were almost acquired by Apple (in fact, they got an offer, but while Be's CEO was stalling as a negotiating ploy, Steve Jobs swooped in and convinced Apple to buy his company, NeXT Computer, instead). In 1999, they went through an underwhelming initial public offering (IPO).[4] Then in 2000, when nobody was buying Be's hardware or OS, the company tried what the team called a "Focus Shift," building an OS for an internet appliance device, which people also didn't buy.

---

[1] There is no company called Be/PalmSource, nor is there one called WebTV/Microsoft. Rather, there was a company called Be, which was acquired by Palm, which then spun out that division into the company PalmSource. Similarly, there was another company called WebTV that was acquired by Microsoft.

[2] Like this.

[3] This book is the story of how Android came to be. This part of the story is how Be came to Android.

[4] Michael Morrissey, who later led the services team on Android, left Be soon after the IPO: "That did not go as well as planned, Red Hat had just had a really big IPO, and it changed the dynamics of the OS industry."

Macworld *went to print one month with a story about Apple's acquisition of Be, which fell through when Apple acquired NeXT Computer instead. (Picture courtesy Steve Horowitz.)*

Finally, in 2001, Be was acquired by Palm (which then spun out that division into a new company called PalmSource), to build the operating system for future Palm devices. To be specific, Palm acquired the intellectual property (IP) of Be and hired many of Be's employees; Palm didn't acquire the company, the debts, or the assets (like the office furniture).[5]

Be is significant in Android history for a couple reasons. First, Be attracted engineers who were interested in all aspects of operating system development, from user interfaces to graphics to device drivers (getting the system to talk to hardware, like printers and displays) to the kernel (low-level system software that handles the heavy-lifting for the basics that the platform needs). Working on these kinds of projects creates exactly the kinds of skills needed to build an OS like Android.

Also, BeOS became a cult classic in operating systems. Engineers all over the world stumbled upon Be during college or in hobby projects and tinkered around with it. Be's advanced capabilities in multimedia,[6]

[5.] Jeff Hamilton, who was at Be and later Android, talked about Be selling the assets: "They had an auction for all of the physical assets of the company; the chairs, the monitors. . . . I went and bought the monitor off my desk, because it was a nice Sony Trinitron. The company that ran the auction (they gathered all the stuff, took the cash, managed all of that) went bankrupt between when they sold all of the stuff and when they were supposed to pay it out. So Be didn't ever see a dime for the physical assets that they sold. It seemed like the canonical Tech Bubble bursting story." So Be did sell its assets, but was never actually paid for them.

[6.] Multimedia = video and audio

multiprocessing,[7] and multithreading[8] made it an interesting playground for engineers interested in OS development. Many of the engineers on Android who didn't actually work at Be had played around with BeOS on their own and developed a passion for operating system development, which they later used on the Android team.

When Be was acquired, half of the engineers went to work for Palm (soon PalmSource).[9] There, they continued working on operating systems, building Palm OS Cobalt, which didn't end up shipping with any devices. Along the way, the engineering team continued honing their skills in OS development, while also gaining experience in mobile devices, which were the target of their Palm OS efforts.

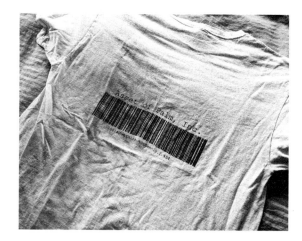

The Be engineers joining Palm made t-shirts that reflected their cynical take on the acquisition. (Picture courtesy Mathias Agopian.)

---

[7] Multiprocessing is the ability to take advantage of hardware to run multiple things in parallel. This capability is common in most hardware these days, from desktop computers with multi-core CPUs to phones, which generally come with at least two, but often four or more, cores.

[8] Multithreading is the ability for a single process to run multiple threads executing concurrently, either on separate processors or on a single, shared processor. BeOS was known for having a multithreaded UI, which was (and still is) unusual. It offered performance benefits for users, at the cost of complexity for app developers. Android originally took a similar approach (implemented by a former BeOS engineer), but eventually scrapped it in favor of a less fragile single-threaded UI model.

[9] Mathias Agopian remembered: "Palm took 50 people from Be, then did a layoff days after we joined and told us that it was only fair that we participated. So they let go of three of us. We were off to a good start!"

PalmSource was itself acquired by ACCESS in late 2005. Uninspired by the direction of the new company, many of the former Be engineers found their way to the Android project at Google. By mid-2006, ex-Be employees made up a third of the Android team.

WEBTV/MICROSOFT

WebTV was founded in mid-1995 and was acquired by Microsoft less than two years later, in April of 1997.[10] The people who came to Android from Microsoft in those early years came specifically from the team that started out as WebTV, as well as other TV/internet groups like IPTV that were part of the same division.

WebTV provided one of the first systems to bring the internet to televisions. This seems silly today, when many of us consume most or all of our television content through internet services on our TVs. But back then, these were very different worlds, and most people's access to the internet was through PCs.

The team at WebTV was creating a platform for users to consume content that wasn't just television, so they needed to create the software platform that ran on the hardware, the user interface layer to build apps, and applications for that platform. The team built an operating system, a UI toolkit (the system responsible for user interaction in applications), a programming layer for writing applications, and applications for an internet-enabled device. All of these efforts resulted in practical experience that would come in handy for the people who later found themselves on Android building very similar things.

DANGER, INC.

Danger, Inc. was founded in December of 1999 by Andy Rubin, Matt Hershenson, and Joe Britt. Initially, the company was building a portable data

---

[10.] WebTV was acquired around the same time that Microsoft also acquired an internet startup where I was working at the time. The details of our smaller company's acquisition were never made public, and I'm not about to do so here, but suffice it to say that when we learned that WebTV was being acquired for $425 million, we felt worse about our own deal. A lot worse. Of course, WebTV had a larger team and an actual product, and this division went on to make products that Microsoft sold for some time, which was a far better turnout than the products my startup worked on. So maybe that higher purchase price was justified. Maybe.

exchange device, nicknamed "Nutter Butter"[11] because it was shaped like the cookie of that name.

Danger's Nutter Butter device. It was made for exchanging data, not for snacking. (Picture courtesy Nick Sears.)

During the dot-com implosion in 2000–2001, the company pivoted to a device that would automatically sync data wirelessly. But it wasn't a phone. Yet. Then, in January of 2001, Andy met with T-Mobile's Nick Sears at CES.[12]

NICK SEARS AND MOBILE DATA

In 1984, Nick was a private in the US Army working an administrative job to earn college benefits. Then he watched Apple's legendary 1984 ad during the Super Bowl. "I knew we were at the beginning of a technology revolution. I walked into ComputerLand, dropped $3,200, and walked out with an IBM PC (one floppy disk drive), DOS, turbo pascal, Lotus Notes, WordStar, and a dot-matrix printer. During the day, I was a 40-words-per-minute machine. At night, I became a mild-mannered computer nerd."

Nick coupled his computer skills with a business degree and joined McCaw Communications in the late 80s. From his vantage point inside McCaw, he watched the growth of both the mobile industry and the internet for the next decade. By the year 2000, he had moved to T-Mobile,[13] where he was a vice president in charge of the company's wireless data strategy.

---

[11] The team also used the name Peanut because it lacked the copyright problem of using a branded cookie name.

[12] CES = Consumer Electronics Show, a huge annual conference where manufacturers would show their upcoming products and would-be manufacturers would meet with would-be partners.

[13] T-Mobile was then called VoiceStream Wireless. It was renamed to T-Mobile in 2002.

T-Mobile had recently dedicated a team to the wireless internet, which they wanted to grow. They were the only carrier in the US with GPRS[14] technology, and their data network was ready about a year before those of other carriers. Nick was tasked with making it happen. This meant going out and finding, or creating if necessary, devices that would need and use this new data network.

Nick and his team realized a richer internet experience wasn't going to happen without a better keyboard experience. Doing anything interesting on the web just wasn't feasible, or pleasant, with the traditional 12-key dial pads on phones at that time.[15] So the team was looking specifically for potential devices with QWERTY keyboards.[16]

T-Mobile was already working with RIM,[17] and had convinced them to add phone capabilities to their previously data-only BlackBerry device. But the form factor of those devices (especially with the belt clip popular with users) wasn't going to appeal to consumers, who were looking for something less business-centric.

Nick went to CES in 2001, hunting for consumer device possibilities. He met with Danger's CEO, Andy Rubin, who showed him a mockup of the latest version of Danger's device. Like BlackBerry, it also was data-only. And like Black-Berry, Nick told Andy that T-Mobile needed it to be a phone, so Danger pivoted to add phone capabilities and partnered with T-Mobile for that first device.

Nick reflected on T-Mobile's push for these new data-enabled phones, "We're the ones that put the phones in smartphones."

In October of 2002, Danger released their resulting *Hiptop*[18] phone . . . but T-Mobile insisted on renaming it. As Nick explained: "Business executives

---

[14.] GPRS = General Packet Radio Services, a data network capability that was new at the time and promised better data connectivity than was otherwise available.

[15.] There actually was a full-keyboard device that Nokia had tried earlier, but it was unsuccessful. When Nick talked to them, they were unwilling to add the appropriate network capabilities to it and reintroduce it into the US; they took the initial failure as a strong signal and declined the offer.

[16.] QWERTY is the abbreviation for the traditional Latin-script (including English) keyboards, whose letters are arranged, starting at the upper left, "q w e r t y . . . "

[17.] RIM = Research in Motion, which made the BlackBerry device.

[18.] Ficus Kirkpatrick, who worked at Danger at the time, explained the name: "It was a joke on a laptop, versus a hiptop is something you hold on your hip, though I would never be caught dead with one of those hip-holsters for a phone. Are you kidding me? My Dockers pulled up to my belly button? No way."

and engineers were wearing BlackBerry devices on their hips like HP calculators, and we didn't think consumers would do that with a phone." The device was released as the T-Mobile Sidekick.

This device occupied a middle ground between the feature phones of that time and the smartphones of the future. For example, the Hiptop offered a real web browser (compared to the very limited mobile browsers prevalent on phones in those days). Also, Danger phones had an app store, which was one of the first of its kind. But that store was curated by T-Mobile; carriers at that time held control over the applications that could run on their network, which was called the *walled garden*.[19]

These features, along with cloud/network capabilities, including the Hiptop's persistent connection for immediate email and chat updates, plus over-the-air updates, would be seen later on Android, as would some of the developers that made it all work on the Danger phones.

Ultimately, the Danger phones never broke through from cult status to mass-market success. The combination of internet email, messaging, and browsing, along with T-Mobile's aggressive unlimited data pricing, created a phone with powerful capabilities for the time. Danger devices garnered a lot of attention, especially in tech[20] and pop culture circles (including the second Hiptop device being featured in the 2006 film *The Devil Wears Prada*). But the phones failed to capture the minds and wallets of consumers. Nevertheless, these devices were important in moving the mobile field forward, from the technology that was created, to the new experiences these devices enabled, to the team of engineers that Danger educated along the way.

ALL TOGETHER NOW

Most of the early Android team worked at one or more of these companies: Be/PalmSource, WebTV/Microsoft, and Danger. Through mid-2006, those people represented at least 70 percent of the team, and continued to be a majority of the team until 2007.

---

[19] That wall had to come down to enable the ecosystem that Android enjoyed later; more on that in Chapter 22 ("Android Market").

[20] Including Google's co-founders, who were big fans of their Hiptops. This helped when Andy pitched the idea for Android to Google years later.

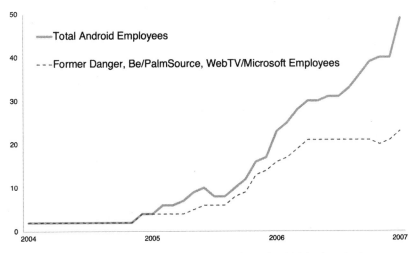

Most of the people who joined the Android team through 2006 had worked at one or more of Be/PalmSource, WebTV/Microsoft, and Danger.

It has always been a fact in tech, and in Silicon Valley in particular, that people move around between companies and end up working together in different places and contexts throughout their careers. It's never a good idea to burn bridges when you leave companies. For one thing, being decent to people is just the right thing to do. But in Silicon Valley, it's a really bad idea to burn those bridges, because the odds are very high that your future self will need to cross those bridges with some of those very same people; it would be handy if the bridges weren't on fire at the time.[21]

In the case of Android, it was much more than this indirect and coincidental effect of people ending up at the same company later on. The early team leaned heavily on their prior company experiences and brought in people who (a) they already had a working relationship with and (b) had experience working on exactly what Android needed: operating systems, embedded devices, and developer platforms.

By joining Android together early on, these people jump-started a tight team of colleagues who knew what they were doing, which allowed them to build this new OS much faster than would have otherwise been possible.

[21.] This is one of the things that makes the valley a good place to work in high tech (ignoring for a moment the traffic and the insane cost of housing). Companies have to try hard to make employees happy, because if they don't, there are other companies nearby doing similar things that might try harder.

Xavier Ducrohet, who joined in 2007 to work on tools, observed, "Those first people came from elsewhere—very few from Google. People who had shipped OSes. How many people have done that? They shipped small OSes and learned from their mistakes."

Dan Egnor, who also joined in 2007 to work on the over-the-air update system, noticed the team dynamic with the people who were there already. "There was this strong sense through shared history: people know each other, they know what parts of each other they were grumpy about, what parts they'd respect, what people could be trusted to accomplish, and they have clear domains of ownership. People's names would roll off each other's tongues even if they'd only been on the team a couple of months. People had this strong sense of knowing what other people did and how they did it."

Not all of these other companies or their products were successful. But the knowledge gained in building them contributed hugely to the Android teams' ability to build a working platform later. Steve Horowitz, who worked at Be and the WebTV team at Microsoft and later managed the Android engineering team, said, "That's part of this world: you learn probably more from the failures than you do from the successes."

Dianne Hackborn, who worked at Be and PalmSource before joining the early Android team, said, "Most of us had a number of failures behind us before working on Android, where the situation or the timing or something else wasn't there for success. I count three to four failed platforms I worked on before Android. But we kept trying, learning from each of those failures, and using the knowledge gained from that to help our work on Android."

Companies Leading to Android

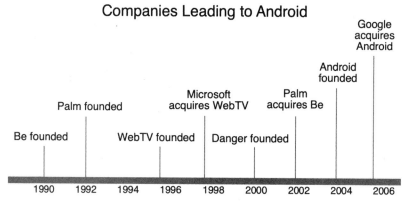

Android already had a long history before it was formed, building on the history of all of the companies that contributed to its early team.

3

GROWING THE TEAM

Toward the end of 2004, the small Android startup needed reinforcements. Andy and Chris provided enough engineering and design wherewithal to get some of the initial vision and technology working. But when they started pitching actual products to investors, they needed an engineering team to help create the platform and technology demos while the founders worked on the business.

Meanwhile, Brian Swetland, who had worked with Andy at Danger, was looking for a new challenge.

BRIAN SWETLAND, ANDROID'S FIRST ENGINEER

From the age of five, Brian Swetland (referred to simply as "Swetland" on the team) had been a systems programmer.

"My father soldered together a Timex Sinclair clone, a single board computer with membrane keyboard, on our kitchen table over two or three evenings and hooked it up to a crappy old black and white TV. You could type things in BASIC. It did stuff—it was this magical thing. And you learn life lessons that stick with you, like which end of the soldering iron to never pick up."

Swetland continued programming through childhood and then college, but didn't finish his computer engineering degree. "Sophomore year I didn't make it to classes for a large chunk of it. Projects with the local ACM chapter, a job at NCSA SDG, and working on the X/Mosaic web browser had distracted me. Then finals happened, and it wasn't pretty." But hobby programming led him to Be, and he captured the company's interest while trying to get BeOS to work on his PC.

When Be released a version of their OS for PCs, Swetland installed the CD on his computer. But it didn't quite work. "It didn't recognize my hard drive, because I only had SCSI[1] drives in my PC. So I found the manuals for the bus logic SCSI controllers I had and thought, 'This doesn't look that complicated.' I emailed Dominic Giampaolo, one of their engineers who was active on Usenet."[2] Dominic emailed Swetland a sample SCSI driver for the BeBox hardware.

"That weekend, I ended up hacking together a SCSI driver for the BusLogic controller I had. I got it booting, but there was some problem; the disk size was coming up wrong. So I emailed him back, told him 'I wrote the driver, but the size is wrong: I think there's an endian[3] bug in the mid-layer.'

"He emailed me back fifteen minutes later and asked me if I wanted a job." After a trip to California and a full day of interviews at the company, including a live debugging session with Dominic, Brian had a job offer. He returned home, packed up his things, and moved to California two weeks later. He had gone to college with the goal of eventually writing operating systems. With the opportunity to start on that immediately, he figured a college degree could wait.

Two years later, in May of 2000, Swetland left Be for Danger, joining former Be (and future Android) colleague Hiroshi Lockheimer. At Danger, Swetland worked on the kernel and other system software, and helped to ship the first couple of Hiptop devices. But after the first few years, most of the work tended to be incremental improvements, or features implemented at the request of the carrier (or killed on their behalf; even sometimes killed based on what product

---

[1] SCSI = Small Computer Systems Interface. SCSI was a common interface between computers and peripheral devices. For example, SCSI was used to connect (using very wide ports and ribbon cables) motherboards with hard drives and printers.

[2] Usenet was a collection of newsgroups that were popular in the early days of the internet.

[3] Endian is a term used to represent the order of bytes in a machine. "Big-endian" means the most significant (largest) byte is first in a multi-byte number, whereas "little-endian" reverses that order, with the most significant byte last. The difference in endian representation between different architectures is a common source of bugs in code meant to run across different machines. In this case, the endian assumptions for code on BeBox (using big-endian) were not correct when that same code was run on an x86 PC (which uses little-endian representation).

managers thought the carrier *might* request). Eric Fischer, who worked on text and other platform features at Danger (and later Android) said, "Everything we did there was in the shadow of the slow, conservative carrier acceptance process that could veto any feature or design."

Swetland was always more interested in building new systems than iterating on existing ones, and he was getting frustrated. Danger had become a much larger organization of about 150 people by 2004, far from the tiny team he joined back in 2000. It had also been four years of long hours, first helping Danger as a struggling startup, and then working to ship the company's first two phones. So in September of 2004, he took three months off to recover from burnout and frustration.

Swetland wasn't planning to quit Danger; he just needed a break. A few weeks into his hiatus, he realized he was pretty happy not being at work. He also realized he'd continue to be happy if he continued to not go back to work. More specifically, he realized he really didn't want to go back to work at Danger.

But he still needed a job. Be and Danger had been decent software jobs, but hadn't paid out in the way everyone imagines every startup doing.[4]

At Danger, Swetland got to know Andy well, since there were only a handful of employees when he started. So when he was searching around for new opportunities, he reached out to Andy. After all, Andy had founded an interesting company in the past; maybe he'd have more ideas. And he did; Andy had started Android with Chris White, and they were looking for their first employee.

At that time, in the Fall of 2004, the startup was focused on an open source camera operating system. Andy pitched the camera OS idea to Swetland, who was intrigued. If nothing else, it was a chance to work on another new operating system, which is what he loved. And at least it wasn't phones again; he had had enough of that tumultuous domain during his time at Danger. So he signed up, planning to start when he finished his break.

[4.] Successful acquisitions and IPOs are highly unusual for startups. Everyone hears far more about the few people who strike it rich than the multitudes who just have regular jobs at these places as they continue to not get acquired by the big tech firms, not to mention the many companies that go bust chasing the dream, and the engineers that then go chasing the new jobs for necessary paychecks.

Before Swetland started, Andy talked with Nick, Rich, Chris, and VCs, and decided to change Android's product focus.

In early December, Swetland came into the office on his first day at Android, excited to be working on something that wasn't phones. Andy said, "What would you say if we were doing phones?"

Swetland started on the same day as another long-time Android person: Tracey Cole. Tracey was hired as Android's first administrative assistant. She remained in that role, and was Andy's personal admin, for many years.[5] Tracey and Brian were the third and fourth people to join Android, and the first two non-founder employees.

ANDY MCFADDEN AND THE DEMO

In May of 2005, Andy McFadden (known to the team as "Fadden"[6]) joined the company. Fadden had worked with Andy Rubin and Chris White at WebTV. When Andy [Rubin] was looking to hire someone else for his startup, he emailed Fadden:

```
WTF?
How are you?
I want to hire you. It's going to be huge™
```

When he was 13, Fadden was programming BASIC and assembly[7] on an Apple II. So it was no surprise that he would later be one of the people on Android working on low-level code for Android's Dalvik runtime. "Some people [later, when Android was a large team at Google] didn't like having parts of the

---

[5] Tracey was Andy's admin until he left the Android team in March of 2013.

[6] Andy McFadden will also be known as Fadden in this book, to make it easier to distinguish Andy McFadden from Andy Rubin. Too many people, too few unique names.

[7] Assembly language is the lowest-level code that programmers use. It maps very closely onto actual hardware instructions on a computer, which makes it very simplistic and verbose, compared to higher-level languages like C++ and Java. Most programmers learn assembly programming along the way, usually in a class on low-level programming. Most programmers never actually use it in their real jobs. But it comes in handy in very performance-sensitive situations, which is why it was used by some of the programmers on the Android team, including Fadden.

Dalvik VM[8] written in ARM[9] assembly. When you've been crawling around in the guts of computers since the 8th grade you have a different perspective."

Andy brought Fadden in to help out.[10] When Fadden started, Android's "product" was nothing more than 3,000 lines of JavaScript,[11] tied together with various open source libraries. It wasn't a platform; it was a prototype to help visualize a nonexistent experience. Fadden's job was to take this concept demo, which Swetland and Chris had been working on, and start adding real capabilities, including applications. The startup had to be able to show potential investors what real users could actually do with this future system.

In the Spring of 2005, the Android team didn't yet have a product, but they did have a clear idea of what they wanted that product to be. Startups have been acquired for far less.

FICUS KIRKPATRICK, THE STARTUP'S LAST EMPLOYEE

The final person to join the Android team before it was acquired by Google was Ficus Kirkpatrick.

Ficus started programming when he was young. Really young. "I have been programming since I was four. I don't have any memory of not having computers and not programming computers. My whole childhood was on and off programming and using computers."

In 1994, at the age of fifteen, Ficus dropped out of high school and went looking for work. A few months later, he got a full-time programming job and

---

[8.] Dalvik was the runtime (or virtual machine—VM) responsible for running code on Android. Dalvik (and runtimes in general) are discussed later in Chapter 8 ("Java").

[9.] ARM = Advanced RISC Machine. Or at least it used to mean that. ARM is a computer architecture that defines the instructions used on chips (CPUs) commonly running on mobile devices.

[10.] Fadden said he wasn't brought in to work on anything in particular, but rather whatever needed to be done. As he put it, it was more a directive of "Glove up and dig in."

[11.] JavaScript is a programming language typically used on websites. There is more about it in Chapter 8 ("Java"). Confusingly, JavaScript has almost nothing in common with the Java programming language, apart from those four shared letters in their names.

has been working steadily ever since. "In 'work age,' I'm like seven years older than people my age who got out of college at twenty-two."

He came to Silicon Valley and bounced around various companies, including Be, usually working on low-level systems software. In 2000, after leaving Be, he joined a startup for all of two days. On his first day at the new company, he realized that it wasn't for him. "My first sign that things were wrong: my computer was all set up and I already had email. They were a startup!" Also, his entire team was at an offsite meeting that day to debate a minor technical decision. Ficus was a firm believer in getting down to work and writing code. This company obviously wasn't his kind of place. His second day of work, he only went into the office so that he could quit.

Hiroshi Lockheimer, who'd known Ficus from Be, heard that he was looking for something new and directed him to Danger, which Hiroshi had recently joined. Ficus joined Danger and worked on the kernel and drivers, helping to build out the platform for the Hiptop phone.

By mid-2005, Ficus had left Danger and moved to Seattle. Andy asked him to join Android. Part of the pitch to Ficus was that co-founder Nick Sears lived near Seattle as well, so Ficus would be allowed to stay there and work remotely.

Ficus joined the team. One week later, Google acquired Android.

Ficus remembered: "When Andy said, 'The company's gonna be bought by Google,' I thought 'Wow, this is the only way I could ever possibly get into Google.' Then he said, 'We have to go in and interview,' and I thought, 'Well, that's it. It's over.'"

Swetland remembered, "Ficus declared that if anyone asked what the Big O[12] of anything was, he was simply going to say, 'I'm far too handsome to answer that question.'"

But the interviews worked out for Ficus, and he joined Google, eventually moving back to the Bay Area to be closer to the team's center of gravity. He had always preferred working on low-level systems software. Helping to build the Android OS from the ground up promised plenty of opportunity for that kind of work.

---

[12] "Big O Notation" is a way of quantifying the performance of an algorithm. It tends to come up in coding interviews where engineers are asked about the performance of a proposed solution. It's something programmers study in school and is annoying to try to think about during interviews.

4

THE PITCH

By mid-2005, Android was acquired and the future looked bright. But just six months earlier, things weren't quite as rosy. In January of that year, the startup was desperate for cash and their main task was the same as for most startups: getting funding. After the pivot from a camera OS to an open source phone platform, they still had the daunting task of actually building a product, which meant they'd need more money to hire a large enough team to do the work.

So the company focused on three things. First, they needed a demo to show what was possible. Next, they needed to articulate their vision and create a pitch deck to help explain that vision. Finally, they needed to take the demo and the slide deck on the road to pitch their story to potential investors.

DEMO TIME

Fadden's first job when he joined was solidifying the demo, a prototype phone system that Swetland and Chris had been working on. It wasn't actually functional (for example, it showed a stock ticker on the home screen which used a set of hard-coded symbols and stale data). But the demo represented a vision of what the product could be when it was actually implemented.

The original demo, written by Brian Swetland and Chris White and later enhanced by Fadden, showing a home screen and several apps (most of which were not implemented). It's a far cry from a modern Android home screen.

One of the apps that Fadden added to the demo was a simple calendar application. This early demo project would come back to haunt him. After many intervening years of working on things throughout the Android platform, he ended up helping out with the Android Calendar app. Time waits for no man . . . but calendar apps do.

THE MOBILE OPPORTUNITY

As the team honed their vision, they created a slide deck to explain it. These slides painted a picture of the opportunities that they saw for Android in the marketplace, as well as a picture of how Android would make money for the investors.

The slide deck in March of 2005 had fifteen slides, which was enough to capture the attention of VCs as well as Google.

The pitch deck got interesting by the second slide, which compared PC and phone markets. In 2004, there were 178 million shipments of PCs worldwide. During the same period, there were 675 million phones shipped; nearly four times as many units as PCs, but with processors and memory that were as capable as PCs were in 1998.

This potential in mobile hardware was a point that Dianne Hackborn, then at PalmSource and eventually on the Android team, was also thinking about. The mobile industry was ready to pop because there was finally enough power for there to be a real, capable computing platform: Dianne said, "You could see the writing on the wall. The hardware was getting more powerful, and the market was already bigger than PCs."

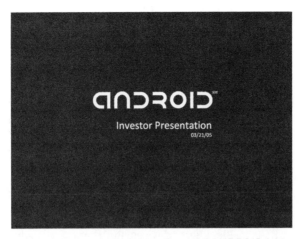

The first slide of the pitch deck. The word ANDROID in that custom font remained the logo for the OS for many years after this startup phase.

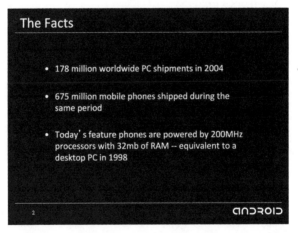

The number of mobile phones already dwarfed the number of PCs being sold in 2004, providing a huge opportunity for phones with more capable software.

The presentation also identified the problem of the growing cost of mobile software. The cost of hardware was going down, but that of software was not, making it a larger and larger proportion of the per-handset cost. But handset manufacturers were not experts in software platform development and didn't have the skill set or interest in providing the increasing capabilities required to differentiate their software from that of their competitors.

AN OPEN OPPORTUNITY

The second major point in the pitch deck was that there was a gap, and an opportunity, in the market for an *open* platform. That is, Android would be an operating system that was free and available to manufacturers through open source. Companies would be able to use and distribute this OS on their own phones, without being beholden to a software provider and without having to build it themselves. This open approach was something that was simply not available at that time.

Microsoft provided a proprietary OS that manufacturers could license and then port to their hardware. Symbian was primarily used by Nokia, with some uptake from Sony and Motorola. RIM had its own platform, which it used only for its own BlackBerry devices. But there was no alternative out there for manufacturers that wanted a capable smartphone without either building their own OS, putting significant effort into customizing an existing one, and/or paying a high licensing fee.

Even more problematic, the systems that were available failed to provide an ecosystem for applications. Symbian provided some of the core infrastructure for an operating system, but the UI layer was left as an exercise for the manufacturer, resulting in an application model for phones where apps written for one flavor of Symbian wouldn't necessarily run on some other variation, even on phones from the same manufacturer.

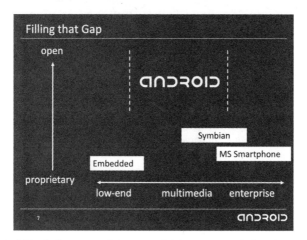

Slide 7 diagrammed the potential for an open platform, providing something that was otherwise not available at that time.

The Java programming language, known in the server and desktop PC world as "write once, run anywhere," could possibly have provided this kind of cross-device application capability, but Java ME[1] fell far short of this in the mobile space. While it did provide at least the same language across devices (much as Symbian provided the same language of C++ for all of its implementations), Java ME addressed the wide variety of form factors and architectures in phones by providing different versions of the platform, called *profiles*. These profiles had different capabilities, so developers needed to change their applications to run on different devices, and often that approach failed when capabilities were drastically different across devices.

Linux to the rescue! . . . Almost. Texas Instruments (TI) provided an open platform based on the Linux OS kernel. All manufacturers needed was Linux itself, reference hardware from TI, and then a huge host of other modules that manufacturers had to acquire, license, build, or otherwise supply to create their own device. As Brian Swetland put it, "You could use TI's OMAP[2] chips to build a Linux phone. So you needed TI's OMAP and then forty

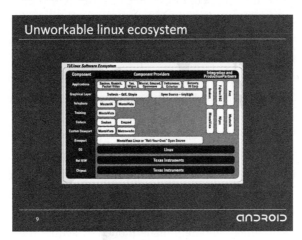

TI provided a Linux-based solution, but many of the details of drivers and other components were left as an exercise to the manufacturer, which wasn't a compelling option.

---

[1] Java ME: Java Platform, Micro Edition. See the discussion in the Jargon appendix at the end for more on Java ME.

[2] Open Multimedia Applications Platform: OMAP was a series of processors from Texas Instruments for mobile devices.

components from forty different vendors of middleware. You put all these together and you integrated them all and then you'd have a Linux phone. And that was just absurd."

Android wanted to provide the world's first *complete* open handset platform solution. It would be built on Linux, like TI's offering but would also provide all of the necessary pieces so that manufacturers would have only one system to adopt in order to build and ship their devices. Android would also provide a single programming model to application developers, so that their apps would work the same across all devices on which the platform ran. By having a single platform that worked across all devices using it, Android would simplify phones for both manufacturers and developers.

MAKING MONEY

The final part of the pitch (and the most important part, for the VCs they were pitching to) was how Android was going to make money. The open source platform described in the slides is essentially what the Android team eventually built and shipped. But if that was all there was, the company would not have been worth funding for VCs. Developing and giving away an open source platform sounds great from a save-the-world standpoint, but where's the payoff? Where's the upside for investors? That is, how did Android plan to make money off of a product that they planned to simply give away? Venture capitalists fund companies that they hope will make more (far more) than their investment back.

The path to revenue was clear for the other platform companies in the game. Microsoft made money by licensing its platform to Windows Phone partners; every phone sold contributed a per-device cost back to Microsoft. RIM made money both on the handsets they sold as well as the lucrative service contracts that their loyal enterprise customers signed up for. Nokia and the other Symbian adopters made money by selling the phones that they manufactured with variations of that operating system. Similarly, all of the other handset manufacturers funded their own software development through the revenue generated by the phones they sold.

So what was Android's play that would fund the development of this awesome platform that they had yet to build and which they would give away free to other manufacturers to build their own devices?

Carrier services.

Carriers would provide applications, contacts, and other cloud-based data services to their customers for Android-based handsets. The carriers would pay Android for providing these services. Swetland explained: "Rather than running and hosting the services [like Danger did for its Hiptop phones], we would build the services and sell them to the carriers."[3]

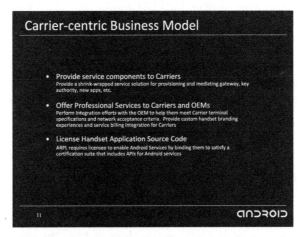

Slide 11 laid out the path to profits, based on services that carriers would license from Android.

PITCHING THE DREAM

The Android team pitched to a few VCs, mostly on the East Coast, far away from Silicon Valley. As Rich Miner put it, "Andy had been up and down Sand Hill Road[4] with the Android pitch as a Camera OS and had already got a bunch of 'No!'s, including from Red Point where he was the EIR [Entrepreneur in Residence]. Part of my joining up was to say, 'I have a bunch of East Coast VCs and other people I can introduce you to.' So we started going to mostly new people who hadn't heard of Android before."

In parallel with these VC meetings, the team was also meeting with Google. In early January, Larry Page[5] asked Andy to come to Google for a

---

[3.] The system that the team eventually built and shipped stayed true to the vision laid out in the pitch deck, except for this part about revenue from carrier services, which went away entirely.

[4.] This street running through Palo Alto and Menlo Park is home to many of the Silicon Valley venture capital firms.

[5.] Google co-founder

meeting. Larry was a huge fan of his T-Mobile Sidekick (the Danger Hiptop) phone, which Andy's previous company had made, so he wanted to talk to Andy about the mobile space. Andy called Nick Sears, who was still working at T-Mobile, and asked him to come to the meeting as well.

It was a small meeting, with just Andy and Nick from the Android side and Larry, Sergey Brin,[6] and Georges Harik (an early Google employee) from the Google side. Nick remembered the meeting as very casual, but also that Google was clearly interested in what Andy and Android were up to. "That meeting started out with Larry saying the Sidekick's the best phone that's ever been done. Larry very much wanted to see an even better phone get made, and he knew that's what Andy and the group of us were working on. At the end of that meeting they said, 'We'd like to help you guys.'"

That meeting was encouraging, but nothing substantive came out of it. In fact, Andy wondered whether they were just using the meeting as a way to pick Andy's brain about Danger, the company he'd founded and left back in 2003. He thought that Google might have been interested in purchasing Danger.

Meanwhile, the team continued pitching to VCs. Then in March, they went to Google for another meeting. This time, they showed a demo and shared more of their plans. Nothing significant happened at that meeting either, but Google made it clearer that they wanted to help the startup.

The team was also meeting with potential manufacturing partners at this time. They took a trip to Korea and Taiwan to visit Samsung and HTC. The meeting with Samsung started with the CEO of the mobile phone unit, K.T. Lee, saying he'd missed his chance with Danger and didn't want to see that happen again, so he was interested in getting on board with Android. Nick described the meeting: "K.T. Lee told his team to make it happen, so we thought it was a done deal. But then we met with his team of 10+ mid-level managers, who said, 'Who is going to build your OS?' When we said 'Brian,' they laughed. They had 300 people working on their own OS."

Samsung asked the team if they were dreaming. Nick said, "'No, really, Brian and a few other people are going to build the OS.' They asked how this would be possible and we responded that not only is it possible, but he already did it on Sidekick."

---

6. Google's other co-founder

After the business meetings, Samsung hosted a dinner to celebrate the new partnership. But the Android team later learned the deal was contingent upon securing an order from a carrier, which Nick admitted, "wasn't really a deal at all. It took about 18 months to convince T-Mobile to become our Android launch partner."

The team didn't come away with a deal, but they did get a device name from it. When they later picked the device that would become the G1, they gave it the code name "Dream" in memory of that meeting.

From Korea, the team flew to Taiwan, where they met with the CEO of HTC, Peter Chou. Nick remembered the meeting: "Peter mentioned something about exclusivity for our first device, which Brian overheard. By the time we got back to our hotel room, Swetland had threatened to resign because 'I didn't join Android to become another Danger.'[7] I was concerned because Brian was so critical to our success, but when I saw him the next day everything was fine."

The team continued pitching to VCs and found some success. Charles River Ventures and Eagle River Holdings were both interested. While they were waiting on paperwork from those firms, Google called them in for a third meeting.

This time, there were more people in the room, and Google was ready to talk specifics. Andy and his team had assumed they were coming to give an update on the company's progress since the last meeting. But in the middle of the presentation, Nick remembered, "They just said, 'Let us interrupt you there. We just want to buy you.'"

Google turned what Andy's team thought was a meeting of Android pitching to Google into a meeting in which Google was pitching to them instead. Google said if Android allowed itself to be acquired, it would do much better than it would otherwise. Instead of having to deal with the requirements of venture capitalists and having to charge customers and carriers for specialized services, they could just give the OS away to the carriers

---

[7] Swetland said, "I don't recall the discussion, but certainly believe it could have happened." His memory of Danger was fresh and strong at that time. The dynamic at Danger of being beholden to the carrier and manufacturer for product decisions was not something he wanted to repeat. He was strongly in favor of Android's vision for an open and independent platform. He threatened to resign several times during his time on the Android team over decisions that would have resulted in a closed platform.

for free. In fact, it would be even better than free: Google had revenue from search that they might be able to share with carriers. So rather than having to sell carriers on something, they'd be able to form partnerships with them. Nick remembered that it was a powerful argument for getting carriers on board: "We were actually going to help them *make* money by doing a partnership deal with us."

The team from Android was game for joining Google, but there were still many details to be figured out. In the meantime, in mid-April, they got term sheets from both Eagle River and Charles River and decided to go with the Eagle River deal. The Google deal was far from final, but had entered negotiations in early May, so they added a carve-out[8] in the term sheet, to account for the possibility that they'd do something with Google instead.

[8] The carve-out was an exception clause that allowed Android to get out of the agreement in the event that they struck a deal with Google.

5

THE ACQUISITION

They bought a team and a dream. I'd like to believe we executed pretty
well on it.

—BRIAN SWETLAND

When Android met with Google, Larry Page observed that it would make
sense for Google to acquire the small company, to help them build a
platform that would enable Google to enter the mobile market.

While both parties agreed in principle, there were many details to be
ironed out. Nick recalled two large issues that Android needed to resolve
with Google. The first was money: they needed to agree on the valuation
of the company and how they would be paid, both initially and in ongoing
milestone payments after the team joined. The second issue was commit-
ment: Android wanted to make sure that they would actually get to accomplish the original goal and not just get sucked up into the larger company
and forgotten. They needed Google to agree to support Android's efforts after
the acquisition and provide internal support on an ongoing basis.

The negotiations began in the Spring of 2005. But Rich Miner had a
problem: a family vacation conflicted with these time-sensitive meetings.
He ended up doing both in parallel, calling in to the meetings from a sail-
boat in the British Virgin Islands. "I had to find ports that had mobile phone

coverage. I'd have to have the boat with everybody off on the beach enjoying themselves during these two-hour negotiation phone calls.

"One of the things we were concerned about was, 'This isn't strategic to Google. You guys haven't even started focusing on WAP[1] or any mobile stuff. We think this is going to be a lot of work, require resources. What happens if you don't want to do this? How do we know we're going to get the resources we need to be successful?'"

Larry Page suggested they go talk with Jonathan Rosenberg, a Google executive in charge of product and marketing. Rich remembered his advice: "'Google's different from other companies. A lot of other companies, when projects aren't going well, they throw a lot of resources at it. At Google, we like to give resources to things that are going well. So if you do what you're going to do and you're executing, you'll get more resources.' That was, in essence, his Leap of Faith talk; why we should, if we believe in ourselves, do this because we'll get the resources if we're executing."

The Android team came back to the table (and the boat), hammered out a deal, and the team started at Google on July 11, 2005.

A few weeks after the Android team started at Google, they were again presenting the pitch deck. This time, it was at an internal meeting at Google, pitching to a group of executives. Andy and others were showing what this newly acquired team was planning to do. Swetland described the meeting: "We showed the demo we had. Andy was running through the deck. I remember when he got to the monetization thing, Larry cut him off and said 'Don't worry about that. I want you guys to build the best possible phone and we'll figure out the rest later.'"

---

[1] WAP = Wireless Application Protocol, which was introduced in 1999. Prior to the iPhone, there was a push in the industry for a parallel web that would work better on mobile devices. Websites use HTML to describe web pages, WAP sites use WML, a much more limited language tuned for the lower capabilities of mobile devices at the time. Most mobile devices didn't offer full web access (Danger's Hiptop phones were notable exceptions), so carriers expected mobile devices to support WAP.

6

LIFE AT GOOGLE

So now the Android team was at Google. All they had to do was hire lots of people, build out the rest of the product, and ship it. Easy!

Not quite. In fact, Android started out at Google pretty much as it had existed outside of Google: it was a small, secret project that nobody knew anything about. They just happened to work on the other side of the badge-access doors. Android wasn't acquired to help fill out an existing group that was already doing this work; they were hired to *start* that effort.

At this point, the Android team was just eight people, only half of whom were actually writing code to build the product. They needed to figure out how to grow from a small startup pitching to investors into a department of people building and shipping products.

Part of that transition included finding their way in the new company. Tracey Cole said, "We were in building 41 in the hallway for a long time. It was weird. They kinda just left us alone."

Swetland concurred: "The biggest thing was, for a month or two, just figuring out how to find our feet. We moved from a ten person startup to a 4,500 person company. We spent the first two weeks camping out in conference rooms because they didn't have permanent offices allocated to any of us. Where do we work? How do we hire people?"

Hiring was the next step: Android needed more people. But hiring Android engineers proved to be difficult at Google.

HIRING AT GOOGLE

Google has always been famous in the tech world for its hiring process. Around that time, there were billboards up and down the main artery of Silicon Valley, Highway 101, displaying a cryptic math puzzle:

$$\left\{ \begin{array}{l} \text{first 10-digit prime found} \\ \text{in consecutive digits of } e \end{array} \right\} \text{.com}$$

This equation greeted drivers at that time along Highway 101 in Silicon Valley.

The puzzle confounded drivers. There was no mention of Google, just a puzzle that would lead successful solvers to a recruiting site for the programmer-focused company.

An engineering candidate lucky enough to get their resume past the recruiter and into the system faced potentially multiple interviews, including a phone screen and in-person interviews with various engineers.

Google has always held the belief that smart software engineers can do any kind of programming work. This is why engineers that are experts in 3D graphics have ended up working on Japanese text implementation. Their skills and experience get them the interview, but the actual job they end up doing is based on the things that need to be done.[1] It's also why Google interviews test general knowledge of computer science fundamentals (algorithms and coding). These interviews skip what other companies view as a required step: grilling candidates about their domain expertise and the shiny items on their resume.[2]

This approach serves Google well in general because much of Google's software is based on similar systems, so engineers can fluidly move from one group to another. It's all just software, and any specific product knowledge is something that smart engineers can pick up on the job. So Google hires

---

[1] It was also typical, at that time, to not even know what you were going to work on until you started at the company. Sometimes it might be days or weeks into your orientation before you were matched with a team.

[2] One candidate that I brought in (many years later) met me for lunch on the day of their interview. They were pretty shaken; apparently the interviews weren't going so well. I asked them about it. "Nobody's asked me about my experience. Nobody!"

clever engineers without looking for particular domain skills, assuming that they can learn what they need to do their job when they get to Google.

This hiring technique didn't work well for Android. The type of engineer that is good at, say, creating algorithms for data analysis on servers may not have any idea about how to build an operating system. Or how to write a display driver. Or how to optimize graphics operations, or UI code, or networking. These topics aren't necessarily covered in the computer science fundamentals that most undergraduates take, and they are also not things that arise in typical jobs that engineers have prior to arriving at the Google interview. Fadden said, "One of my interviewers told me that Google likely wouldn't hire me because I was 'too low level.' We had a lot of trouble hiring device UI people because it's very different from web UI."

The skills needed to build a platform like Android are those developed through jobs and hobby projects that people took on because of their passion in these particular areas. The engineers that write operating systems are engineers *that want to write operating systems*. There are courses taught on the subject, but they are not taken by everyone and are necessarily cursory; only those who really love OS development will end up learning what they need to do in jobs and projects that they take on outside of classrooms.

Android needed specialists; there was not enough time to train a large team of generalists. For the project to have a hope of succeeding in a world with such strong competition as the mobile field had at that time, Android needed to deliver a finished product as soon as possible. They needed to build the platform quickly, which meant they needed to hire domain experts who could dive right in and get to work. But specialists who excel in writing an operating system don't necessarily sail through Google's generalist interviews.

Another problem was that Google, at that time, also expected an academic pedigree; the company preferred candidates from top engineering and name-brand schools. Specialists coming in with great experience, but a non-traditional education didn't fit the mold and had a hard time making it through the process. This created problems with many early-Android team members, who didn't have the academic credentials that the Google recruiters expected. Many of them didn't have a college degree at all, much less one from a top-tier engineering school. Fadden said, "One 10+ year industry veteran had his hiring stalled because his undergraduate GPA wasn't high enough. For a company that favors Stanford PhDs, it was quite a shift to buy a startup where only one of the engineers graduated from college."

Chris DiBona, who was working in Google's open source office, was brought in to help fix the hiring problem.

CHRIS DIBONA AND THE HIRING SOLUTION

Chris had a checkered academic past himself; he'd dropped out of college with one class left[3] when he moved to California years before. He had become a community organizer for Linux user groups in the area, which eventually got him noticed by Google in 2004. Thirteen interviews and three days later, Chris started at Google.

Chris became a regular contributor to Google's hiring committees, which make hiring decisions based on feedback from applicants' interviews. "I was seen as a useful person. If it was too permissive, I was the hard guy. If they were too harsh, I was the easy guy. So they would bring me in to balance out a hiring committee. And I was friends with the recruiters and the admins."

Chris's manager asked him, "Can you help Andy figure out hiring?"

Chris had already been through this difficulty with another group at Google: the "systems and platforms" team. That team also looked for specialists, like Linux kernel developers, so Chris had an idea of how to fix the problem.

"We'd spun up this 'platforms' hiring committee that was the source of unusual hires—people who were deeply specialized, but not very broad. But we needed them."

Chris took Andy to that hiring committee, telling him jokingly, "When the recruiter says, 'No, no, no, this person's too specialized, we need someone who can go do all kinds of things,' then you say to her, 'If they want to leave my team, I'll just fire them.'"

Andy didn't actually say that to the recruiter, nor did he fire people for being too specialized. In any case, there wasn't going to be a problem; Google was growing, and there would be an increasing need for all kinds of engineers, on Android and on other teams. So they encouraged the recruiter to accept those people anyway, and it worked. In the first year, that committee

---

3. Chris eventually completed his bachelor's as well as a master's degree much later, while working at Google.

hired about 200 people for Google, many of them for Android. People with the skills that the Android team needed were routed through that more specialized hiring committee.

But getting people through the hiring process was only part of the problem. There was also the added complication of just getting the right people to apply. Google was known at the time for search and ads, along with some web applications like the new Gmail app that launched the previous year. As Dianne Hackborn put it, "I'd never thought about working at Google, because I don't care about search and web stuff." Joe Onorato (who worked with Dianne at PalmSource and later joined her framework team at Google) agreed: "When I applied to Google in 2005, my girlfriend asked why Google has so many people. 'They have a website with one text box and two buttons!'"[4]

Also, Android remained a confidential project. Even inside of Google, most employees didn't know about it.

The Android group at Google couldn't advertise that it was looking for developers to help write an operating system, or a developer platform, or even a mobile phone. Sometime later, the company was rumored to be working on a "Google phone," but that's about all the rumor mongers knew, and the team wasn't allowed to talk about it. Instead, they would quietly reach out to former colleagues and tell them that they should apply.

Mathias Agopian (another person from Dianne's team at Be and Palm-Source who joined Android in late 2005) talked about the word-of-mouth recruiting process: "The few ex-Be people who were at Android were like, 'You have to come!' but couldn't tell us what they were working on. 'Just come!'" Once Mathias and others from Dianne's team were at Google, they recruited her with similar vague offers: "They came to me and said, 'You should come over to Google—there's really cool stuff going on here!'"

David Turner, who joined the project in 2006, was able to discern more when he interviewed: "Many of the interviewers I had were engineers on the Android team. They didn't want to tell me why I should join the company, so I asked them what they had done at previous companies, and . . . they told

---

4. Google still has that same text-box-and-two-buttons search page, although there are now a large variety of other projects that Google is known (and rumored) to be working on that attract a wider variety of software developers. But in 2005, search, ads, and web apps were about it.

me. So after six or so interviews, I had a good feeling that Google was indeed starting a new project for a smartphone or a PDA."[5]

TOM MOSS AND HIRING IN TOKYO

The difficult hiring situation for Android wasn't specific to the Mountain View headquarters. Nor were the creative solutions.

Tom Moss (who was working on business development for Android) spent several months in Japan. Tom said, "We knew that the race was to get to scale, and to do that we needed to go international. Japan was picked as our first proof point." Tom's role in Japan ranged from cutting deals with OEMs[6] and carriers to evangelizing to local developers and sourcing local content for the platform. He was also responsible for hiring, to bring developers onto the team that could handle localizing the platform for Japan, plus related engineering work.

He took on this role both to help some of the partner relationships in that part of the world and to get more engineering talent for the team. In addition to the normal hiring difficulties, the candidates in the Japan office had to be not only top-notch engineers, but also fluent in English. The language requirement made the pool even smaller than it would have been otherwise. External hiring in Japan for Android just wasn't working.

To encourage internal employees to apply to Android's open roles, Tom gave a tech talk at the Google office in Japan. He described Android and the team's culture and pointed out that Android was a top priority project for Google. By engaging engineers directly, he was able to quickly hire several engineers from other teams like Maps and Chrome.

Despite the difficulties finding the right candidates and getting them through the process, the hiring story wasn't all bad; Google was willing to be creative to get the right people on board. Mathias Agopian was actually planning to go to Apple when he interviewed at Google. "I interviewed at Apple at the same time as Google. They even made an offer, which I took. It was going

---

[5.] PDA = Personal Digital Assistant. This type of device, of which the Palm Pilot was probably the most successful incarnation, carried useful information like a calendar, contacts, and note-taking apps. PDAs basically went away once smartphones became common and provided a superset of PDA functionality plus communications.

[6.] OEM = Original Equipment Manufacturer, a company that makes the actual hardware.

---

to be for the graphics team, before the iPhone. I was really happy because I thought I'd finally be able to work on Desktop again. BeOS was a desktop OS. I didn't really like that mobile stuff.

"But because of my visa situation, they retracted their offer. I was at the end of my six years on the H1-B.[7] To stay, they would have had to do a green card, and it was complicated.

"Google had the exact opposite approach. I told them initially that my visa situation was complex. They said, 'Whatever—let's do the interview first.' I did the interview, they made an offer, then I explained the situation. They said, 'We never did that before. That's challenging.' Instead of saying 'That's too hard,' they were saying, 'Something cool to do!' They said if it didn't work out, I could work from Europe for a year. I even got a fallback offer letter from the Zurich office!"

---

[7] Mathias said, "Actually the 6 years were expired. I was only allowed to stay because the green card process was pending. I couldn't leave the country for any reason. It was a very stressful time."

PART II

BUILDING THE PLATFORM

The Android platform was built, necessarily, from the bottom up.

Much like it is tricky to build the penthouse apartment in a skyscraper before having the foundation and fifty stories below it, it was difficult to build Android applications without having the underlying OS kernel, graphics system, framework, UI toolkit, APIs, and other fundamental layers that those applications would need. Because there's nothing worse than walking into your new penthouse apartment and falling down all the way to street level.

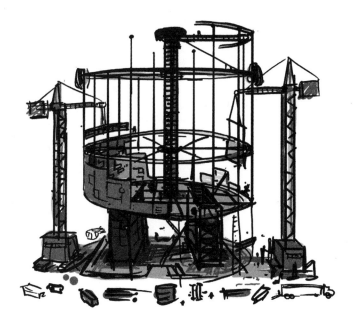

7

THE SYSTEMS TEAM

The systems team is responsible for the lowest layers of the software stack. You can think of their work as connecting the phone hardware (the Sooner, Dream/G1, Droid, and every other device that the team worked on) to the rest of the software running on each device.

At the bottom layer of everything running on Android (or any operating system) is the kernel. The kernel is a combination of the interface between the actual hardware and the rest of the system, plus everything that an OS has to do to make everything run (like boot up the system, create processes,[1] manage memory, and handle communication between processes). If a phone were a house, the kernel would be the foundation, the wiring, and the plumbing running through the walls, making that "drip, drip, drip" sound keeping you from getting back to sleep in the middle of the night.

Hardware communication is handled by *device drivers* in the kernel, which are software modules that talk to the actual hardware on a device. For example, in order to display pixels on the screen, a driver translates between the information from the graphics software (which figures out what color each pixel in the display should be to show, say, images, text, and buttons) and the physical screen hardware where those pixels live. Similarly, when

---

[1] Processes are essentially different programs. Each app runs in its own process, as does the system, the system UI, and every other separate software piece on the device.

the user touches the screen, that action is turned into raw hardware signals indicating the affected locations. These signals are sent into the system as *touch events*, which are then processed by software, including applications that want to handle those events.

One of the fundamental tasks of the systems group is *bringup*, which is the process of getting from simply having a piece of hardware (a phone, or even a prototype of a phone, with a collection of chips, circuitry, and a display) to one that boots the Android operating system.

BRIAN SWETLAND AND THE KERNEL

With Swetland's background in low-level systems, and the fact that he was the first person to join, it was only natural that he headed up the Android systems team from day one. Brian was already working and leading the systems efforts pre-acquisition; he continued in that role after moving over to Google and as the team grew.

The main work of the systems team was to get the kernel working, for the early Android devices and for every new Android device since.[2] When Android was a startup, the kernel needed to be just good enough that the demo could run. But after the team started at Google, they had to shift toward building a real product: a full OS and platform on top of a solid kernel.

Fortunately, Swetland ensured that the early prototype kernel provided a decent starting point: "Everything I was building was toward something that would eventually be a product. I'm not a believer in doing total one-off demos. We didn't have process separation,[3] but we knew where that was going to go. We still needed the kernel, the bootloader,[4] the graphics drivers, and

---

[2.] Or at least those devices that Google ships or assists with. This included the G1, the Droid, and all of the later Nexus devices. In the early days, the systems team also helped out with bringup for other manufacturers' devices, although these days those other companies have sufficient experience with Android to handle it on their own.

[3.] If processes are not completely independent, then stability of one application can affect stability of other, unrelated apps (or even the entire system). Also, you generally want separate processes for apps for security reasons; one application should not be able to access the memory (or data) of other applications.

[4.] The bootloader is the piece of software that starts the whole system—it loads the kernel and verifies that the filesystem is in a good state. It also runs that splash screen animation that you see as your phone is starting up.

---

everything. We did some demo-y things along the way, but we always tried to chart a path where it wasn't pure demo. It was progress towards a system."

Swetland's feelings toward demo-ware came from experience in previous companies where people on the business side misunderstood the difference between a great demo and an actual product. "The dangerous thing of building purely demo-ware is someone decides you're going to ship it. Then you're screwed."

So Swetland worked on the kernel that Android would build on top of: "We kept working with it [the kernel from the demo]. It's basically Linux off-the-shelf and then driver work on top of it. There are some patches in mainline Linux[5] from F-Sample[6] with my name on them that I submitted after I went to Google. We weren't thinking a lot about upstreaming[7] stuff in the early days."

Meanwhile, Swetland and his team started to see some tangible advantages to being part of Google. Prior to Google, "It was a little painful, as a tiny company making progress with TI [Texas Instruments]. The level of support was not what we got later." Then after starting at Google, "It became massively easier to get support from the vendors. Surprise, surprise. People stopped talking about how much we would have to pay to get development boards. They'd bring us hardware, which is kinda nice. That's one of the big advantages of Google, being this recognized name instead of this unknown tiny startup. People will pick up the phone and answer your questions. We still had to fight for support in places, but it could have been a lot worse."

One of the legends of Brian Swetland was how he "found" extra memory on the G1 shortly before it shipped. He submitted a fix in the run-up to the release, expanding the available RAM on the device from 160MB to 192MB, giving the OS and all applications 20 percent more memory to play with, which was a significant boost on this very memory-constrained system.

The trick was that he knew where to find that memory because he had hidden it in the first place. The kernel is responsible for making memory available for the rest of the system to use. When he first brought up the

---

[5] Contributions to the open source version of Linux.

[6] Texas Instruments hardware that early prototypes were based on.

[7] "Upstreaming" refers to pushing code into the open source repository. The team was more focused on just getting things to work at that time.

kernel on the G1, he configured it to report less memory that it actually had. To the rest of the system, there was effectively 32MB less memory for use than was physically available in the hardware. He did this with the certain knowledge that every developer would use all available memory if it was there, but they'd work within a tighter budget if they had to.

Everyone got their software working in this much smaller pool of memory, because that's all they had. When he freed the rest of the memory before the G1 shipped, that meant more was available for running more applications simultaneously, because he had forced the entire system into an artificially smaller space than necessary.

Nick Pelly, who joined the team later to work on Bluetooth, remembered that not everyone was happy how this worked out: "OMG the drama this caused. The Browser team had been pulling extra Sundays to fit into the (false) memory budget. I remember one of them storming into Brian's office with some loud and choice words when he 'found' that extra memory."

FICUS KIRKPATRICK AND DRIVERS

The kernel itself didn't need extra hands working on it. This might be surprising, given the complexity of the kernel and its importance in the overall system. But Linux was there already, and where it wasn't sufficient, Swetland was on it. But kernel *drivers*, on the other hand, were in serious demand. The system required all kinds of different hardware which had to be handled by the kernel. So when Ficus Kirkpatrick joined Swetland's team, he got busy writing drivers, starting with the camera.

"I was into OSes and low level stuff, which is the core thing that I was best at coming into Android. The first year or two [on Android] it was low level systems stuff. We had decided to use Linux, so there wasn't a lot of kernel work. So I was doing a lot of driver stuff. I did the first camera driver, got that working on OMAP.[8] Also got audio working." Once audio was possible, "We can pass buffers, or we can get camera data in, what are we going to do with it?" So Ficus moved onto the media framework, creating APIs[9] and

---

[8] The display hardware from Texas Instruments

[9] API = Application Programming Interface. APIs are the layer between applications and the operating system, the pieces that apps call to get to the functionality in the Android platform. See the discussion of APIs in the Jargon appendix for more information.

---

functionality for applications to be able to access the new audio and camera capabilities of the device.

ARVE HJØNNEVÅG AND COMMUNICATION

One of the missing drivers early on was for the radio[10] hardware; there was no way for the new phone OS to make a phone call. So Swetland brought in someone who excelled at communications drivers.

Arve Hjønnevåg joined Swetland's systems team in March of 2006. He was well known on Android for his . . . silence. His teammate Rebecca (who enters the story in a few pages) said she would sometimes ask him for help on a system they used for managing their source code. She got used to responding to his answers with, "Again, with more words."

Once Arve got the system talking to the radio hardware, he focused on power management. Specifically, now that the hardware was able to make and receive phone calls, it also needed to not fall asleep when the system was in the middle of a call.

At the time, Linux was great for servers and desktop systems, including laptops. But it wasn't built for phones, and it needed new functionality to handle this new use case. When you close a laptop lid, you want the laptop to go to sleep, completely. You don't want or need anything running on the system until you open the lid later.

But a phone is quite different. When the screen turns off, you don't want it doing everything that it might be doing when you're actively using it, but you do want it awake enough to, say, continue a phone call[11] that you are in the middle of, or to keep playing music that you are listening to.

So Arve added the concept of *wake locks* to Android's Linux kernel, to ensure that screen-off didn't mean completely-off. Android would aggressively put applications and most of the system to sleep when the screen turned off (because battery consumption was always a huge concern), but wake locks ensured that the system could stay in a wakeful state if there was something happening that needed to continue even if the screen turned off.

---

[10] Just to be clear, "radio" here doesn't mean FM, AM, and ad-filled morning DJ shows. Radio is the term used to describe the hardware in the phone that communicates with the carrier network and cell towers.

[11] Depending on whom you are talking to

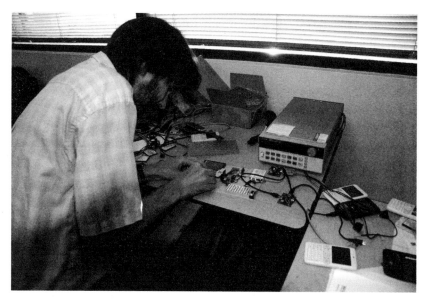

Arve debugging G1 prototype hardware in October of 2007, with a TEK battery emu-lator and several pre-G1 devices ("Sooners") (photo courtesy Brian Swetland)

Arve submitted the wake lock feature into Android's version of Linux. This feature caused a bit of a stir in the Linux community, as some stalwarts of that open source community saw this feature as an example of Android forking[12] the Linux kernel. Chris DiBona (who dealt[13] a lot with open source projects) remembers talking to people from the community at a Linux conference around that time. "There was one guy who was spitting mad, 'I can't believe you're doing this!'

"I was like, 'Three years from now, this won't be a problem. In between now and then, either the Linux community will accept our patches in the shape they're in right now, they'll modify them slightly, maybe they call them something different, or you'll leave behind every mobile device in the

---

[12] Forking is a common term in software, where a particular version of some system is copied and then altered, essentially causing a fork in the road where there are now two (or even more) versions of the system with different features and functionality. It's an unpopular approach in the open source community, because everyone should contribute to the one-true version instead. But sometimes, as in the wake lock example, you may need to fork just to make progress while the larger community decides what to do.

[13] And continued to deal; Chris went on to become the Director of Open Source at Google.

market. So work with us to make something that's acceptable. Otherwise we're going to keep shipping because it's very important to us that this has a decent battery life.'"

In the end, Linux didn't take Android's wake lock implementation directly, but they did implement something that solves the same problem.

ILIYAN MALCHEV AND BLUETOOTH

Display drivers were another problem that the systems team had to solve. It doesn't help having a powerful operating system if you can't see what it's doing. Iliyan Malchev got to work on this problem when he joined the team.

Iliyan learned to program when he was eight years old in Bulgaria, using a language he did not speak. His parents got a computer for their home and Iliyan started playing around with it. "It was amazing; I'm banging on the keyboard and things are happening on the screen—that's what really got me interested in it. I didn't know what I was doing. It's not like I immediately became a programmer. In Bulgaria, everything was Cyrillic alphabet. Everything [in program code] was in the Latin script, like program listings. I didn't speak English or know the Latin alphabet, so I'd just copy it, letter by letter."

Iliyan made his way to the US for college and ended up working at Qualcomm for a few years. This experience was incredibly helpful to his later work on Android, and for the systems team in particular, since Android devices use a lot of Qualcomm hardware.

Iliyan joined Swetland's systems team in May of 2006. His first project was getting a secondary display to work: "[Swetland] tosses me a flip phone with 2 displays. He said, 'make the peripheral display work.' Being Swetland, he booted Linux on this without any docs. I guess he just wanted to give me something to get me off his back."

After that project, Sooner devices[14] started arriving on the team. Iliyan worked on getting hardware input working on the device: a D-Pad (up/down/left/right arrows) and a trackball. In the meantime, he noticed that Android was getting too big to fit in the device's limited storage space, and the system was constantly growing, so he spent time optimizing the size of the system to make things fit.

[14.] Sooner was the original device that Android was targeting for 1.0, with the G1 (codenamed "Dream") being the second device. The Sooner was eventually dropped, which is described in Chapter 37 ("Competition").

The Sooner device, complete with hardware keyboard, D-Pad, and many, many buttons

He then worked on Bluetooth. This included making the driver work for the Bluetooth hardware, as well as the Bluetooth software that applications could use to talk to the device. "This was the first Bluetooth software on Android and it was . . . not very good. [Bluetooth] is a terrible standard. They invented something of the scope and complexity of the internet to essentially support wireless headphones. It's so over-engineered. I did that, then I handed it over to another engineer, Nick Pelly. Nick took the Bluetooth stack and made it work. He deserves all the credit."

NICK PELLY AND BLUETOOTH

Nick studied computer science at university in Australia but didn't think he'd end up programming for a living. He lined up a job at Telstra in communications engineering that was going to start after returning from a post-graduation gap year, traveling around the world.

But while he was traveling in California, his Telstra job fell through, so he needed another option. He was always curious about Silicon Valley, so he quickly put out feelers for interviews in the area. Only one company responded: Google. Fortunately, he got the job and started in 2006 on the Google Search Appliance (GSA) team.

Ficus and Iliyan debugging . . . something in August of 2007 (photo courtesy Brian Swetland)

GSA was one of the products that Google thought they'd make their money on early on, when their main product was the search engine. They sold a rack-mounted piece of hardware to companies that would index their internal documents. It extended the power of Google's internet search into companies' internal websites. But then Google got into the ad business, and GSA quickly became less of a focus. By the time Nick joined the team, the product was not being as actively pursued as it once was, but Nick admitted that "It was a fantastic way for a new engineer to learn the Google search stack."

In the Summer of 2007, he attended the first presentation from the Android team to the rest of Google on what they were doing. Nick was hooked. "I had no relevant background. I was one of the first people who joined the team who had not worked on consumer electronics before, who had not worked on platform level stuff like San and Rebecca and Mike,[15] who came from the Google platforms team. I only had one and a half years of serious professional experience.

[15.] San, Rebecca, and Mike, who also worked on the systems team, are introduced in upcoming sections.

"But I came to them, and I was like: 'This is awesome. I'll work on anything. What do you need help with?'

"Brian said: 'Bluetooth!'

"I knew they were too ambitious, and that they'd fail. I told my girlfriend and my Mum: 'No way it'll work. But the people are great and I'll learn a lot.'"

Nick took on Bluetooth and quickly owned it. "It was such a steep learning curve that once I began to catch on, I was stuck with it." He had to make Bluetooth work not only as a driver, but through the platform and application layers of Android. One of the hardest, and continuous, parts of the job was to make it work correctly with the wide variety of peripheral Bluetooth devices in the world.

"Most Bluetooth peripherals ship with oodles of 'quirks' (bugs), and never see a firmware update. So we had to work around the issues. I came up with a simple policy—every time a Bluetooth interoperability bug was found, I would purchase the device, add it to the collection at my desk, and include it as part of my manual testing. Pretty soon I had two extra desks jam-packed with Bluetooth devices. I'd keep them all plugged in charging—this ensured I didn't lose obscure chargers, and that I never had to wait to charge a device before running a test. On more than one occasion I had to clear them all out when we got word of a fire warden inspection, due to all the daisy-chained chargers.

"The car-kits were a bit harder since you can't fit a car in an office. But I soon discovered the major automotive manufacturers would happily ship me Pelican cases containing the guts of a car's infotainment system so that I could test against the relevant hardware from my desk. They overflowed my desk and into various corners of the hallway."

Nick's manager was Brian Swetland. Swetland was, like many managers in those early Android days, not very hands-on. This included resisting sync meetings with the people on his team, as Nick recalled: "I remember a few weeks in, asking if we'd ever have a 1-on-1. He didn't seem too happy with the question, but said I was welcome to schedule one. I did. He turned up ten minutes late and his first words were 'I $#^&()# hate 1-on-1s. . . . ' We didn't have 1-on-1s after that.

"Yet I remember Brian as one of my favorite managers to work for. His systems knowledge was second to none. He was generous with scope and responsibility and did not micro-manage. He was dedicated to building the phone and was tremendously loyal and good to his people. Working for Brian was a highlight of my career."

Nick catching a nap in the office in March of 2008. In the upper left is a car infotainment system, in the protective case shipped from the auto manufacturer. (Picture courtesy Brian Swetland.)

SAN MEHAT AND THE SD ROBOT

It's a hundred degrees, it's summertime, I'm looking at this phone and I'm listening to this person say garbage over and over again.

—SAN MEHAT

More help for drivers, and system bringup overall, arrived in the form of San Mehat. San joined Swetland's team in 2007, around the same time as Nick, in the run up to the SDK[16] release.

San learned programming when he was a kid by typing randomly on a keyboard. His parents had a computer store in their basement, where he'd play around on the machines. "I was frustrated one day and I just mashed on the keyboard. By accident, I hit ctrl-C, and that dumped me to this prompt, and I had no idea what that was. Start typing stuff, it says 'Syntax Error.'

[16.] Software Development Kit: This is a general term for application development. It's a bundle of whatever tools, libraries, and APIs developers need to write, build, and run their applications. Android's first public SDK was released in the Fall of 2007.

I'm like, 'What does that mean?' I type something else, it says, 'Undefined Function Error.' I'm like, 'What does that mean?'" His cousin suggested that he type 'LIST,' and the BASIC code for the game he was playing printed out on the screen.

San's approach to learning programming ended up being a great experience in building drivers. A lot of the work in writing hardware drivers is figuring out what the hardware can do and how to get it to do it. Much of that work is experimentation, to understand how the hardware works and what the rules and protocols are to talk to it. San was figuring out how those rules worked from the beginning, by typing randomly onto the computers in his parents' basement just to see what happened.

He continued his programming education in childhood with hobby projects, like cracking software copy protection schemes. He did this as a workaround for having limited access to games, since Canada didn't have a strong software marketplace at that time. He kept programming through high school and afterwards by working on kernels and drivers for chips and other hardware systems, always learning more about how to make the software talk to the hardware.

San didn't go to college. Ironically, it was an internship created to show kids the advantage of going to college that convinced him not to.

He got an internship (which led to a summer job) working with Bell Northern Research (BNR) on a CPU simulator, where he learned new programming languages and internals of processors. He was so enthusiastic about the work that he wanted to eventually work at BNR, but he realized that his grades in high school would never get him into the kind of college he needed to go to to get a job there. So he decided to skip that step and do it all on his own instead, and started an Internet Service Provider (ISP) with some friends. Along the way, he kept hacking on operating systems and random pieces of hardware, building up the skills that make a good driver developer.

"Give me a weird piece of hardware that you don't really know how it works, and give me some piece of software that can make it work. Between taking apart the software and analyzing the hardware, I can reverse-engineer and create another driver that works."

In 2005, San joined the platforms group at Google, where he wrote drivers for custom hardware. In 2007, he moved over to Android to work on Swetland's systems team.

"I joined to work on the G1. Initially, that was in the form of the 'franken-board,' the Qualcomm 'surfboard,' which was this big, crazy prototype phone board, which was the MSM chipset[17] on a big breakout. It was like a phone, but exploded out with all kinds of test points, so they could load code into it and do all kinds of stuff."

San performing thermal testing on a battery (with a lighter), in February of 2008. The Qualcomm "surfboard" for the processor in the G1 is on the desk, in the background. (Picture courtesy Brian Swetland.)

When he started on the team, San's main job was bringup. "Bringup at that time was the really, really low-level stuff. The clock control and power rail, power control." That first system, the G1, was unusually complicated. There were actually *two* CPUs on it, one controlled by Qualcomm's controller chip (an ARM 9), and one controlled by Android (an ARM 11). Booting the G1 required first booting the Qualcomm chip, then booting the Android chip.

"My job was to figure out how to build the drivers. I had to figure out how to have these two things talk to each other. Then get the clock control hooked up, get the power rails hooked up so we could start turning on peripherals,

---

[17.] MSM = Mobile Station Modem, a Qualcomm System on Chip (SoC) that integrated all of the mobile hardware needed.

like the SD[18] controller so that the SD card could come up, and the graphics controller. So I did all the low-level nitty-gritty stuff, and then moved on to the SD Card."

The SD card on the G1 presented an interesting problem. First, the SD card was useful for two separate things: storage and Wi-Fi. SD cards are mostly thought of as removable storage. But at the time, SD was also sometimes used to provide Wi-Fi (the card would have a Wi-Fi chip instead of memory hardware).

Getting SD to work was important, because it controlled both of these areas. But it was difficult. "No one [on the Android team] knew how SD cards worked. You couldn't get the specs on SD cards, because to get the specs you had to join the SD association, and they wouldn't let you do anything open source.[19] So I had to reverse-engineer the SD card, the SD card protocol, and the SD IO protocol [for Wi-Fi], and reverse-engineer a bunch of drivers, to figure out how to write my own driver. I spent months figuring out how to make it work."

San got SD working (for both storage and Wi-Fi), but there was a problem. The SD card on the G1 was very accessible to the user, so it could be popped in or out at any time. "Someone had decided that having the SD card on the side, hot-swappable, was a good idea. If you try to pull a hard drive in and out of a Linux system, you're gonna have a bad time. This was the worst: device ripped out with almost no warning. You could be writing to the disk. Maybe you took a picture thirty seconds ago, so those buffers were still in the OS page cache, and they're not gonna get written out for another thirty seconds."

There was a cover on the G1's SD Card slot that users had to open before popping the card out. Opening that cover sent a signal into the system, which could be used as a cue to quickly get everything into a stable state in case the user popped the card out. But it was difficult to find all of the places in the code where this needed to happen. To make things worse, debugging the situation required a lot of tedious card-popping. Over, and over, and over. Eventually, San asked for help.

[18.] SD = Secure Digital, an abbreviation for SD Card, which is still used for removable storage in things like cameras (and some phones).

[19.] This was an overall requirement for Android that spanned everything the team did. If the code couldn't be open sourced, then it couldn't be part of the platform.

He reached out to Andy: "'Hey, you're into robots. Do we have someone that could make me a robot that could do this?' He hooked me up with someone. I told them what I needed: a little bot that allows me, through software, to control how it goes in and out, and then I would create a little closed-loop test. That allowed me to track down all of these bugs." San used the SD card robot to chase those bugs one by one until the system worked reliably.

San's SD Card robot, which continuously popped the card in and out of the slot to force crashes that San could debug (picture courtesy San Mehat)

POST-G1: SAPPHIRE AND DROID

After the G1 shipped, San started work on the device code-named "Sapphire," which would become the T-Mobile G2 MyTouch. The main work for that device was performance. "It was slow as shit. It was a little bit faster than the G1, but at the same time, Romain,[20] bless his heart, and all these other turkeys [in the platform and apps teams] were putting all this crazy thicker software on top of it. So switching apps, it was always janky and laggy. I spent a lot of time on that project optimizing the kernel. So it was really lots of performance improvements. It was kind of rinse and repeat."

After the G2 shipped, San's next challenge was the Motorola Droid. One of the problems that he had to deal with was handling power-off scenarios, which was . . . complicated. "These little bastards have like thirty different

---

[20.] San is talking about Romain Guy, whom we shall see more of in Chapter 14 ("UI Toolkit").

power domains in them, and they're all individually controlled. To turn the thing off, it's a delicate dance of: *this* off first, wait so long, *this* off, then *this* off, then *this* off . . . All the way, as you're going down, the phone is getting dumber and dumber.

"The failure case on Droid was this: the phone would idle to sleep, or you would turn it off, and you would get a phone call at the same time and your phone would never ring. We would be going down these power states and we would stop listening to the modem because we would turn that off. The modem would try to wake us up, but we're not listening to the modem anymore; we're committed to going to sleep. So we go to sleep, and the modem's like 'But, but, but, but . . . !'

"We realized eventually that the hardware was missing a wire between the modem and the CPU to actually tell it to wake up." It was way too late[21] to change the hardware, so they ended up hacking around the problem by sending the wakeup signal on wires used for other parts of the system.

Another part of working on the Droid involved a bug that San chased in the Wi-Fi system, which was causing hiccups in video. "There was that Miss America pageant with that very controversial comment about marriage between a man and a woman. Hiroshi comes into my office and was like, 'We got this big problem. YouTube videos are glitching, only over Wi-Fi.' I'm like 'Okay, no problem, it's probably a DMA[22] thing. Give me a reference video.'"

Hiroshi gave him the video and the time at which the glitch occurred, which happened to be that awkward segment of the Miss America pageant. San spent 2 days debugging it, listening to that same video segment over and over. "Whenever I hear someone mention Miss America, I get this visceral [feeling of] being in Walnut Creek, it's a hundred degrees, it's summertime, I'm looking at this phone and I'm listening to this person say garbage over and over again."

---

[21] This is a fundamental difference between hardware and software development. If you find a bug late in the cycle before software ships, you can still fix it. In fact, you can even fix bugs after it ships, as long as you have a way to get that update to your users. But with hardware, that bug is there to stay; you cannot usually re-spin a piece of hardware, at least not without causing massive delays and costs to reproduce the hardware. So usually, hardware bugs are handled by figuring out software workarounds.

[22] DMA = Direct Memory Access, a type of memory that can be accessed without directly involving the CPU. This is useful for memory-intensive hardware subsystems such as storage and displays, which can read and write memory directly while the CPU is busy with other tasks.

REBECCA ZAVIN AND THE UNLOVED DEVICE

We built this safe. We just forgot the walls.

—REBECCA ZAVIN

The systems team needed more reinforcements for the push to ship 1.0. Rebecca Zavin joined the team in early 2008.

Rebecca started programming much later than many of her teammates on Android; she didn't really get into it until college. She always figured she'd become a doctor, so she went to college to get a pre-med degree in chemical engineering. That's when she discovered that she hated chemistry. In the meantime, she got a job in the computer science department at the college, helping set up a computer lab. She started hanging out in that department more and more. Once she started taking classes in CS, she was hooked.

After college, Rebecca went to grad school, and eventually joined Google, working with San in the platforms team. About a year after San left her team to join the Android team, Rebecca was also up for something new. "I wanted to be a little uncomfortable. A little bit challenged." She joined Swetland's systems team in January of 2008, two months after the SDK shipped, and just in time for the long push up to 1.0.

The first day on the new team, she was in the office debugging a problem in the kernel until after 9:00 pm. "Swetland was like, 'Alright, this is going to work.'"

The team had just shipped the SDK; now they needed to make everything work on a real device. Rebecca initially worked on display drivers for Android. Swetland gave her a minimal driver to start with. After banging on it for a while, she complained to him that it was really buggy. He told her it was just a prototype; she wasn't supposed to actually use it. She said, "I wish you would have told me that. I assumed you knew what you were doing."

After getting the driver to work, Rebecca moved on to work on the memory subsystem, which she continued working on for the next few years. Her goal was getting bits to flow through the system with the minimum number of copies (because copy operations are expensive). For example, if the camera takes a picture, there are a lot of pixels in a buffer somewhere that need to be sent to the GPU (the graphics processor), then to the video decoder, and finally to the display memory. The simplest implementation copies the pixels to each new subsystem along the way. This takes a long time, and a lot of memory, especially since pictures tend to be large (even with the more limited cameras of that time). Eventually, she made the system work with zero copies.

After the G1 shipped in late 2008, Rebecca started working on the next device: the Motorola Droid.

The Droid was an unloved project and device. The rest of the team was working on the device code-named Passion, which became the Nexus One. Passion was going to be a Google phone, with all the latest and greatest features, and the team was really excited about it. And then there was this Motorola device.

Rebecca said, "No one wanted to touch it. It was ugly. Everybody was really excited about Nexus One. And the Droid thing? We were left to our own devices. Shortly after, it became a big deal for the team, because it became the first Verizon launch."[23]

The chipset was from TI, which had drivers for the chips. But there was an alternate implementation of those drivers from Nokia, which Rebecca recommended that they start from.

"We had a three-way meeting with Motorola where I told them, 'I don't think we should use this TI kernel; it's a mess. I think we should use this Nokia Kernel.' I got a call from our TI sales guy who said, 'Motorola called me and they said that you said our code was shit.'

"I said, 'I don't think that I used any expletives in the meeting.'"

THAT EMBARRASSING ROOT BUG

One of the hallmarks of early Android development is the raw speed at which the team executed. Going from nothing to 1.0 in three years was astonishing, especially when that first release contained most of the fundamentals that would ensure that Android would soon become one of the most widely distributed operating systems in the world.

I have found that the probability of spilling coffee on myself is proportional to the speed at which I'm moving. There are trade-offs that come with execution speed. In those early days, everyone was running so fast that they sometimes failed to notice things that might have been caught in a

---

[23.] That launch involved a lot of marketing dollars, a lot of publicity, and, eventually, a lot of Android devices being sold and used. There's more about the Droid story later, in Chapter 45 ("Droid Did").

---

more cautious and slower-paced environment. One of the examples of this dynamic was the famous (at least internally) "feature" of being able to reboot the phone from the chat app.

Jeff Sharkey and Kenny Root were external developers when 1.0 launched (they were both hired onto the Android team later on). They were tinkering with Android, even before that first release. Kenny had developed an SSH client (an app that allows you to log into a remote computer). Kenny's version had been built against an earlier, pre-1.0 version of the SDK. Jeff updated it to work against later builds of Android and added more functionality. They eventually published it as ConnectBot, one of the first applications on Android Market,[24] where it is still the top SSH client.

When they were first working on ConnectBot, they received odd bug reports from some of their users. Jeff said, "We got this weird bug from someone saying they'd SSH into their server at home, type reboot, and their phone would reboot. We thought they must be smoking something, and closed as Not Reproducible."[25]

But the bug turned out to be totally valid, and more than a little scary for Android.

Rebecca Zavin said, "People discovered if you typed root[26] in Gchat[27] you could get root access on your phone. And then people realized that it also worked when you typed shutdown. Or reboot."

[24.] Android Market was the name of the original application store. It was later renamed to Google Play Store.

[25.] Bugs for a software product are filed in some kind of bug database. That's where the engineer(s) add more information to the bug that helps diagnose the problems. Bugs are ideally closed (eventually). In the best case, they are closed as Fixed. In the worst case (for the person that filed the bug), they are closed as Working As Intended (meaning, "Yes, you are correct, that's the way it behaves. And we think that's the correct behavior."). But the most frustrating closure case, for everyone, is Not Reproducible, which means, "We believe you . . . but we can't see the problem on our devices, and we can't fix it if we can't cause it to happen in the first place."

[26.] Having root access on a computer allows you to do things that you can't as a regular user, like delete important files, or shut down or reboot the system. You can't usually get root access by just typing root (hackers love a backdoor security hole in a system, but being able to get root so easily is less of a backdoor and more like a front door which has been left ajar).

[27.] Gchat was the informal name used for Google Talk. Gchat was eventually replaced by the Hangouts application and, more recently, Google Chat.

Rebecca explained how the bug came to be. "The keyboard events were sent to a console that was left open. You always wanted to have some serial console.[28] It was convenient. So we put the root console there for debugging... and should have made a note to turn it off.

"At some point, we had this ongoing bug where we used to have the framebuffer console support there, so you could switch to a mode where you could see the log, same as you can on your Linux PC. We had this recurring bug where you'd get a black square in the upper left corner. It was a timer issue. Some race condition[29] would cause the cursor to blink when you came back to graphics. So I'd get Steve Horowitz [telling me], 'That black square. I got a black square!'

"After spending a lot of time trying to fix the problem, I was like, 'Let's just turn off the framebuffer console. Why do we need to see the kernel log on the screen on the device? This is stupid. Let's just turn it off and then we don't have to deal with this problem.'

"But when we turned off the console, it was still there [just invisible]. We all were like: 'Uh-oh, oops!'

"We built this safe. We just forgot the walls."

Jeff said, "The person typing reboot into ConnectBot was effectively typing it into both their remote server, and into their phone, which explains the surprising reboot."

Nick Pelly remembered the bug: "We thought it was some subtle, clever hack that someone had figured out. No, no, no: every single keyboard press you made was going into root shell."

Kenny Root added, "This probably opened the way for the first 'root' of the G1, but I promise it wasn't named after me."

[28.] A serial console is a terminal window, like the DOS window on Windows or the Terminal application on a Mac, where you can type commands into the system.

[29.] Race conditions are a common cause of software bugs. The underlying problem is two different, potentially unrelated, parts of the software (or of the whole system) trying to access the same resource at the same time. But since they are running independently (on different threads in the same process, or even in different processes), it's impossible to predict which one will get there first. The general approach is for the code to be flexible enough to handle any possible ordering of accessors. The problem is that it is easy to not think about ordering problems in random spots in the code, and race conditions can be infrequent, so you might never see them occur, they just happen elsewhere, when you don't happen to be watching the device screen. Which is also a type of race condition.

Rebecca debugging in March of 2008 (photo courtesy Brian Swetland)

There are other examples where Android missed some of the details along the way; everyone was running very, very fast and there was a lot to do to just get things working. Fortunately, the platform has survived long enough that the team has been able to go back and fix the problems over time. At least the ones we know about.

MIKE CHAN AND THE B TEAM

We felt we were going to change the world. And we did.

—MIKE CHAN

The final member to join the systems team prior to 1.0 was Mike Chan.

Mike first wanted to become a programmer as early as middle school. When he saw the game *Lode Runner*, he wanted to write video games when he grew up. That dream didn't last long, however; in high school, he was more interested in administering computer systems. But in college, he took programming classes and returned to his original plan of becoming a programmer. Landing his first job out of school at Google sealed his fate.

He started at Google in 2006, joining the platforms team that San and Rebecca worked on. Like them, he also eventually transferred to the Android group, arriving a month after Rebecca, in February of 2008. The SDK had already launched, but there was still a lot of work to do to get the product to 1.0.

SECURITY BLANKET

Mike's starter project was to make Android secure prior to shipping 1.0. No pressure.

Android was built from the start with security in mind. Swetland specifically wanted to implement a more secure model for Android than he had worked with at Danger. Those Hiptop devices were even more resource constrained and didn't have hardware facilities to protect apps from each other, so they relied on software mechanisms. Brian insisted that all Android hardware had to have an MMU[30] to provide hardware security instead.

Another important aspect of security on the platform was treating all applications as separate "users" on the device. On other operating systems, users would be protected from each other, but not from themselves. So, for example, you could create a user account on a PC and the data that you created in that account would be protected from other users on the system. However, any application that you installed would run as you, so all of your applications would have access to all data in your account. There was an implicit trust between any user and all of the applications they installed.

But the Android engineers felt (rightly so) that the applications on the device should not be inherently trusted. So rather than having apps running as the user who installed them, Brian's design had each app run as a separate, unique user on the device. This approach guaranteed (through the Linux kernel mechanism of user IDs, or UIDs) that apps had no automatic access to the data of any other application on the same device, even though those other applications were installed by the same device owner. Brian provided a low level service to create, destroy, or run-as-a-user. Dianne Hackborn, on the framework team, integrated this service with higher-level application permissions and built out the policies for application UID management.

---

[30] MMU: Memory Management Unit. This piece of hardware translates from the memory addresses used by a process to the actual physical memory on the device. This approach ensures that one process cannot read or write memory (intentionally or not) in any other process because it has no physical access to it.

This system of hardware-protected processes and applications-as-users was mostly set up and working, but there were many details that needed to be polished. For example, although the application processes were protected from each other, many of the built-in system processes were running as users with elevated permissions, giving them access to more than they strictly needed on the device.

In the meantime, the iPhone had recently been jailbroken,[31] which was a good reminder to complete this security work before they shipped 1.0.

Mike thought the project was not only a great introduction to Android and security models of operating systems; it was also an introduction to Swetland's management style, "Brian has an interesting way of throwing you into the deep end and figuring out if you can sink or swim."

As starter projects go, it was . . . a big one. Not only was there pressure to get it done, because it clearly had to happen before shipping the first device, but it was something that affected everyone else building the platform and apps on Android at the time. The pressure was on. "As I was trying to make changes, I was breaking stuff left and right. It was super painful. All the teams would be complaining that something's broken and I'm trying to fix this as fast as I can, trying to anticipate it.

"Steve Horowitz [Android's engineering director at the time] was all over me. 'You broke the build!' I'm like, 'I know, Steve. I know I broke the build. I'm trying to fix it now. Having you stand there is not going to make me fix it any faster.'

"That was a trial by fire. Learned a bunch of stuff, touched all parts of the system, and broke everything."

Mike's next project was improving battery life. At that time, coming up to the launch of the G1, the battery life was awful. To make things worse, all of the teams were blaming the other teams for the problem. "Apps team would blame the framework team. The framework team would blame the systems team. The systems team would blame the apps team."

Andy didn't care whose fault it was, he just wanted it fixed. He gave the problem to Swetland, who gave it to Mike.

[31.] Jailbreaking refers to modifying the OS to remove or change software restrictions on the device, enabling things like installing applications not available on the App Store (known as sideloading).

Brian asked, "How much do you know about power management?"

Mike said, "I don't know anything, Brian."

"Well I suggest you start learning, because you're in charge of this thing now."

Mike quickly realized that part of the problem was one of expectations. "The problem I explained to everyone was: You're telling me we have to have just as good battery life as the iPhone. We have this capability to run all these apps in the background,[32] the hardware that we have has a bigger screen, we run background tasks, we were the first to do 3G, and we have a physically smaller battery."

One of the main things that Mike did was add instrumentation to the system to know where the power was going. Prior to this, they could see the battery was being drained, but had no idea who was doing what, so it was difficult to find and fix the root problems. Once they knew where the problems were, they could go address them.

Mike also had ongoing debates with Dianne, on the framework team. Many of the battery problems were coming from poor behavior in apps, which would do things like hold a wake lock[33] too long, but the users would just blame Android overall. "I was pushing for a more explicit system where if an app goes into the background, you force-release the resource. So basically a less flexible platform. Dianne was under the firm belief that it's not the platform's fault, it's the developers', and the right fix is to educate all these app developers.

"This was a battle we had for years."

The other project that Mike worked on was the *governor.*

A governor in an OS is the mechanism by which the speed, or frequency, of the CPU is changed to save power. For example, if your CPU is running really fast, it is consuming more power and thus more battery. But if the device is idle at the time, that's a large and unnecessary waste of battery power. The governor exists to detect these different runtime modes and scale the CPU frequency accordingly.

---

[32] At the time, the iPhone did not allow this. It was a distinguishing feature of Android in the early days.

[33] Wake locks (which are discussed earlier) keep the system from going to sleep. They are a powerful and necessary part of the system, but can cause serious power problems when used incorrectly, because they keep the system awake when it would otherwise go to sleep and use less power.

When the G1 launched, the only governor in effect was the *ondemand* governor that was part of core Linux. It was a simple system with just two settings: full-speed and idle. This was better than nothing, but wasn't good enough for Android's purposes, especially since the heuristics for that governor were tuned for Linux running on server or desktop machines, not for the more constrained world of mobile devices.

Mike started playing with the governor in the late stages of 1.0, but had to put that project aside after an unfortunate incident of a demo that Andy gave to the Google execs.

Mike had checked in a change that inadvertently made the phone painfully slow. "I was experimenting on master[34] with the conservative governor, which skewed very, very heavy towards saving power at the cost of performance. The phone was pretty much unusable."

Meanwhile, Andy had a monthly review with Larry and Sergey to show them the status of this project. Andy flashed[35] a build of master onto a phone and went off to his meeting.

At the meeting, he showed a demo using that build, which . . . did not go well.

"He came back, he was pissed off."

This incident was a great learning experience for Mike. On one hand, he learned the importance of testing his changes before pushing them on everyone that might use that build. But also, he learned how important it is to have a supportive manager.

"Brian stood toe-to-toe with Andy in the hallway, screaming back that it was his fault for using master without any testing. We're doing all of this stuff to launch Android on time, we don't have the time to make sure your

---

[34] The "master" branch is the main one into which all code changes go. There are often other branches of the build, for specific devices or situations, but master is where the main product code is checked in, built, tested, and released. Checking a change into master is how you ensure that everyone gets it in their builds and devices (for better or worse).

[35] Flashing is the term used in Android to mean installing a build (Android devices use "flash memory," thus the term). If you had a build on your computer, you could flash from the computer to a phone (with the phone plugged into the computer on a USB cable). There were also "flash stations" set up in the Android building where you could flash any of the recent builds onto a device. It was useful to be able to install different builds for testing purposes, or sometimes because the build you flashed previously was . . . not a good one, as this story illustrates.

demos are perfect. I never saw anyone yell at Andy. He never brought my name up. He knew it was my code.

"He later came back to my desk and calmly told me to revert all my changes and not touch this until after we shipped."

THE B TEAM

Mike joined Rebecca on the Droid project. The systems team was split between the people working on the Passion (which became the Nexus One) and the Droid. Swetland remembered, "I had decided that we needed to split the systems group into two teams to distribute work between N1 and Droid, and introduced this at our team meeting by saying, 'We'll need like an A team and a —'. Before I could back that up and reword it better, Erik[36] completed 'B Team!' and much to my horror they adopted it as a badge of honor (possibly also because it embarrassed me)." The people on the Passion project were mostly those people who had more familiarity with that hardware. But Rebecca joked that the Droid project had the "B Team," because they were working on the device that the team wasn't excited about. Passion was getting all of the love and, well, *passion* from the team at the time.

Mike said, "Everyone assumed Nexus was going to be the big phone that was going to land: the first Google-branded phone, no keyboard, really slick design, OLED screen. It was a good phone."

Meanwhile, the Droid hardware design was underwhelming at the time. "It was always hyped up that the design was going to be so amazing. When they finally unveiled the design, it was this ugly square thing. I remember thinking, this is just the initial prototype. There's a new one coming with the final design. Right? No, this is the design we're shipping with."

In the end, Verizon's branding and marketing for the Droid overshadowed anything that Google did for the Nexus One. More on that in Chapter 45 ("Droid Did").

BUILDING A ROBUST SYSTEM

It's worth reflecting on the approach and accomplishments of the systems team before moving onto the rest of the software stack. For one thing,

---

36. Erik Gilling was another member of the systems team at that time.

everything they built was fundamental to the rest of the OS even being able to power up, much less function. But also, the approach they took to their work was indicative of an overall theme in Android of doing a complete (if quick) job, beyond the immediate needs of the day and looking forward to what they envisioned (or hoped) Android would eventually become.

For example, they didn't just work on the one or two devices currently in the pipeline. At the same time that the rest of Android was focused on the Sooner and Dream phones being developed prior to 1.0, the systems team was getting Android to work on completely different devices, making it more robust and flexible for the future world of manufacturers with completely different hardware.

Also, the team didn't just plug together drivers from hardware manufacturers and ship the result; they wrote everything from the ground up to be solid and robust.

Nick talked about this dynamic on the team: "Why wasn't the systems team just an integration team? Integration is more about plugging things together to make them work, taking the drivers from manufacturers and getting Android to work on them, rather than writing the drivers themselves.

The port of Android to this Nokia device was what Swetland called "the holiday port," which happened over Thanksgiving weekend of 2007. (Picture courtesy Brian Swetland.)

"We were writing a whole bunch of device drivers that many other companies wouldn't have written; they would have just taken the reference Linux driver that the silicon provider hands over. Back in that day, those reference Linux drivers were total shit. It was a key decision that we weren't just going to take those reference drivers; we were going to rewrite them to be at a quality that could be upstreamed and that we could stand by, maintain, and support. The rest of the ecosystem could follow our lead and fork our drivers or just reuse them.

A port of Android to a PC, in March of 2008. Landscape laptop screens don't show the portrait-mode phone screen in the best light. (Picture courtesy Brian Swetland.)

"We ended up with much higher quality drivers. Sure, we had some bugs, but we got to stability. If you have shitty drivers, it costs you stability— peripherals will randomly fail, the device will reboot. And it's very hard to do power management correctly without good drivers and without wake locks and things like that; you just destroy the battery life.

"That was one of the key decisions that I think largely Brian was responsible for that set us on the right path. We're building out a high-quality codebase here, and we're doing things the right way."

8

JAVA

We came back from Christmas break. I got in pretty early, bright eyed and bushy tailed, and talked to Rubin. He informed me that he and Brian had dinner during the week off and that they'd decided that we were going to write everything in Java.

—JOE ONORATO

LANGUAGE CHOICES

The choice of a programming language for Android was probably more tied to Android's growth than might otherwise be obvious. After all, a programming language is just the medium to input the information to the computer: Does it really matter?

Yes, it does. Experienced programmers can and do pick up new languages all the time. But even these experts develop patterns that make them more efficient with languages that they know well. And the effect of middleware, or utility libraries that developers can carry from project to project, can't be discounted. The fact that a programmer can depend on some library[1] in one

---

[1.] The concept of libraries is discussed in the Object-Oriented Programming section of the Jargon appendix.

project and then use it to bootstrap other projects means that they can be more efficient and productive on every new project because they don't have to keep re-inventing the world.

The choice to use the Java programming language[2] was important, because at the time Android was released, Java was one of the major languages used by software developers around the world. The fact that Android allowed these developers to use their existing language skills to write applications on Android meant that many developers could avoid the ramp-up time that learning a new language would have entailed.

But this language choice was not obvious or immediate in the early days of Android. There were actually three languages being debated internally.

First of all, there was JavaScript. In fact, in the beginning there was *only* JavaScript, because Android, at the start, was a desktop app written on and around the web's programming language.

JavaScript is the programming language that developers use to write the code that is on the web pages that we visit. When we see something moving on a browser page, that animation is usually powered by JavaScript code. But JavaScript is a bit, er, messy, as real programming languages go. It's easy for a developer to get things basically working with JavaScript, but some of its fundamental concepts[3] make it more difficult to program larger systems.

After work began on the real platform for Android, there was a choice of which language to use: JavaScript , C++, or Java.

C++ was attractive because many developers know it and it's used in low-level programming tasks to this day. C++ developers have a lot of control

---

[2] Hereafter written as simply *Java*, because "the Java programming language" is entirely too long and cumbersome. The distinction to understand, and the reason that we tend to use the longer form when we talk about the programming language of Android, is that there is a *Java platform* offered by Oracle, which includes the language, the Java runtime (*hotspot*), and the implementation for the set of libraries that Oracle (previously Sun Microsystems, which was acquired by Oracle) developed. But the only one of these used by Android is the language itself; the runtime is completely different, as is the set of libraries implemented in the Java language that developers can use in their applications. But rather than bog down the readability of the book, and artificially bulk up its word count, by writing the *Java Programming Language*™ everywhere, I'll simply write Java. Just know that I mean the language.

[3] I always enjoy reading the foreword of a book, because I like the context that it provides about the author and the topic. My favorite sentence out of all of the tech book forewords I've read was this bit from Douglas Crockford in his preface to *JavaScript: The Good Parts*: "Thanks to XYZ [the inventor of JavaScript], without whom this book would not have been necessary."

---

over important aspects of their application's operation, such as memory allocation. But the flip side is that developers have to manage this kind of information in their applications. If they allocate memory to store an object (say, an image), they have to make sure they deallocate it when they are finished. Failing to do this (an all-too-common problem in software) can lead to *memory leaks* where memory is dribbled away and the application simply grows without bound until it uses up everything available in the system and fails when the system has no more memory to offer.

Java is a programming language built around the concept of a *runtime* or *virtual machine (VM)*, which handles all of the tedious bits about memory management that C++ programmers have to handle on their own. In the image example above, the Java programmer simply loads an image, which causes the memory to be allocated. When the image is no longer being used, the runtime automatically *collects* that memory, which is known as *garbage collection*. Java developers can ignore details of memory collection (and leaks) and get down to the business of writing their actual application logic.

Another reason for the team to consider Java was the existence of J2ME,[4] the Java-based platform that ran on various devices already. Ficus Kirkpatrick said, "At the time, to be on a phone and to get these carrier deals, you had to have support for J2ME." Choosing Java provided some ability to run J2ME code on the platform, which was considered useful at the time that Android was first being created.

Finally, powerful tools for writing Java code were available for free, including Eclipse and NetBeans. On the other hand, C++ didn't have good free IDE[5] support. Microsoft offered VisualStudio, which was a great tool for C++ development, but it wasn't free, and Android wanted to appeal to all developers without requiring expensive tools.

The first plan was not to have just one language, but to offer a choice. Again, Ficus: "Our original idea was that we were going to do everything in a language-independent way. You were going to be able to write your apps in JavaScript, C++, and Java. Eventually we realized there were like twelve of us

---

[4.] J2ME = Java 2 Platform, Micro Edition, also called *Java ME*. See the discussion about Java ME in the Jargon appendix.

[5.] IDE = Integrated Development Environment, discussed in the Jargon appendix.

and we were never going to make that work. So we said 'OK, we have to pick a language.'"

Andy Rubin saw the choice of just one language as a simplification for developers. Swetland said, "We were toying with some concepts of doing Java and C++. Andy felt very strongly that we needed one language, one API, so as to not confuse things. He saw Symbian[6] with their n different toolkits[7] as confusing."

These were the technical details and merits that factored into the debate. The actual decision was a bit less formal; Andy made the call and told Swetland over dinner one evening.

The language choice was a good example of how quickly decisions were made on Android. In part, it was because it was Andy's call, and Andy tended to make hard decisions that the organization would then scramble to execute. But more important, decisions were made quickly so that the organization could simply move on and do the rest of the infinite set of things that needed doing. The language choice had been debated internally for a while, and there was no right answer, but simply having a decision was more important than everyone being happy with whatever decision that was. So Java was it, and the team moved on.

Ficus said, of the decision: "It didn't really feel like much of a choice, given that the carriers wanted to see support for J2ME[8] apps and this kind of ecosystem that existed at the time. And some of us had worked at Danger before, on the Hiptop, and we knew that we could make Java perform on a low-end device."

Dianne Hackborn remembers when the decision was made: "Andy, very rightly, said, 'We cannot do three different languages. That's ridiculous, and we need to pick one. So we're going to do Java.' There was a lot of drama about that. No one cared about JavaScript, but a lot of people cared about C++."

---

[6] Symbian was the operating system used by Nokia and some other manufacturers. There were different flavors of the platform available, which made it difficult to write applications for it, since it wasn't clear which capabilities a given Symbian device would have.

[7] *Toolkit* is often used to refer to the visual/user-interface capabilities of a platform. The terms toolkit and framework are further described in the Jargon appendix at the end of the book.

[8] Android never ended up supporting J2ME applications. By the time Android was released, J2ME was no longer a factor (this was not related to Android, but there was simply no interest in that platform in the post-iPhone smartphone world).

The choice of Java made sense for various reasons, including team expertise. For example, the engineers from Danger had learned how to write an operating system with that language in an efficient way for those earlier, very constrained devices. In the end, with this and many other decisions, the team took a pragmatic approach. As Dianne said, "Not because anyone loved it, but because it's what made sense to make the platform successful, and then the team adjusts."

Although Java was chosen as the primary language for Android development, there was (and still is) a lot of code written for Android in other languages. Much of the platform itself is written in C++ (and even some limited parts in assembly language). Also, most games are written in C++, as are some other apps, in full or in part. C++ is a popular language with many developers, because it offers some performance advantages for low-level code, as well as integration with existing C++ libraries and tools. But the main language, especially for most non-game applications, became Java, and that's what all of the Android APIs were written in and for.

Not everybody was happy with the language decision. San Mehat wasn't a big fan of Java, especially for the low-level systems programming that he did. "I didn't have a problem with the language itself. Well, maybe I did, inasmuch as it hid all the details that were important to writing code that scaled and ran well." He ordered a new license plate for his car, JAVA SUX. "When you go to get the license plate, they [the Department of Motor Vehicles] ask you what it stands for. I said that I used to work for Sun and we made this Java thing, and it stands for Secondary User Extensions, and they said 'Okay.'"

San's license plate. San was not a fan of Android's language choice. (Picture courtesy Eric Fischer.)

RUNTIMES

To understand runtimes, you need to understand something about programming languages. Programmers write their code in whatever language they choose (C, Java, C++, Kotlin, Python, assembly . . . whatever). Computers don't understand these languages; they understand binary code (0s and 1s) . . . and that's it. The binary code represents instructions that the computer executes, like "add these two numbers." In order to convert from typical programming languages into the binary-encoded instructions that the computer understands, programmers use tools called compilers.

Compilers translate from whatever language the programmer uses into binary instructions that the computer understands. So, for example, you can take a chunk of code written in C and compile it into a binary representation for a PC such that that compiled C code will run on that PC.

That same compiled code may not run on a different kind of computer, like a Mac, or a Linux server, because that other computer may not have the same kind of CPU, so the binary instructions the compiler generated won't make sense on that other system. Instead, the original source code needs to be compiled into a different binary version for each different type of hardware you want to run it on.

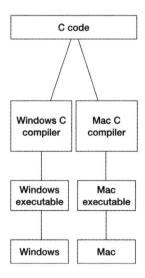

Separate compilers create unique executables for every type of machine on which the code will be run.

Along comes Java. The Java compiler translates source code not into machine-readable code, but into an intermediate representation called *bytecode*. This code can be executed on any computer platform that has an additional piece of software running on it called a *runtime*. The runtime interprets the bytecode and translates it into the binary representation of that computer, essentially compiling it on the fly. This ability to run on different hardware is what Sun Microsystems (the company where James Gosling was working when he created Java) called, "Write once, run anywhere." Code would be compiled into bytecode that could then run on any target computer with a Java runtime.

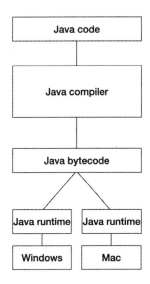

Java code only needs to be compiled once. This produces a single executable that can run on all target machines that have a Java runtime.

Since the Android team wanted to use Java, they also needed a runtime. In fact, they went through several of them.

At first, the team simply used existing runtimes. The first of these was Waba.[9] Later on, the JamVM[10] virtual machine was substituted for Waba.

---

[9] Self-described on its open source website (*waba.sourceforge.net*) as "a small, efficient and reliable Java Virtual Machine (VM) aimed at portable devices (but also runnable on desktop computers), written by Rick Wild of Wabasoft."

[10] JamVM, by Robert Lougher, is also open source, available at *http://jamvm.sourceforge.net*, where it is described: "JamVM is an open source Java Virtual Machine that aims to support the latest version of the JVM specification, while at the same time being compact and easy to understand."

Mike Fleming had joined by this time and helped get JamVM going: "Dan Bornstein's VM wasn't going to be ready for a while and we were going to write an awful lot of code. If we were going to be a Java platform, we needed to have something to run with for a while. Swetland and Fadden helped me out." JamVM was used by Android until, in 2007, the Android runtime (Dalvik) was up and running.

DAN BORNSTEIN AND THE DALVIK RUNTIME

Open a file, bang a few keys at random, then debug until complete.

—DAN BORNSTEIN (ACCORDING TO ANDY MCFADDEN)

Although Waba and JamVM were sufficient for prototyping and early development, the team wanted their own runtime that they could control and customize as they needed. Brian Swetland was involved in the runtime that was written at Danger, but he had his hands full with kernel and systems work for Android. So the team hired Dan Bornstein, whom Brian had worked with at Danger.

Dan (known to the team as "danfuzz") had taken over the runtime from Brian at Danger. "Not long after I was hired, I started referring to myself as 'Brian Jr.' He really didn't like it ... which is why I kept saying it."

Dan was introduced to programming at the age of seven. He and his brother just wanted to play video games, so they eventually talked their parents into getting an Apple II, which the parents thought would be both a game and an education machine. The parents apparently won, because Dan didn't just play games; he started programming them: "I totally wrote crappy video games, mostly text and low-res graphics." Both Dan and his brother eventually became software engineers.

Dan worked at various companies in Silicon Valley through the 90s and early 2000s, including Danger, where he worked on (wait for it ...) a runtime for the Java programming language. So he was a natural candidate for that work on the Android team when he joined in October of 2005.

Dan's first task was to evaluate the possible options. It wasn't obvious to the small team on Android at that time whether they could simply use something that already existed (either open source or some technology that they could acquire) or whether they needed to build something in-house.

Dan started working on both of these options in parallel, evaluating existing runtimes while also building a runtime from scratch.

Although Waba and JamVM worked well for quickly enabling the team's use of Java, they were not seriously considered as long-term options. Both runtimes interpreted Java bytecode directly. But the team felt that there were performance and memory gains to be had by converting the Java code to another, more optimal format. A new bytecode format meant a new runtime, so Dan got busy making that happen.

Dan began work on a new runtime, which he named *Dalvik*: "I had just finished reading an issue [of *McSweeney's*], which consisted of English translations of modern Icelandic fiction. So I had Iceland on the brain. I looked at a map of Iceland and tried to find something that was short and pronounceable, and didn't have any of the weird characters, and I found Dalvík[11] (or 'Dal-veek,' as it's pronounced). It sounded like a nice little town."

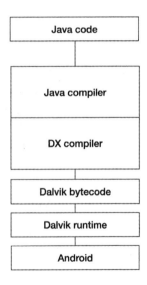

Java code written for Android went through two compilation steps: one to create Java bytecode, and the next to convert that to Dalvik bytecode, which would then run on Android's Dalvik runtime.

Instead of running Java bytecode, the Dalvik VM ran another form of bytecode compiled from Java bytecode. There were efficiencies in size to be gained in having their own bytecode format, and space on the device at that time was at a premium. The Dalvik bytecode required an additional

---

[11] Dan said, "An Icelandic guy once berated me for misspelling it. I told him the town is spelled 'Dalvík' but the VM is spelled 'Dalvik.'"

compilation step (using another compiler, called DX) to get it into the form readable by Dalvik, called dex.[12]

Dan Bornstein, outside of the town of Dalvík, Iceland. In the period between finishing work on the G1 and the device actually shipping, Dan took a break from working on Dalvik to visit Dalvík. (Picture courtesy Dan Bornstein.)

Eventually, Fadden pitched in to help with the runtime. "Danfuzz had the bytecode converter working reasonably well and needed someone to step up and write the VM. I volunteered, but pointed out that I knew very little about Java and VMs, and wasn't quite sure where to start. He said, 'Open a file, bang a few keys at random, then debug until complete.'"

Dave Bort, another engineer on the team, wrote the first version of the Dalvik garbage collector. That garbage collector shipped with the runtime in 1.0 and was the basis for several years of refinement and optimization.

Throughout this time, the runtime was constantly changing out from under all of the Java code being written for the platform. From Waba to JamVM to the nascent Dalvik runtime, major shifts were happening, but code kept running. Romain Guy remarked that even though the team was changing a huge and critical part of the system,[13] "I don't remember running into showstopper

---

[12.] dex = Dalvik Executable, the bytecode format understood by the Dalvik runtime on Android.

[13.] Changing the runtime while the rest of the team is writing software that runs on it is somewhat like brain surgery, except instead of fixing the patient's brain, you replace it with a different brain, sew them back up, and have them drive back to work immediately.

---

bugs, or even bugs at all. I don't remember anything else on Android being that stable." Dan replied, "Some amount of the nature of that layer of the system helps with that—if the VM's not working, shit just falls over."

ZYGOTE

One of the things that the Dalvik team created to make Android work for 1.0 was (and still is) called Zygote.[14] Zygote is like the loaf of bread you slice when making a sandwich. You could, of course, bake the bread from scratch every time you made a sandwich, but that's a lot of effort and time spent every time you want a sandwich. It's obviously much faster and easier to have a loaf that you can just cut slices from to jump-start each sandwich. Zygote is like sandwich bread for applications.

Dan had this idea, which came from a feature of Emacs[15] (a popular text editor on Unix systems), where it would allow you to dump the state at any time and then start up Emacs later from this saved state (cleverly called *undump*). This meant that Emacs could start much faster because it just sucked in the state from disk instead of running a bunch of code logic at startup time. "My idea was that we implement an undumper-type system as made most 'famous' (at least to me) by Emacs. Mike [Fleming] said, 'How about we skip the part where we dump to disk and reload?' And he ran with it." Mike got the system up and running, dramatically changing the way that applications started. Instead of each app loading in all of the code they required, and initializing it as it was loaded in, the Zygote system created a single process with much of the core platform code, essentially pre-loading and initializing all of it. Whenever an application launched, the Zygote process would be *forked* (duplicating itself into a new process), resulting in an almost immediate launch to that early stage of the new application.

Bob Lee (who worked on core libraries, the subject of the next chapter) said of Zygote, "It was just so simple! It's like one API call! The reason we

---

[14.] Wikipedia defines zygote as, "A eukaryotic cell formed by a fertilization event between two gametes." Which helps not at all. But it later says, "contains all of the genetic information necessary to form a new individual," which is a little closer to its meaning in Android.

[15.] Emacs is a classic text editor favored by a certain segment of programmers. Other programmers favor one called vi, and still others feel strongly about the one that comes with their IDE. A very tiny portion of programmers don't care, and prefer to save their religious fervor for non-text-editor-related issues. Like the use of spaces versus tabs when indenting code. Don't get me started.

were able to do that was that the memory was copy-on-write.[16] So as long as you didn't touch those memory pages from that initial Zygote process, all that memory would be shared across the whole OS. It was just such a clever, beautiful solution to leverage stuff that was already there."

The system didn't quite work as intended at first. Bob chased down a problem with the garbage collector: "After one garbage collection, I was like, 'My app's taking up so much memory again!' It was because the garbage collector would touch every memory page." That is, the normal efforts of the runtime would write to pages in memory that needed to stay read-only for the shared-memory approach of Zygote to work.

Fadden came in with a fix for this. Each new process would separate the heap from the garbage collector after the Zygote stage, excluding it from the memory that the garbage collector examined. The shared memory portion didn't even exist in the new app, so it wouldn't get touched.

After this, Bob and Fadden continued to work on Zygote, to figure out which classes[17] needed to live in Zygote to get optimal sharing out of all applications. Bob said, "I modified the VM and added some instrumentation, so I could say, like, how long every class initializer is taking, and figure out how much memory each class is allocating, and then an algorithm would decide which classes to preload. You don't want to take up too much memory for the shared processes that's only ever going to be used by one app."

Bob credits Zygote for Android being at all functional at that time: "The Zygote thing helped a lot, just being able to share memory, going from having just a couple Java processes running to having dozens running on a really small device. And rather than having to wait for a whole VM to start up, our apps actually looked faster; they would launch instantly, because we'd just fork a process and start right there. Everything was already warmed up." Eventually, Zygote contained not just code, but also shared data such as images, and continued providing memory and startup benefits to Android as the platform grew.

---

16. Copy-on-write is an optimization where a common resource can be shared by completely different clients as long as none of them writes to it (making a change). So as long as everyone was simply reading Zygote data/memory and not making changes to it (which was the general idea), it never needed to be duplicated, avoiding an expensive copy operation.

17. The concept of classes is discussed in the Object-Oriented Programming section of the Jargon appendix.

9

CORE LIBRARIES

H aving a programming language for the platform is one thing. And it's a pretty big thing, especially when it's a language that most developers already know. But programmers also want to have standard utility functions so that they don't have to reinvent everything every time they write an app. A programming language gives you the ability to encode logic (like condition statements, loops, equations). But higher-level functionality like data structures, or networking, or file reading and writing is the job of the core libraries.

Although the Android team adopted the Java language, they were explicitly not using the implementation of the libraries that shipped with Sun Microsystems'[1] version of Java, called the Java Development Kit (JDK). The JDK comes with, say, an ArrayList class that implements a simple data structure that is common in programming. But Android didn't use those classes, so they needed to provide their own.

BOB LEE AND THE JAVA LIBRARIES

When Android needed standard Java libraries, they brought in a Java expert working elsewhere at Google: Bob Lee.

---

[1] Sun was acquired by Oracle in April of 2009. But the company was still independent at the time of this work on Android, so I'll continue to refer to it as Sun.

Bob (also known as "Crazy Bob"[2]) started programming in middle school, in the early 90s, mostly because he wanted to write video games. He soon picked up various programming languages and in high school moved on from video games to building a website for a nearby college. The college was so impressed that they gave him a full ride to the school to continue that effort. But college didn't suit Bob, so he left and started consulting, along with writing books and popular Java libraries, which eventually landed him a job at Google in 2004.

Bob wanted to work on mobile technology, so after a couple years on the Ads team, he switched to the Android team, starting in March of 2007.

When Bob joined, Android was still using the JamVM runtime, before the Dalvik runtime came online. The *core libraries* were basically a collection of random utilities that people wrote for one-off purposes. "They were totally incompatible. Somebody would need something and they would just implement what they needed. They kind of resembled the Java libraries, but they were obviously missing a lot."

Fortunately, there were a couple existing options for more standard libraries, so Bob and the team evaluated them. "We looked at GNU Classpath, but we ended up going with Apache Harmony.[3] There was a lot of stuff that wasn't great about it, so it was a matter of rewriting parts of it, and we would contribute those back. Like we rewrote ThreadLocal [and] Runtime .exec(). Rewriting that stuff and merging it back was a big part of it.

"There were also APIs added to the core Android platform by other engineers on the team just because it seemed like a good idea at the time. If someone thought something might be potentially useful, they would put it in there. And there was some really bad stuff."

An example of this was WeakHashMap, a data structure class that developers use in memory-constrained situations, like Android at that time. It offers an advantage over the traditional HashMap class by automatically cleaning up (garbage-collecting) objects which are no longer used. Like a Roomba for your memory heap, cleaning up the trash you leave behind. Note that "weak"

---

[2] Bob had used this nickname since high school and even used it as his corporate email address.

[3] GNU Classpath and Apache Harmony were both open source libraries for the Java programming language.

here is taken from the term "weak reference," which is an object that can be garbage-collected when it is no longer in use.

Joe Onorato, on the framework team, added the WeakHashMap API. Sort of. He said, "I had this library that depended on WeakHashMap, and I needed to link[4] it, so I created a class called WeakHashMap." The problem was, Joe's class wasn't a "weak" HashMap, it was just a standard HashMap. It subclassed HashMap and didn't add any of the logic that would have made it weak. Sometime later, Jeff Hamilton (also on the framework team) was writing code that needed the functionality of WeakHashMap. He saw that the class existed in the core libraries, used it, and had memory problems that required a lot of debugging until Jeff discovered that Joe's WeakHashMap class wasn't cleaning up memory at all. It was just a regular HashMap, which didn't do the garbage-collecting work that Jeff expected.

Bob continued, "I know the Android APIs could be a lot better . . . but they could also have been so much worse." Much of Bob's time was spent preventing these APIs from becoming public. "I would find and just remove all that stuff from the API. If there was a class that was only used by one app, I would move it back out into that app—if you weren't going to use it [from multiple apps], it didn't belong in the framework libraries."

As part of making the core libraries work, Bob implemented significant networking functionality, fixing bugs along the way. One of those problems prevented every phone from starting up at all. "The first time you started a phone, it had to connect to a time server, but the time [on the device] was set to sometime in 2004." The phone would try to connect to the server through a secure connection, which requires a security certificate on the server. But the initial time on the phone was before the time that the certificate was issued on the server, so the connection would fail and the phone wouldn't boot. Bob's fix was to catch that failure condition and set the initial time on the phone to the day that he fixed the bug.

Bob also tracked down a networking problem that was specific to mobile data. Android phones were experiencing severe outages that seemed like a problem with bad carrier network infrastructure.

[4.] Compiling code involves a *link* step, in which the code is built along with all of its dependencies. So if code refers to a class, then that class must be reachable by the compiler for compilation to succeed.

Networking protocols have built in fault-tolerance, because networks can go down, or packets of data can get lost or delayed. Android was using the *congestion window* approach in Linux that responds to an outage by halving the size of the data packet, and halving it again, and again, until it gets a response from the server that packets are going through. Then it doubles the packet sizes each time they succeed until packets are eventually back to the full size.

This algorithm is reasonable for regular internet traffic, where latency (the delay between sending a message and receiving a response) is measured in milliseconds and outages are infrequent. But it doesn't work well for cellular data, where it's common to have high latencies of a second or more, and where brief outages are common. Bob did some profiling and investigation to track down the problem. After failures decreased the packet size, "it would double the size of the buffer every time it had a successful packet. But with high latencies over mobile networks, you had one or two second round trip times over 2.5G or 3G back then. So it was only scaling up the buffer every time it made a successful round trip. It'd take like 30 seconds to scale the buffer back up after you had some kind of outage."

JESSE WILSON AND THE TERRIBLE APIS

We spent a long time taking these APIs and re-implementing them from scratch to be good, while maintaining their existing terrible APIs.

—JESSE WILSON

Bob worked by himself on core libraries for a while, but eventually, after 1.0 shipped, he got some help. Josh Bloch[5] joined his team in late 2008, and Jesse Wilson joined in early 2009.

Jesse Wilson was working on the Google AdWords product with Bob before Bob joined Android. "Bob got out of AdWords to go work on Android

---

[5] Josh is famous in the software world for a couple of reasons. For one thing, he is the father of many of the APIs in Java itself, having worked at Sun Microsystems during the early days of Java's development. Also, Josh wrote *Effective Java*, which is perhaps one of the last programming books that people still buy and read (programmers having moved to a model of online search/copy/paste for most software problems).

when Android did not seem like a responsible job decision. I followed him there, more to work with Bob than to work on Android."

Bob and Jesse would eventually leave Android and Google. Bob became the CTO of Square. Jesse followed Bob once again and joined Square.[6] "He's got something on me, I guess."

Jesse described life on the core libraries team: "In the first year of Android, people just brought in whatever libraries they thought they needed, and put them in the public APIs. We have something called kXML, which is the pull parser. We have the org.json JSON library. The ApacheHttp client. We basically have 2006-vintage snapshots of all of these libraries, which have since gone on to introduce ten thousand features that make them too big for Android. Their current versions are incompatible in big, meaningful ways. If you're shipping a web server, you can control which version of the thing you're including; if you change it in an incompatible way, your client just changes it. Android's versioning is such that if we change an API in, say, the JSON library, even if the new API is better, the apps don't get to opt in or out of the API change, and so you have to be 100 percent backwards-compatible. So we spent a long time taking these APIs and re-implementing them from scratch to be good, while maintaining their existing terrible APIs.

"We inherited all the Apache Harmony code, and Apache Harmony was never really a shipping product. It was much more of an inventory to build a shipping product with. There was so much work to take something that was half-baked and make it correct.

"It was a lot of re-implement-and-optimize. The org.json code in the standard library, 100 percent of it was brand new. One day Dan Morrill came to me and said, 'Hey, heads up, the open source library for the JSON library we're using has this, 'The Software shall be used for Good, not Evil' clause[7] in it. That means it's not open source because open source has no discrimination against any endeavor.' So I got to go and re-implement it."

---

[6] It's only fitting that in this chapter Jesse once again follows Bob.

[7] *https://www.json.org/license.html*

10

INFRASTRUCTURE

One of the non-obvious parts about any software project, particularly a project that is being worked on by more than just one or two people, is the infrastructure that you need to actually build the product. *Infrastructure* can refer to a number of things, including:

BUILDING   How do you take the code that random engineers are constantly submitting and build the product? What if the product needs to run on various different devices and not just one? And where do you store all of these builds for testing, debugging, and releasing purposes?

TESTING   How do you test the product once it's built? And how do you test it continuously so that you can catch bugs that have crept in before they cause serious problems (and while you can more easily trace them back to when they were first submitted so that you can find and fix them)?

SOURCE CODE CONTROL   Where do you store all of the code? And how do you allow a team of people to make simultaneous changes to the same source code files?

RELEASE   How do you actually ship the product to the devices that need it?

Android needed people dedicated to solving these infrastructure problems.

JOE ONORATO AND THE BUILD

In the beginning, Android builds were cobbled together by a fragile and time-consuming system that built all of the constituent pieces for the kernel, the platform, the apps, and everything in between. This system was fine in the early days when there wasn't much to build, but Android was getting too big for it to work any longer. So in the Spring of 2006, Joe Onorato attacked the problem.

Joe figures he was destined to be a programmer, since both of his parents were MIT grads. "They met at the Tech Model Railroad Club;[1] it was love at first chat. It was pretty much obvious that I was going to be a computer scientist."

In high school, Joe worked on the yearbook with his friend Jeff Hamilton (a future Be, PalmSource, and Android colleague), making the first Jostens[2] yearbook that was entirely digital. Their system included a custom search algorithm and a digitizing system that simplified publishing while decreasing the cost for the students. Joe later worked (again, with Jeff) at Be, and then PalmSource, on operating system projects that were similar to what he would work on later at Android.

In late 2005, Joe wasn't excited about where PalmSource was going, so he reached out to a former colleague from Be. That person knew Swetland and got Joe routed over to the Android team. Joe got an offer, but wasn't sure what he was signing up for, so the recruiter got him in touch with Andy. After assurances of confidentiality, Andy told Joe, "We're going to make the best phone ever." That's when Joe joined the Android team.

Joe worked on several projects in those early times, including the framework and the UI toolkit. But in the Spring of 2006, he saw that the build system needed a serious restructuring.

"We had a big recursive[3] make build system, and I was like, 'Let's have a real build system.' It was somewhat controversial: is it even possible?" Fortunately, Joe had experience from Be. Be used a similar build system, which was written by a group of people including future Android engineer

---

[1] The club is a hacker community at MIT that dates back to the 1940s.

[2] Jostens sells school-oriented memorabilia like class rings and yearbooks.

[3] Definition: recursion: See [recursion].

Recursion is a common technique in software, in which a given function calls itself. A very simple example is that the sum of all integers up to some given integer x can be solved by adding x to the sum of all integers up to $(x - 1)$. Recursion is a powerful technique, but can be tricky to think through, and to ensure that it will actually terminate.

Jean-Baptiste Quéru (who was known to the team as "JBQ"). Joe remembered, "I think some of the Danger folks [who had also worked at Be] had left before that happened and thought that was an impossible thing to do. How could you have one make file that knows about everything? Like it's going to get all confused. But . . . it worked."

Joe dove in and made the build system work for Android, speeding it up and making it more robust in the process. The whole project took a couple months, resulting in a system called Total Dependency Awareness.

ED HEYL AND ANDROID INFRASTRUCTURE

The first monkey lab was my laptop and seven Dream devices. I wrote some scripts and tools to beat the shit out of them till they crashed.

—ED HEYL

The build system that Joe wrote worked sufficiently for a while. But as the team and the number of code submissions grew, there was a need for a system that could automatically build the product as developers submitted their changes. For example, if someone submits code that causes a bug, it's better to be able to build and test the product with just that change than to wait until after many other changes have piled on top of it, obscuring the root cause of the problem.

In September of 2007, to get the build and test infrastructure under control, the team brought in Ed Heyl, who was then working at Microsoft.

In college Ed studied computer science but couldn't wait to graduate. "I was looking to get out as fast as possible and get into the workforce. I did okay in school . . . but I excelled at work."

Ed joined Apple in 1987, where he worked for five years. "The company was in a really weird state. They were still making all their money off the Apple II, but all the mindshare was going into Mac." A few years later, Ed joined the Taligent[4] spin-out, followed by General Magic soon after, "right when they did their IPO. It set the record for IPO gain, and then nose-dived

---

[4.] Taligent was a company formed by Apple and IBM with the goal of providing a new operating system, at a time when Apple was trying to come up with a successor to the aging MacOS. Taligent eventually failed and Apple continued its attempts internally before eventually acquiring Steve Jobs's NeXT Computer and adopting NeXTSTEP OS instead.

in the months after. The company itself was not very healthy at that time. All the people were already kind of disenchanted. There was so much hype building up to the IPO that there was a lot of letdown."

Ed lasted at General Magic for about ten months, then joined WebTV. He stayed through the acquisition by Microsoft and another ten years until joining the Android team. At WebTV and Microsoft, Ed worked with future Android people, including Andy Rubin, Steve Horowitz, Mike Cleron, and Andy McFadden.

Ed started on the Android team around the time that the Android SDK was first released, in October of 2007. At the time Ed joined, Android already had an automated build system called *Launch Control*. Three times per day, it would take whatever code had been submitted and build it, producing a result that was then available for the automated testing system.

Launch Control was better than nothing, but it was nowhere near what Android needed. "It was something for QA to test, as opposed to a dashboard to show the state of the world. There wasn't a lot of traceability. Continuous integration[5] tries to build and test as much as it can to give you as many data points as it can."

The team needed a system that would build and test far more often. It also needed to scale up. At the time, it was only building for a single device: Sooner. But soon the team would have Dream devices (which launched with 1.0 as the G1), and the system would have to build for multiple targets.

Ed started on his own, but eventually led a team of people who worked on the build. Ed said, "It was Dave Bort that took it and actually made it good enough to base products on. Made it really solid, with a good design and a good layout of how things worked. Dave Bort took it from a good but sloppy build system to a product.

"At the same time he reorganized the build system, he reorganized the whole source tree. He set all of the fundamentals in place for open source and architectural level things. Even though he worked on the build system,

---

[5] Continuous Integration, or CI, is the practice in software development of integrating all of a team's changes as often as possible for building and testing. It helps maintain a constant measure of the quality and stability of the product so that it doesn't spin out of control before someone notices.

it was architectural; it rippled through the whole system. He laid all that groundwork. He basically got Android ready for open source."

TESTING, TESTING

Another area that had to be figured out was testing. How do you verify that all of the random bits of software landing in the build constantly from different engineers on different parts of the system are not actually breaking things? It's necessary, in any software system, to have some kind of automated test framework,[6] to catch problems quickly. Android didn't have automated testing at that time, so Ed got some monkeys to do it.

"At WebTV, we had this thing called the monkey,[7] which would find links on web pages and just go nuts surfing everywhere.

"I can't remember if Dianne had already done it [for the Android platform], or whether we were talking to her about it and she did it. But she put in the system for randomization and event injection into the framework, which we call 'monkey' today.

"I built the first monkey lab, which was my laptop and seven Dream devices. I wrote some scripts and tools to beat the shit out of them till they crashed, grabbed the crash [report] and put them back to work. I'd analyze those reports and I'd summarize them all. So every day we could have the number of events that it would handle, and what crashes it hit. Jason Parks and I, and eventually Evan Millar, hooked up a set of tools to help create our first stability numbers. That ended up living for years and years, as bad as it

---

[6.] Ideally, you have tests that run automatically, all the time, to make sure that changes don't break things. Manual testing is much more expensive, time-consuming, and infrequent, so automated testing is preferable.

[7.] Bruce Gay, who eventually ran the monkey lab, said the name came from the Infinite Monkey Theorem, which states that an infinite set of monkeys hitting keys on a keyboard will eventually produce the works of Shakespeare. Which seems like a slightly different goal than finding crashes in an OS.

The monkey didn't just come from WebTV; Dianne also used a monkey system at PalmSource.

Andy Hertzfeld's enjoyable book, *Revolution in The Valley: The Insanely Great Story of How the Mac Was Made*, also talks about monkeys, which apparently have a long history in platform testing. The original Mac had a desktop utility also called "The Monkey" that would similarly generate random input events to pound on the system and test its robustness. Who knew monkeys were so useful, so ubiquitous, so good at testing, and so very random?

was. It was just Python[8] scripts analyzing bug reports and writing out HTML reports. In late 2008, I hired Bruce Gay [also from Microsoft]. He took that and turned it into a real lab environment."[9]

Bruce grew the lab over the years from an initial set of seven devices to more than 400. He said there were some unanticipated problems to resolve over that time. "One day I walked into the monkey lab to hear a voice say, '911—What's your emergency?'" That situation resulted in Dianne adding a new function to the API, isUserAMonkey(), which is used to gate actions that monkeys shouldn't take during tests (including dialing the phone and resetting the device).

Early monkey tests would run for up to 3,000 input events before crashing. By 1.0, the number was up around 5,000. Bruce said, "'Passing' was 125K events. It took us a few years to meet that goal."

The monkey test lab in May of 2009 (photo courtesy Brian Swetland)

[8.] Python is a programming language, used for many things including small utility programs like the ones Ed is describing here.

[9.] The monkey testing lab continues to be an important part of Android testing. Somewhere in a quiet lab are racks of devices being hammered by a horde of virtual monkeys until they crash, at which point they collect a log of the crash and file a bug.

Damn monkeys.

Romain Guy talked about how critical monkey testing was in the run up to 1.0. "We used to rely on the monkey a lot back then. Every night we would run those monkey tests and every morning we had a lot of crashes to fix. Our goal was to get the monkey number up; how long can we run the monkey without crashing? Because they were crashing everywhere, from the widgets down to the kernel or SurfaceFlinger.[10] Especially once we switched to the touchscreen, things were a lot more complicated."

In addition to monkey tests, other people on the team were working on different kinds of tests to verify that the platform had the correct behavior. Evan Millar, who joined the team out of grad school in early 2007, worked on early performance testing frameworks, timing how long it took for applications to launch. He also worked on an early system of automated testing called Puppet Master, which allowed test scripts to drive the UI (opening windows, clicking on buttons), measuring correctness against golden images.[11] The results were mixed, given the difficulty of comparing against golden images, in addition to the asynchronous nature of the tests and the platform. A test script would request a particular UI action, like clicking a button or launching an application, but it might take a while for the platform to process that event, making correctness-testing tricky and error-prone.

Chiu-Ki Chan dealt with some of these inherent difficulties in testing when she joined the Maps team after stints on the services and Android Market teams. She had been working on a system to automate testing of the maps app, but was increasingly frustrated with the difficulties of testing her app on a system that not designed for testing. She said, "Testing? There was no such thing as testing."

An important part of overall Android testing is the Compatibility Test Suite (CTS). This was a system built initially by external contractors (managed

---

[10.] SurfaceFlinger is part of the low-level graphics system, which is described in Chapter 11 ("Graphics").

[11.] Golden image testing works by saving a visual result from some known-correct run, then comparing that image to future runs. Some variation is typically allowed to account for minor differences that don't indicate failure. This technique tends to be effective for very low-level tests (for example, verifying that a graphics API can draw shapes consistently), but can be rather fragile the more that's involved with each test, because so much variation can be introduced that is not indicative of failure.

by Patrick Brady[12]). CTS tests are important because they not only test specific pieces of functionality in the system and catch regressions[13] when tests fail, but they are required for partners to pass as well, guaranteeing that the Android devices they ship conform to Android's defined platform behavior. For example, if there is a test that colors the screen white and tests that the result is, in fact, white pixels, it should be impossible for a device to reinterpret "white" as red and still pass that test.

LEAN INFRASTRUCTURE

Android build, test, and release infrastructure, like much of the rest of Android, was created by a small team with limited resources. This was a conscious decision about where to invest limited budget given the priorities of getting the product out the door. Ed Heyl said, "We had no idea whether what we were doing was going to be successful or not. We were just trying to make a new device and be relevant. Apple was getting all the mindshare, Microsoft was not going to let go, and they were actually in the best position at that point. So everything was of the mindset: whatever we can do to make forward progress. We did not prioritize investing in really good solutions, it was just 'we gotta get this going, prove that we can deliver and iterate.' We never stopped and said we really need to invest in a build infrastructure, Python scripts are not going to get us very far, so we should really think about how we're going to use the Google back-end infrastructure. We never stopped to think about that. It was just full steam ahead.

"If it was part of the core product, we invested more into it. But if it was just test, or build, it was minimum stuff to get it going. That's the way we operated."

---

[12] Patrick went on to become the VP of Android Auto.

[13] Regression is a term often used in software testing. Tests are used to catch failures in software in general. A regression is a new failure on existing code; the software used to work (and the test used to pass), but now there is a failure in the software that is causing the test to fail. This tends to indicate that code checked in recently is buggy (or the test is flaky and reports failures randomly, which is depressingly more common than you would hope).

11

GRAPHICS

When people on the Android team say "graphics," they may mean vastly different things, because there are many layers of graphics functionality that are implemented by very distinct teams for very different reasons. For example, there are 3D graphics systems using OpenGL ES,[1] and more recently, Vulkan, for supporting anything from games to mapping applications to Virtual Reality to Augmented Reality. There are graphics capabilities in the UI toolkit, which is responsible for drawing things like text, shapes, lines, and images, so that application developers can populate their user interfaces with, well, graphics. And then there is the lowest level of graphics on the system which provides the fundamental capability for pixels and windows to appear on the screen.

We'll start with this lowest level of graphics, which came about through the work of Mathias Agopian, another hire from Be and PalmSource, who started on the Android team in late 2006.

---

[1] OpenGL is an API for performing graphics operations (typically 3D, used by games, but also 2D). Graphics operations are essentially a combination of shape and image drawing, and OpenGL handles those operations, executing commands on a GPU to do the work. OpenGL ES is a subset of OpenGL that is specifically targeted at embedded devices like smartphones.

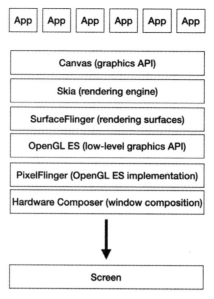

A vastly simplified view of Android's graphics system. Applications call into the Canvas API to draw things. The Canvas API is implemented underneath by the Skia rendering engine, which turns things like shapes and text into pixels. SurfaceFlinger provides a buffer, or surface, into which these pixels are drawn. SurfaceFlinger calls into OpenGL ES, a low-level graphics API that renders triangles. OpenGL ES uses PixelFlinger to draw the buffer. Note that PixelFlinger was eventually replaced by a GPU (Graphics Processing Unit) when GPUs became standard in smartphones. Finally, all of the surfaces that need to be drawn onto the screen (including the foreground application as well as the status and navigation bars) are composed together in the Hardware Composer and then displayed on the screen for the user to see.

MATHIAS AGOPIAN AND ANDROID GRAPHICS

Software rendering, in my opinion, was going to die.

—MATHIAS AGOPIAN

Mathias is a calm and quiet person who arrives at the office late, stays very late, and focuses almost exclusively on coding (avoiding email and meetings as much as possible).

In the early days, Mathias had a temper[2] that would occasionally surface. Something would upset him and he would storm out, sometimes staying away

---

[2] I haven't actually seen this in action; it might have been related to the stress of those early days and all of the hours that everyone was putting in to ship the product.

for several days or even weeks. In one episode, Mathias was upset at Brian Swetland. He threw his phone and marched out of the office, only to return a few minutes later to ask for his phone back, since he needed its memory card.[3]

Mathias spent his childhood learning how to program various computers, from the Armstrad CPC to several Atari computers, to the BeBox. He wrote graphics and audio applications for his Atari Falcon (including a sound tracker app for the Falcon which he sold under the name Crazy Music Machine[4]) and he became known[5] for programming articles that he wrote for French computer magazines. He also, as a hobby, wrote Epson printer drivers for the Atari and the BeBox, which those companies shipped with their systems. His work on the Be printer drivers resulted in a job; he left France to join Be in 1999.

Mathias stayed at Be until they were acquired by Palm and continued on with the rest of the team at PalmSource, working mostly on graphics software, until he decided he'd had enough of wherever PalmSource was going. He left around the same time as Joe Onorato and joined Google to work on Android in late 2005.

THE BASICS

When Mathias joined Android, he started on system fundamentals. The operating system essentially didn't exist yet, so everyone who joined at that time helped out with building basic necessities.

For example, the platform didn't yet have core data structures for C++ (Vector and HashMap). In a desktop or server world, these pieces wouldn't have been needed, because they come with standard libraries that developers typically use. But on Android, especially at that time, the platform only

---

[3] Swetland remembered: "To be fair, he threw it past me; there was no need for me to dodge. I was fighting some nasty pre-1.0 ship thing too and said, 'I don't have time for this right now,' that I think was the last straw for him that day."

Hiroshi would regularly send devices that had hardware issues back to HTC for evaluation. Swetland remembered putting that thrown device into the next round: "I followed the normal process and left Mathias's G1, with a shattered display, on Hiroshi's desk with a post-it describing the suspected issue: 'Poor anger management.'"

[4] Published by Application Systems Paris.

[5] Nicolas Roard, a French developer on Android's browser team in the early days, knew Mathias's name before he got to Google because of Mathias's articles Nicolas had read during high school.

included code and libraries that were absolutely necessary. Adding standard libraries would have pulled in too many unnecessary pieces, taking up storage space that simply wasn't available. So Mathias wrote versions of these data structures that everyone could use for Android development.

Mathias also worked on optimizing memcpy[6] and memset, low-level utilities for manipulating chunks of memory. Memcpy is a critical piece of software used by the entire system,[7] and is often a performance bottleneck in memory-intensive situations. Bob Lee commented on this work, "He hand-wrote this assembly language for memcpy, made it insanely fast and had a huge performance improvement. It was brilliant."

PIXELFLINGER[8]

Mathias's main goal for the graphics system was to implement something he called SurfaceFlinger, which was needed to display the buffers (*surfaces*) full of graphics that were produced by all of the applications on the system. But this system depended on lower-level functionality that did not yet exist, so he started there instead.

One of Mathias's assumptions was that SurfaceFlinger would need a GPU[9] to do its work; it would use OpenGL ES to perform the low-level operations required to get the graphics data from the application into buffers, and then to display those buffers onto the screen. The problem was, Android

---

[6.] Unix commands are typically abbreviated and often cryptic. It's not obvious, especially today, why "memcpy" is more useful than fully spelling it out as "memcopy." But there were probably multiple reasons for abbreviating things when Unix was created in the early 1970s, including storage space constraints as well as transmission time for characters on teletype machinery. Brian Swetland also attributed it to "just good old fashioned programmer laziness—I recently built a little program to test a radio interface and I called the binary *rctl* not *radio-control*—regarding things one expects to type over and over again."

Ken Thompson, one of the designers of Unix, in the book *The UNIX Programming Environment*, replied to a question of whether he'd do anything differently if he were redesigning Unix by saying, "I'd spell *creat* with an *e*."

[7.] This doesn't apply to just Android; memcpy is a fundamental piece of every OS, because copying memory around tends to be an important thing in software systems.

[8.] Mathias chose the name PixelFlinger as an homage to some graphics code called Bitflinger written at Be by Jason Sams, a colleague at Be and Android.

[9.] GPUs speed up graphics operations. They have been standard in desktop computers since the late 1990s, but were not standard in phone hardware when Mathias was doing this work.

---

wasn't running on a device with a GPU. The device that Android was targeting at that time, and all the way through the launch of the SDK, was Sooner, which had no GPU and therefore no OpenGL ES.

But Mathias saw a future in which GPUs would be standard on smartphones. "Before joining Android, I had a little bit of experience with mobile platforms. And it was really, really obvious to me that in the future we would be rendering using hardware.[10] Software rendering, in my opinion, was going to die.

"My idea was: I want everything to be ready for when we get hardware. The problem is, we don't have hardware. We don't really know when it's going to happen. So I thought, I'm in charge of graphics, I'm going to pretend I have a GPU. So I wrote a GPU, essentially. This way, I was able to write SurfaceFlinger using 'GL.' It was using real OpenGL ES, but it defaulted to software. And then, little by little, real hardware started to show up."

When Mathias said that he wrote a GPU, he meant that he wrote a *virtual* GPU; software that performed the same work as a GPU would, but in software instead of dedicated hardware. A GPU is not magical; the dedicated hardware in a GPU is not doing anything that cannot be done by software running on the CPU instead. It just does that job much faster, since it has hardware that is optimized for graphics operations.[11] In writing his fake GPU, Mathias provided a software layer to handle graphics operations normally handled by a GPU, translating those commands to low-level information that the existing Android display system could understand.

The OpenGL ES layer that he wrote issued commands to a lower layer that handled drawing textured triangles,[12] called PixelFlinger. This extra layer of abstraction of using OpenGL ES on top of PixelFlinger added work and

---

[10.] To clarify, all rendering happens on the phone's hardware. But there's a big difference between CPU rendering (where a general-purpose system computes pixel values) and GPU rendering (where a dedicated graphics processor computes those pixel values). GPUs are much better and faster at that job. That's what Mathias is referring to as *hardware rendering*.

[11.] Specifically, GPUs at that time optimized texture mapping, which draws geometry overlaid with image data. Most graphics that we see on the screen, from complex games to simple 2D buttons, can be boiled down to image data on geometry.

[12.] GPUs, and therefore underlying rendering engines for OpenGL ES, are essentially triangle renderers; they draw triangles that usually contain some kind of image data (textures), which, when drawn with many other textured-triangles, can create a visually complex scene. There is a lot more to it, of course, but rendered scenes, even complex 3D ones in games or movie effects, are essentially collections of textured triangles.

overhead and wouldn't have made sense if it were the only device Android was targeting. But in a world where Android was aiming at the future, and the future almost certainly included GPU hardware, this meant that Surface-Flinger had to be written only once, to target OpenGL ES. As soon as the future matched Mathias's vision and GPUs were available, it would continue working as-is, but faster (using hardware, instead of the software-based PixelFlinger).

Mathias's approach of writing PixelFlinger's virtual GPU was an example of the *product versus platform* approach that Android took in the early days.[13] A *product* approach, where the team simply got the initial phone to work as quickly as possible, wouldn't have taken as long. But the *platform* approach that Mathias took, building up layers of software that scaled way beyond that initial release, proved useful to Android in the long run. "It was necessary to go through that step to be ready for when the hardware was there. But also to convince people that that's what needed to happen."

This long-term approach to the graphics system, and other parts of the platform, was an element of the team's approach in those early days. Overall, the team was very scrappy, preferring small, hard-working teams, and making quick, pragmatic decisions as they drove toward 1.0. But several of the decisions that the team made early on, and the extra work those required, happened because they were the right thing for the future of the platform, even though that future wasn't assured. So although the team was focused on the goal of shipping 1.0, they were trying to do so with a platform that would live beyond that single ship date, into the future that Android eventually achieved.

PixelFlinger had a limited shelf life in terms of Android phones. It was critical for the Sooner device that the team used during early development, but the G1 that shipped with 1.0 already had the GPU capabilities[14] that Mathias had wanted and predicted. The importance of PixelFlinger wasn't in the capabilities that it provided for specific products, but in what it meant for the platform, to build in forward-looking capabilities that drove an architecture and ecosystem into a hardware-accelerated future.[15]

---

[13] See Chapter 29 ("Product vs. Platform") for more on this.

[14] The G1's GPU had a serious limitation, however; only a single process at a time could use it.

[15] In fact, PixelFlinger was still used for a long time after 1.0: for the boot animation seen when the phone starts up, for the device upgrade UI, and for the emulator. The emulator, which runs on developers' computers, had no access to a GPU, so it used Mathias's virtual GPU for many years.

SURFACEFLINGER

Once PixelFlinger and OpenGL ES were working, Mathias could implement SurfaceFlinger. Applications draw their graphics objects (buttons, text, images—whatever) into a buffer in memory and SurfaceFlinger posts that buffer to the screen, visible to the user. SurfaceFlinger was essentially the glue between the higher-level graphics operations happening in applications and the OpenGL ES layer that he had written previously, responsible for copying buffers around and displaying them to the user. The separation of app rendering from displaying the pixels on the screen was intentional; one of Mathias's design goals was to enable smooth graphics by ensuring that no app could cause rendering performance problems for any other app (this was related to Android's overall approach to security on the platform, where there was always a clear separation of applications from each other). So applications would draw into buffers, and SurfaceFlinger would take it from there.

HARDWARE COMPOSER

The other part of the graphics system that Mathias wrote was the Hardware Composer (HWC). SurfaceFlinger handles drawing UI graphics into a window on the screen. But there are several windows that need to be combined together to make up the final pixels on the screen.

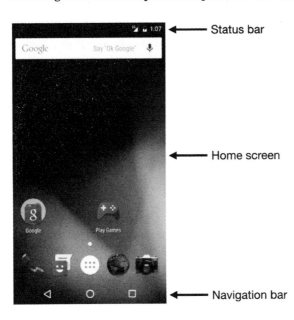

Status bar

Home screen

Navigation bar

A sample Android screen, showing the typical status bar, navigation bar, and home screen

Think about a typical Android screen that the user sees. There is a status bar (where the current time and various status and notification icons show up), a navigation bar (where the back and home buttons reside), and finally the actual foreground application (or the home screen). There may be other windows as well, like popup menus on top of the foreground application.

All of these are separate windows, often running in separate processes. For example, the navigation and status bars are managed by the system process, whereas the application window is owned by the application process. All of these windows need to be displayed together in some sensible way, which is the job of the Hardware Composer.

Mathias's idea for HWC was to use specialized graphics hardware called hardware overlays,[16] which provide display memory dedicated to each application, avoiding the overhead of all applications sharing the same video memory. Using overlay hardware also saved power and provided higher performance for applications. By using dedicated overlay hardware, the system avoided using the power-hungry GPU for these simple and frequent windowing operations. Also, using overlays left the GPU available for use by applications,[17] for accelerating games or other graphics-intensive operations.

Rather than drawing each of these windows manually on the screen, or telling the GPU to draw them through OpenGL ES, the HWC would send each of the windows to a different overlay. The display hardware would then compose these overlays together onto the screen to make it all look like one seamless screen of information, rather than the several completely different processes that they actually are.

The problem was that overlays were difficult to use in practice, since every device tended to have different numbers and capabilities of overlays. But given the GPU limitations of the G1, plus relatively good overlay support on that device, Mathias and Jason Sams came up with a novel approach. Instead of trying to handle the infinite variations of overlays directly in HWC, their software would tell the underlying hardware what HWC needed

---

[16.] Overlays are specialized display hardware for displaying different windows of graphics, especially windows with fast-moving images, including videos and games.

[17.] Using overlays was actually a requirement for the G1. Only one process at a time could use the GPU, so if HWC used the GPU, apps could not. Using the overlay hardware was a good workaround for this constraint.

and either the hardware could support their requirements or HWC would back off to using OpenGL ES. Over time, hardware vendors saw the benefit of handling these overlay operations directly and it became an area for vendors to offer extra performance on their devices for this critical area of the platform.

MIKE REED AND SKIA

All of Mathias's work was predicated on having something to display on the screen: graphics content from the applications. The system for applications to draw graphics content for their UIs also needed to be created. For that, Android used a rendering system called Skia that was acquired early on from Mike Reed.

If "serial graphics entrepreneur" is a real thing, that's what Mike Reed is.

Mike started programming late in life, at least compared to many of the early Android engineers. Mike got college degrees in science and math. But in 1984, the original Macintosh was released and showed up on his campus. "That changed everything. I wanted to do graphics, because that's what the Mac was really showing off. So I got a math degree, but taught myself programming."

Mike managed to get hired at Apple after grad school ("I just squeaked into that job"), where he met Cary Clark, future co-founder of Skia.[18] After several years at Apple, Mike left and started HeadSpin, creating a game engine used by CD-ROM games. HeadSpin was acquired by Cyan, makers of the game *Myst*, and Mike left to start a new graphics technology company called AlphaMask. AlphaMask was acquired by Openwave, a company providing browser software for mobile devices.

Mike left Openwave in 2004 and started Skia with Cary, his former Apple colleague, where they created a graphics rendering engine. Skia licensed its engine to various clients, including several in California. For one of Mike's trips to California, Cary suggested that Mike should meet with a startup called Android, which had been founded by a couple of Cary's former colleagues at WebTV: Andy Rubin and Chris White.

---

[18] Cary was also an engineer on the Skia team at Google for many years.

In late 2004, Android was quite small, with only the two co-founders plus new employees Brian Swetland and Tracey Cole. Android was in the midst of a pivot from building a camera OS to a phone OS. Nevertheless, Andy knew that they would need a rendering engine to display the UI, so he paid Mike for an evaluation license of Skia and agreed to get back in touch. But Mike didn't hear back from him: "Andy just fell off the map and he didn't respond to emails."

Months later, in the Summer of 2005, Andy finally contacted Mike. "He says, 'Sorry I dropped out, but I'm emailing you from a new email address.' And sure enough, it's something@google.com. He says, 'Hey I got acquired. We should probably finish that license.'"

But instead of just being another licensee of Skia's rendering engine, Google acquired Mike's company. Android was, after all, in hiring mode, and acquisitions can be an effective way (if you have the money) to hire multiple people quickly.

The acquisition was announced on November 9, 2005, and the four engineers from Skia (Mike, Cary, Leon Scroggins, and Patrick Scott) started in December.

One of the points of negotiation was location. Mike and Cary had, years earlier, made the decision to leave California and settle in North Carolina, and they weren't wild about returning to the Bay Area. Google agreed to leave the team in North Carolina, where they established the new Chapel Hill office.[19]

After the team started at Google, they got to work making Skia the graphics engine for Android. The underlying rendering software itself was fairly complete; they had full support in C++ for the kinds of 2D drawing operations that Android needed (lines, shapes, text, and images). In fact, the raw graphics functionality of Skia in Android has changed very little since those early years (though major improvements have happened along the way, like hardware acceleration). But given Android's choice of Java as the main programming language for applications, they needed Skia to be callable from Java, not C++, so the team wrote the Java bindings.[20]

[19.] The Chapel Hill office continued to expand over time, as the Skia team grew and took on graphics rendering projects beyond Android.

[20.] Bindings are functions in Java that wrap underlying C++ functionality. Calling a binding function essentially transfers execution from Java code down into C++ code.

Writing bindings for Skia and integrating the engine into the rest of the Android platform wasn't too difficult, so the Skia team soon picked up a couple other projects. One of the projects, the new UI system, was short-lived. Mike's team proposed that Android use Skia's existing system for displaying UI. They had a system working already that developers programmed using a combination of JavaScript and XML. But the move to Java, plus some late-night work from Joe Onorato,[21] sent the team down a different path.

---

21. We'll see more about Joe's efforts in Chapter 14 ("UI Toolkit").

12

MEDIA

When software engineers talk about media, they're usually referring to *multimedia*, meaning audio and video. These technologies are very distinct from each other and both require deep domain expertise. So engineers usually work on one or the other, not both. Nevertheless, audio and video engineers are usually collected into the same "media" team. Maybe it's because they both require such power and memory from the device—and such extreme optimizations in the software—in order to work reliably for the user.

DAVE SPARKS AND RINGTONES

Dave Sparks only took one programming course in his life, a Fortran class when he was a sophomore in high school. Writing programs in that class consisted of typing the code onto punch cards, which were then wrapped with a rubber band and couriered to the district office, where they would be executed on the computer there. Students would get the results of their program on a printout a few days later.[1]

Dave was more intrigued by the old Monrobot XI system in the back of the classroom, a circa 1960 machine that used a rotating magnetic drum for storage. He learned how to program machine code on that old system, nearly failing the Fortran class in the process.

His programming career began after high school, while he was working in a RadioShack. Ray Dolby[2] came into the store one day looking for help; he

---

[1] Developers complain about the speed of compiling large Android applications today, which can take several seconds, or sometimes longer for very complex builds. It could be far, far worse.

[2] Inventor of Dolby Noise Reduction and creator of Dolby Laboratories. That Ray Dolby.

wanted a program to download his stock data into a spreadsheet. The manager pointed at Dave as someone who could help. One program and $50 later, Dave was a professional programmer.

In the early 2000s, carriers required mobile phones to support a variety of ringtone formats. Complicating the requirement more was the fact that different carriers used different formats, so phone manufacturers would have to support multiple formats in order to be able to sell their devices into different markets.

Yamaha offered a dedicated synthesizer chip that could handle the requirements, for a cost of a couple dollars per handset. Manufacturers are always looking for ways to cut costs, so a company called Sonivox introduced a software-based solution instead, selling it for just a dollar per handset.

Dave Sparks was in charge of that product at Sonivox when Andy Rubin came calling.

With Android's plans to open source the OS, Andy's needs were different from Sonivox's typical customers; he wanted the product, but also to publish the source code for it, effectively eliminating future sales. Dave remembered the deal as, "This is going to be open sourced in the future. Here's a pile of money."

The deal happened in early 2007. In March, Dave came to Google and spent a couple hours with Ficus Kirkpatrick to integrate that software into the system. Suddenly, Android could play ringtones.

Months later, Andy called Dave, who was still at Sonivox, and asked him to join Android to build a media team. Dave joined Android in August of 2007.

MARCO NELISSEN AND AUDIO

After Ficus got ringtones working with the Sonivox software, he also got a single MP3 ringtone working: "Crazy" by Gnarls Barkley. Joe Onorato explained, "mp3 playback was a ton of work. As soon as he got that working, we needed a ringtone. He checked in an MP3 of 'Crazy' and that was The Ringtone."

With all Android phones playing that same ringtone for every phone call, the song was driving everyone . . . well, you know.

The team needed help generalizing the ringtone system, so they hired someone that had been writing audio software for years: Marco Nelissen.

When he was in high school in the Netherlands, Marco's parents bought him a Commodore 64. Initially, he just played games on it, but he soon started programming on it, learning BASIC and then assembly. He wrote text editors and then began playing with multimedia applications as well, including a music sequencing app called SoundTracker Pro.[3]

After college, he continued working in multimedia, first at a company writing software for Philips CD-i platform, and then at Be. Like many colleagues at Be, he joined Palm after its acquisition of Be. He stuck around at PalmSource longer than most of his team, who had mostly joined Google to work on Android by early 2006. Marco finally joined the Android team in January of 2007.

Marco dove into Android's audio functionality. His first project was to add the increasingly important ability to select a different ringtone. "Not that I didn't like that song, but when you heard the same thing every few minutes when someone's phone rang, it got tiring."

He continued working on sound and multimedia in general. He added sound capabilities to the simulator (which was used by the team for debugging their software), and eventually wrote the first music app for Android. He also later wrote a couple of the first Live Wallpapers (sound and music visualizers) for the Eclair (Android 2.1) release, which shipped with the Nexus One.

AUDIOFLINGER

Another audio problem that had to be solved was for the G1. The original HTC audio drivers for that device were so buggy that even doing something as simple as trying to play a second sound while one was already playing would reboot the device. The Android team didn't have access to the source code for that driver, so they worked around the problem by introducing a layer on top of the driver called AudioFlinger.

Mathias came up with the name, based on his experience writing SurfaceFlinger. SufaceFlinger solved a related problem on the graphics side, where many applications produced buffers of pixel data that SurfaceFlinger displayed on the screen. Similarly, AudioFlinger combined multiple audio

---

[3.] SoundTracker Pro is still available for download and has YouTube tutorials for all of the Amiga users out there. Anyone? Anyone?

streams across the system into a single stream which would then be sent to the driver without (and this is the key part) causing the device to reboot. Mathias worked with Marco, Arve, and Ficus to get it working for the G1. It was only supposed to be a temporary workaround in the platform for that specific device, but as often happens in software, it lived on far past its usefulness until it was finally rewritten so that the system could talk more directly to drivers that didn't have those historical problems.

THE VIDEO CODE NOBODY LIKED

Handling video is complicated. For one thing, video needs codecs[4] to load and save video files. Video software also needs the capability to play content that has been loaded by a codec. And once you have all of that working, you need to optimize it to happen quickly, because a video that can't play smoothly is less "video" and more "frustrating."

Meanwhile, the software needs to be able to talk to the hardware, which is tricky because video-specific hardware can vary widely between devices.

With such a small team, it would have been difficult to implement everything that video required. So Andy made the decision to buy the necessary technology instead of writing it in-house. He asked Ficus Kirkpatrick to check out some options, but had him focus on a company called Packet-Video. PacketVideo, at the time, licensed an entire suite of software to do all of what Android needed.

The deal was going to happen; Ficus's investigation was more like a sanity-check than a deep analysis. Ficus remembered, "Andy told me he was going to do the deal no matter what." Like the rest of the team, he was busy with other things at the time, and it seemed like a foregone conclusion, so he didn't spend a lot of time evaluating the situation: "I didn't think it mattered. I didn't think the code was good, but didn't speak up."

He briefly investigated other options. He vetoed one of the alternatives because of the state of their code. That other company was so focused on making their product work on Windows that they baked assumptions into the software that made it unusable on any other OS (such as Linux, which

---

[4] Codec is short for "encoder-decoder," software that can save (encode) and load (decode) files of some format. For example, video systems typically need to be able to save and load MP4 files.

was what Android needed). Comparatively, PacketVideo was a better choice. "It was probably the least awful of the media frameworks I looked at."

The deal that Andy was proposing was awkward for PacketVideo; he was proposing to give away the core of their business. The company made its money from licensing their video software. Android needed not only the functionality of their code, but also the code itself. Android was planning to open source all of the code for the platform, including PacketVideo's code. So the deal Andy proposed was that Android would take their software and publish it in the open, essentially destroying any future licensing possibilities they might have had, because any potential clients could just copy the Android code. Ficus said, "Andy's pitch to them was, 'Your business is going to change from licensing to professional services. We will give you some money to bridge the transition.'"

The deal was done (with the help of Tom Moss[5]), the code was integrated, and the Android team was . . . not happy.[6] Ficus remembered, "The code was not very good. Optimizing it was really hard."

Mathias Agopian agreed. "It was a disaster, from a technical standpoint. PacketVideo on paper was really good: tons of codecs, playback, recording, video, audio. On paper, problem solved. But we spent many, many, many years fixing and eventually rewriting everything."

Ficus continued: "Probably my only good contribution was refusing to ship their API and only shipping the extremely simple MediaPlayer/MediaRecorder [APIs]. This was a low complexity, low capability API that made it possible to move a lot of the stuff around under the hood." That is, by offering only simple and generic video capabilities to application developers, instead of exposing more advanced PacketVideo features directly, Ficus ensured that the details of how video was implemented could change later, when the team had more time to deal with the problem.

[5.] Tom Moss did business deals for Andy. We'll read more about Tom in Chapter 28 ("Deals").

[6.] An important element of software development is that a project is not done when it ships (at least not if the project is successful). The code has to continue to be supported by the team for as long as that functionality remains in the product. So even if the video code did what it needed to do, it was still a burden on the team because of ongoing bugs, performance issues, additional feature requirements, and general maintenance for years to come.

In fact, this was what eventually happened. Years later, this layer of the system was completely rewritten as a component called *stagefright*. Andreas Huber, an engineer on the media team at the time, had been steadily rewriting portions of the PacketVideo code. Eventually he realized that the old code wasn't being called anymore, so he deleted it and the PacketVideo code was no more.

13

FRAMEWORK

Whenever Dan Sandler visited the Mountain View offices, he'd usually leave behind some whiteboard art in his wake. This one showed up in the framework area on one of those trips.

F ramework[1] is the term that the Android team applies to a large chunk of the core platform that encompasses the internal operating system level stuff (the bits of software that underlie almost everything else on the system except the kernel), along with the APIs that applications use to access those features. Examples of framework functionality include:

- The package manager, responsible for installing and managing applications on the device.

- Power management, controlling, for example, the brightness settings of the screen (the screen being the heaviest user of power on any device).

---

[1] *Framework* is a very overloaded term in software (and on the Android team). The word is further discussed in the Jargon appendix at the end of the book.

- Window management, displaying applications on the screen and animating them in and out as they open and close.

- Input, receiving information from the touchscreen hardware and turning it into input events that are routed to applications.

- Activity manager, handling the multitasking system on Android, deciding things like which applications to kill when memory is getting low on the device.

When the framework engineers started arriving onto Android in late 2005, none of this existed, so the people who started on the Android team back then had to build the framework, piece by piece.

DIANNE HACKBORN AND THE ANDROID FRAMEWORK

The person whose work defines most the shape [of the Android platform] is clearly Dianne. I'm sure she would probably downplay her influence here. But she's wrong.

—FICUS KIRKPATRICK

By the end of 2005, some of the pieces of what would become the framework were started, but there was still a long way to go, including APIs for applications to use and all of the other capabilities that the system required. Then Dianne Hackborn joined the team.

Dianne (also known to the team as "hackbod"[2]) is, as most people on the team would agree, the person who best understands the entire breadth of the Android framework and the overall platform. For one thing, she has a comprehensive understanding of how all of the pieces in the platform fit together, along with an extensive knowledge of operating systems and APIs in general.

Also, she wrote most of the framework code.

Dianne came from computer royalty. Her father started the printer division at Hewlett-Packard and was under consideration for CEO at some

---

[2] Dianne's nickname came from the account name automatically generated for her in the CS department at college. The system used the first six characters of the last name plus the first character of the first name. The superhero-esque quality of the result is purely coincidental.

point. At an age when other kids were experiencing computers through playing video games, she was into system design. "I would look into the way the system works, and the ways that it worked with applications and threading."

After college, she worked at Lucent Technologies, while playing with BeOS in her spare time ("writing frameworks, some applications. UI layout frameworks . . . that kind of stuff"). Eventually, she wanted that work to be more than a side interest, and moved to the Bay Area to work for Be.

"That was at the time of the dot-com boom. You're working at a company that isn't making any money, not sure how you're going to make money, but everybody wants to work on operating systems. That's why they're there. It's not about making money."[3]

Dianne started at Be in late 1999, joining a group of people there that she would work with later at PalmSource, and then again when she joined Android. She worked on the framework at Be and then again at PalmSource.

At Be, Dianne worked on the next version of BeOS, but that was the end of the line for that operating system. "They were trying to compete with Microsoft. You can't compete with the entrenched platform. Unless they shoot themselves in the foot, it is impossible because their ecosystem has so much momentum that anything you do better than them, they have years to react to you for it to matter.

"And it's chicken and egg. You have to get users to get app developers interested in you, and you have to get developers to get users interested in you. You can get some users, but anywhere you try to gain momentum, the dominant platform can go address that particular market and kill you. It's just impossible."

Eventually, Palm acquired Be, because Palm had plans to build a more robust OS for their devices and needed engineers with the right expertise to make it happen. It was Dianne's introduction to mobile computing. "I had never thought about mobile at the time. But once I started looking at Palm,

---

[3.] Dianne's experience at Be contrasted with that of many other people flooding into the Bay Area, and to tech in general, hoping to strike it rich in a dot-com startup.

Life in the Bay Area was more affordable back then (though still not cheap), so it was more possible to not care too much about the money. But still (at least in the ideal situation), engineers tend to be driven more by interest in what they work on than in the compensation for that work. There are (at least in the current and recent environment) plenty of tech jobs; why not find ones that interest you for the thing you'll do for most of your waking hours?

that's when I got really interested. That seemed like the way you compete with Microsoft. It's a new kind of device, so if you can be the platform on that device, then you have a bigger ecosystem than Windows and you have a chance. You could see the writing on the wall. The hardware was getting more powerful, and the market was already bigger than PCs."

But PalmSource was struggling. The original idea with their spinout from Palm was that they would provide the OS that Palm (and other companies) would use. But by the time PalmSource came up with Palm OS 6,[4] Palm had decided to just continue using the OS they began with when Palm and PalmSource split. Then a deal fell through when the team was nearly done with a product-quality OS on a potential Samsung device. After that, there were no other buyers in sight for the OS, so the company started shopping itself around to be acquired.

There's an interesting dynamic of mobile OSes that Dianne and the team were forced to deal with at the time, which would resurface (more successfully) later on Android. "It was really hard to get phone manufacturers interested in someone else's platform. They did their own software and they were terrified of phones becoming the same as PCs, where there's one software vendor that owns the platform that commoditizes the hardware."

That model of hardware companies creating their own OS worked when software was simpler. Handling phone calls and contact information for a flip phone was well within the capabilities of all of those companies. But when the required capabilities and feature sets kept increasing, especially after the iPhone launched, it was difficult for those companies to keep up. The companies that needed an OS in the wake of the iPhone launch were looking for something far more complex than they could create on their own, and were therefore more willing to work with Android.

"The software becomes more valuable than the hardware. Most of your investment is now in the software. And if that's the case, then whoever can invest the most in the software is going to be the most compelling, and that's probably someone dedicated to a platform that works across different hardware."

---

4. Palm OS 6, after years of development by PalmSource, never shipped. Wikipedia has a nice quote about this version of Palm OS: "Palm OS 6.0 was renamed to Palm OS Cobalt to make clear that this version was initially not designated to replace Palm OS 5."

Ouch.

Part of Palm OS 6 was a powerful UI framework. Motorola, a potential suitor of PalmSource, was interested in that framework and in Palm OS 6 in general for its own devices. But Motorola's acquisition attempt failed, and PalmSource was acquired by ACCESS Co., Ltd. "It would have been really interesting to get acquired by Motorola. We were all hoping for that. They wanted to take what we were doing and use it." ACCESS, on the other hand, was not on board with the current direction.

After the acquisition, ACCESS changed the team's OS strategy. Dianne and her team were done. "PalmSource was over. Handset manufacturers didn't want to touch someone else's platform, because they didn't want to be an enabler. I was seeing my team out the door (I was managing the framework team there). Mathias and Joe were leaving. They came to me and said 'you should come over to Google—there's really cool stuff going on here.' They gave me hints: 'It's a platform ... it's open source ....' Work at Google doing an open source mobile platform where you don't have to worry about money? How can you say no to that? It's, like, perfect."

Dianne joined Google and started on the Android team in January of 2006.

She was introduced to Google's take on the Android strategy early on. "When I joined, the way Larry and Sergey were talking about it, and the way Andy was presenting it, they didn't want just a product. It was grander than that: the future survival of Google. They didn't want a company with a closed proprietary platform to own and control the space, like Microsoft owns the PC platform. It wasn't about needing to make money."[5]

ACTIVITIES

It's hard to out-code Dianne when she's on fire. She had a vision of what she wanted, and she just sat down and typed it out.

—JEFF HAMILTON

[5.] I talk about this earlier, in the chapters on Google's acquisition of Android, and later, when I discuss the factors of Android's success. There were a few reasons behind the acquisition of Android and the things that Google was hoping to achieve. But it could be summed up by saying that they wanted an even playing field. That is, they wanted potential users of Google services to be able to access those services. Dominant players could have made that very difficult. So, for example, if Microsoft had done in the mobile arena what it did in the PC space, then they might have made it difficult for users to have had open access to Google services on those devices.

After she joined Android, Dianne started working on many of the fundamental pieces of what's now called the framework. One of those pieces was Activities, which she took over from some initial work by Joe Onorato.

Activities, which evolved from longer-term ideas that the team was thinking about earlier when they were at PalmSource, are a uniquely Android way of managing applications. On a more traditional OS, an application starts, calls its main() method, and then just starts doing things in a loop (drawing, polling for input, doing any necessary calculations, and so on). On Android, an application is broken down into one or more "activity" pieces, each of which has its own window. Activities (and applications) have no main() method, but instead are called by the OS in response to events, like activity creation/destruction and user input.

Another important element of Activities is that they define specific entry points that can be called from other applications, like notifications or shortcuts in the system UI that can take the user to a place inside of the application.

Dianne said, "Palm had a really good understanding of mobile devices. One of the things we learned there was that mobile apps are fundamentally different from desktop apps: the user can only be in one at a time, and they tend to be small and focused on a particular task. Out of this grew a need to easily have apps work together. Palm OS had this hack called 'sublaunching' that allowed one app to effectively call in to another app, to do something like show a UI for the user to add a contact. We viewed this as an important feature for mobile apps, but needed to formalize it into a well-defined concept so it would be more robust and work in a complex multi-process protected memory (and app-sandboxed) environment. Thus Activities, which define the ways apps can expose parts of themselves for other apps (and the system) to launch as needed."

Activities were a powerful concept for Android. They were also at the heart of one of the first big disagreements on the engineering team. There was certainly more complexity associated with Activities than the more traditional approach that some people preferred. In particular, Android's application lifecycle (handling activity creation/destruction/etc.) continues to be difficult to understand, and dealing with its complexities tends to be a hard and error-prone chore for many Android developers.

As Jeff Hamilton (a framework engineer that we'll read about soon) told it, "In the early days of Android, there were two competing visions of what the OS should look like. One was around the fuzzy nature of Activities, and one where there's a main() that gets called. Dianne and Joe were pushing on the notion of the more modular app setup with Activities.

"There were a bunch of other people, like Mike Fleming,[6] in the other camp that were pushing more for a simple model. There was a big conflict there for a while."

Mike Fleming said, "I was a skeptic of the application lifecycle. I was concerned that it was too complicated." Wei Huang[7] agreed: "There are certain points where I think the activity lifecycle is overly complicated. It grew a little bit out of control."

But the team decided to go with the Activities approach. Jeff explained how that happened: "Dianne had a vision of what she wanted, and she just sat down and typed it out. That's the way it worked, because she was productive and got things done."

This model of decision making happened elsewhere as well, such as the initial View system that Joe implemented. The team didn't have a lot of time for meetings and committees and debates on how things should work, so eventually someone would simply bang out a solution and things would move on from there. As Dianne said, "There were so few people that if you do it, you just do it. There was lots of discussion between people, but it was instigated by the person working on the thing." Romain Guy (who joined later to work on the UI toolkit) added, "What was most respected [at Android] was someone just making something happen." And often, that someone was Dianne.

RESOURCES

Dianne also worked on the resource system,[8] which is another very Android concept. On Android, application developers are able to define different versions of text, images, sizes, and other elements of their apps, in what are called *resource files*.

---

[6] Mike worked on telephony and the Dalvik runtime.

[7] Wei was working on the Android Browser, covered in Chapter 17 ("The Android Browser").

[8] Fadden implemented the original resource system, which was a simple system that allowed language-based selection of files. Dianne said she "took that and made it ... complicated."

For example, you might have a button in your application that should say *Click* so that the user knows to click that button. But the word *Click* only makes sense if the user speaks English. What if they speak Russian instead? Or French? Or . . . any other non-English language? Developers use resource files to store different versions of that string for different languages. When the button is populated with a string, the resource system chooses the version that is appropriate for the language that the user has selected on their phone.

Similarly, developers can define what the UI looks like for screen configurations, and can use different image sizes based on different screen densities. Again, the resource system loads the appropriate variation when the application launches, depending on the user's device.

Resources, and the way that they are used to solve the variable-density problem in particular, are a great example of how Android was developed as a software platform, not just as a single phone product, even in those early days before 1.0. If the team was just targeting a particular device, with a predefined screen size (as most manufacturers did at that time), none of this would have been necessary. But then applications would have been written with those initial assumptions firmly in place. When different sized screens came along later, those apps wouldn't look right.

Dianne: "These devices were different from the desktop because the device has much more impact on applications than on desktop. On desktop you can have a bigger screen, but it doesn't really matter for apps, you may just be able to resize the windows. But on these devices, if the screen gets bigger, then the apps need to draw correctly on that bigger screen."

Another factor was screen density.[9] "On the desktop, the density never changes. But we knew that the density [for mobile devices] would change. We saw this happen at Palm. We needed to design something that would let us evolve the platform over the long term, because we had seen what happened with Palm OS and its more minimalist approach. Getting it to support different screen densities was a disaster. We've always [for the Android platform] approached this as: 'We're building this for mobile devices, but we want this thing to scale and address other use cases in the long term.'"

---

[9] Density is the number of pixels per inch. Two phones can have the same size screen, but if one has a higher density, it will have smaller, and more plentiful, pixels than the other one. If the system only supported a way to draw in raw pixel sizes, items on a screen with higher density would be smaller, which is not generally what developers or users would want.

In contrast, iOS and the iPhone didn't take density into consideration in the beginning. "Apple didn't think about this stuff. Apple is one of the few hardware companies that can also do high quality software development. Most hardware companies are focused on the hardware product, and the software is just something needed for the hardware. Apple is able to approach the software as something that they invest in long-term, separately from a particular hardware product. But you still see stuff where they are hardware-oriented, like 'We want to change the size of the screen . . . we didn't think about that.'"

WINDOWMANAGER

> Dianne says, "I'm gonna make a window manager," and typity-type-type, there's a window manager.
>
> **—MIKE CLERON**

Dianne also, long before 1.0 shipped, wrote the WindowManager, which handles windows opening, closing, animating in, and animating out. It's notable because of both the complexity of the problems it had to solve and the fact that Dianne wrote it all as just one of the many things she was doing.[10]

SOFT KEYBOARD

After 1.0 shipped, there was still plenty of work to do. One of the things that Dianne worked on at that time, along with Amith Yamasani on the framework team, was support for the *soft keyboard*, or the on-screen keyboard that touch-only devices needed.

The original G1 had a hardware keyboard. Entering text into an application required flipping that keyboard out. This mechanism worked fine (and in fact many smartphone users continued to prefer hardware keyboards for years after that, especially BlackBerry fans). But the demand for larger screens and smaller devices meant that support for an all-touch device, with an on-screen keyboard, was critical. In fact, the device that was going to launch with the upcoming Cupcake release would have no hardware keyboard.

---

[10] Dianne originally wrote and maintained the window manager code alone. That code is now being maintained by an entire team of people.

In typical Android development fashion, the soft keyboard wasn't just hacked into the framework. Android was known for making trade-offs to get performance or to hit ship dates, but the team always prioritized creating general platform capabilities instead of hacks for specific product features, which was the case for their keyboard solution. The team created a system to provide extensible and flexible support for generalized input. For example, the keyboard support wasn't just called *keyboard*, but rather Input Method Editor (IME). It wasn't sufficient to simply provide support for typing on a regular keyboard, but rather the system needed to accept input from any kind of input mechanism, including speech.

At the same time, input support was built not just as an internal mechanism for the framework to use, but also as an extensible feature that developers could take advantage of. Android supplied the Input Method Framework (IMF) that would accept input from any user-supplied IME, not just the keyboard that shipped with the Android system. That is, Android didn't just supply a soft keyboard for users; they also provided APIs for developers to create their own keyboard apps that users could use instead. The short-term need was for an input system that was good enough for most use cases. But the team recognized that there might be other experiences out there, or other capabilities, that users wanted and developers could help out with, so they built the system to allow it. Even when there were only a couple of Android devices out on the market, the team was playing the long game, anticipating a potentially large and diverse ecosystem of devices and users.

Dianne said, "I don't recall it ever being much of a consideration to go down the path of hard-coding it into the platform. From a practical matter of being able to address the needs of different languages, we thought this should be a user-selectable component."

IME support is a great example of what attracted many developers (and users) to Android early on. The early devices like the G1 weren't the most beautiful smartphones available, but the power and flexibility of the open ecosystem was attractive to many users and developers. The iPhone eventually offered the ability to have keyboard apps besides the one that came bundled with iOS, but that was much later, long after Android developers could offer those apps.

In 2009, Shumin Zhai was working in research at IBM. He was investigating alternative input mechanisms, using an app he built called

ShapeWriter.[11] Rather than typing in each letter, his app allowed a user to slide their finger around the keyboard, tracing out a shape as they navigated between the letters of each word. His keyboard interpreted these shapes as words, using probabilities and heuristics to determine the words the user was tracing out.

Shumin built the ShapeWriter with Per Ola Kristensson in 2004, releasing it originally on the Windows Tablet PC. They later released ShapeWriter for the iPhone in 2008, but it would only work with a note-taking app that they also supplied, because the iPhone had no equivalent of Android's IMF at the time, so it could not take the place of the system keyboard. When Android released support for the IMF, in the Cupcake release in mid-2009, Shumin switched Shape-Writer's focus to Android, releasing the app on Android Market later that year.[12]

He particularly liked developing for Android[13] because it gave him the ability to experiment, to swap out the system keyboard for his own so that he could provide this new capability. Shumin was a researcher, which might not seem like a huge target market to go after. But around the same time, a company released a popular app on Android called Swype, which had similar gesture-typing capabilities.

Shumin eventually joined the Android team and led the team that implemented Gesture Typing for Android's standard IME. Now that capability of tracing out words is built into Android's keyboard by default. But Android still allows developers to supply their own keyboard apps for customizations and capabilities that developers want to create.

JEFF HAMILTON WORKS HIS WAY UP THE STACK

Despite Dianne's legendary productivity, there was still much more that needed to be done to make the entire framework come into being than she

---

[11] *https://www.shuminzhai.com/shapewriter*

[12] ShapeWriter was also one of the winners in the second Android Developer Challenge contest, in late 2009. There's more about the Android Developer Challenge in Chapter 39 ("The SDK Launch").

[13] I know this because he told me so at the time. I was giving a talk at IBM Almaden Research Facility, and he took me aside to show me his project. I didn't know anything about keyboards, or input research, or even Android at the time; I was just a graphics engineer at Adobe. But I remembered the excitement that that researcher had about this platform that allowed people to experiment and go beyond the core capabilities of the product.

could handle on her own. A few other people were also writing copious amounts of framework code. One of those people was Jeff Hamilton (known to the team as "jham").

Jeff started at Google on the same day as Dianne. They had worked together on framework code at Be and PalmSource, and were about to do so again on Android.

Jeff's work on platforms began when he landed at Be for an internship during college. He actually failed his interview, because of his answer about how interrupt handlers[14] worked on BeOS, which was different from how they worked on Linux. He went home to research the difference and sent in an explanation, along with the correct answer, and the team changed their mind. They hired him for the summer, and for the next year while he was at college . . . and eventually for a full-time job when he finished college.

At Be, Jeff was on the kernel team, working on drivers for hardware like the touchscreen display and USB. He also got a good introduction to getting started at a scrappy Silicon Valley company: "First day, they showed me to my cube and it had a case and keyboard. They said, 'There's a motherboard over there, go ask George for a CPU.' They didn't have any RAM, I had to buy some at Fry's."[15]

After college, Jeff joined Be full time, and eventually joined PalmSource after that acquisition in 2001. But like other members of the team, including Joe, Dianne, and Mathias, Jeff eventually tired of PalmSource. "By August 2005, it seemed pretty clear that they had no customers." He had moved to Austin, Texas, so he looked for jobs in that area and found an opportunity at Motorola that looked perfect. "It'd be a local job. They wanted to build a new, modern smartphone OS, ship on all the phones instead of a one-off. The group I was joining had signed a deal to acquire PalmSource;[16] they said I'd fit right in. It all sounded really good, so I quit PalmSource, joined Motorola in August of 2005."

[14.] Interrupt handlers are used to transition from one part of the system to another; they are signals in the system that pass control elsewhere. For example, typing a key causes a hardware interrupt that passes control over to the input software to handle that key event.

[15.] Fry's Electronics was a Silicon Valley staple; it was the place geeks went to buy geek stuff or just to gaze in splendor at geek stuff on the shelves. Then online shopping took over and you could get your fix more easily without leaving your computer.

[16.] Jeff didn't know that at the time; he only found out after he joined Motorola.

But before the PalmSource deal closed, ACCESS swooped in and offered more money, and PalmSource took the higher bid. With the smartphone OS possibility at Motorola shut down, Jeff wasn't very inspired to stick around. Fortunately, his colleagues from Be/PalmSource were in the process of interviewing with and joining the Android team at Google. Jeff heard about the opportunity from his friend Joe. "I said I didn't know anything about search or the web, and I don't want to start a new job remotely, not knowing anybody on the team. Joe said 'Don't worry about the first one, and you already know over half the team. Just come interview.'" Joe repaid Jeff's favor of getting Joe in the door at Be years earlier by getting him hired even though he was remote: "He convinced Andy to hire me when I was in Austin and working from home."

When Jeff started on the team, Android wasn't so much a *platform* as a collection of random pieces of code, prototypes, and technology demos. "Joe had a demo of the window manager drawing a square—basic shapes on the screen. There was a guy[17] working on telephony. Mathias was working on graphics. But nothing was functional. There wasn't really an operating system."

One of Jeff's first tasks came from Brian Swetland, building a protocol[18] for debugging Android applications running on a device. Rather than implement his own system from scratch, Jeff got gdb (a standard debugging tool) up and running. This meant getting a bunch of other things working on the OS that gdb needed, like threading and support for debugging symbols.[19]

Once debugging was working, Jeff started work on Binder.

---

[17] Mike Fleming

[18] Protocol is a very geeky way of saying *language*. A protocol is essentially a standard way for systems to talk to each other, so that each side knows how to send information that the other will be able to understand. In this case, Jeff was building a debugging protocol that would allow someone using a desktop computer to debug applications running on an Android device; the protocol established standard mechanisms for communicating information between the systems.

[19] *Debugging symbols* are the collection of information about the code that is necessary to know when debugging an app. They are like the dictionary for the language of your binary application code, that can translate between the 0s and 1s of machine code and the readable names of functions for the humans that need to understand them. For example, if your code is crashing in a particular function, it's useful to know the symbolic name of that function—for example, myBuggyFunction()—rather than just the address of the function on the system (which is the only information that exists otherwise). Symbols are the extra pieces of data that the system doesn't require, but which humans need for debugging purposes.

BINDER

Binder was a concept that the engineers from PalmSource were familiar with from that previous company and OS.[20] Binder is an IPC[21] mechanism. Whenever something happens on an operating system that needs to involve more than one process, IPC is a system for sending these messages between those different processes. For example, when the user types onto a keyboard on a PC, the system process sends a message with that information to the foreground application process to deal with that key event. An IPC system (Binder, in the case of Android) defines that communication mechanism.

On an Android device, many processes are running at all times, handling different parts of the system. There's the system process, handling process management, application launching, window management, and other lower-level operating system features. There's the telephony process, keeping the phone connection alive. There's the foreground application that the user is actually interacting with. There's the system UI, which handles the navigation buttons, the status bar, and notifications. And so on—there are many, many processes, and they all need to communicate with other processes at some point.

IPC mechanisms are typically simple and low-level, which was something that the former Danger engineers wanted. As Wei Huang put it, "Danger liked to do things fast. Simple and fast. But mostly simple." But the team from Be, including Jeff, Joe, and Dianne, preferred the more full-featured (and complex) mechanism of the Binder approach that they had implemented at PalmSource. And since Binder was open sourced, it was available to use for this new platform.

This disagreement caused a problem between the teams. Mike Fleming was on the Danger side of the fence: "I was a Binder skeptic. I didn't think it

---

[20.] In fact, the original concept of Binder dated back much earlier, to Be. George Hoffman, who led the graphics and framework team at Be, needed a mechanism to allow the JavaScript UI layer of Be's ill-fated Internet Appliance to talk to lower-level system services. Binder was the result. It continued to evolve when many of those Be engineers worked on Palm OS at PalmSource, and evolved further when they got to Android. George did not end up working on Android, but worked with many future Android engineers at Be, and then PalmSource, designing with them many concepts that would eventually end up in Android, such as Activities and Intents.

[21.] IPC stands for Inter-Process Communication, which is a standard element of any operating system that allows different processes to send messages to each other.

---

had been very well thought through. It's true that they had done it at Palm. It was also true that they had never shipped it in a product.

"I was particularly upset with the fact that you had to make a blocking call[22] to the Binder that would then make a blocking invocation on the other side. I felt that caused a lot of unnecessary threading, and it didn't provide any value for my use case. Also, the original Binder Linux kernel driver was not fully robust. It took a lot of work to get it fully bullet-proof."[23]

The Binder skeptics didn't win that battle: Jeff and team forged ahead and implemented Binder, which became a fundamental part of the Android framework architecture. In the meantime, Mike ignored Binder for his telephony work: "I opened a Unix domain socket[24] between the Java process and the native interface layer process."

DATABASE

After Jeff got the initial Binder module working, he moved on to databases. Applications generally need to store information. If that data is anything non-trivial, they need something robust and full-featured; they need a database. At PalmSource, Jeff had worked with databases, but that company had wanted to create something new. Android wasn't trying to invent anything; they just needed a solution. "I had looked at SQLite[25] and thought, if we're trying to build our own phone and get it out the door ASAP, we probably shouldn't build our own database system from scratch. SQLite is there—it works." So Jeff ported the library to make it work on Android, creating APIs for app developers to be able to access it, and then moved onto the next project.

---

[22] A blocking call is a call to some function that must complete before the caller can continue. Blocking calls imply that the function being called must be quick and must complete successfully, so as to not cause the caller to be stuck waiting. Binder eventually (prior to 1.0) supported non-blocking calls as well.

[23] Arve Hjønnevåg later rewrote that driver completely, addressing the robustness problems.

[24] A socket is a much simpler mechanism than the Binder, more like a network connection through which information flows between the two processes.

[25] SQLite was an existing, open source database engine.

CONTACTS AND OTHER APPS

Because he was already dealing with application data, Jeff got pulled into a project to define how applications would share data. The data in someone's contacts needed to be available to other applications on the device (to be able to, say, call or message a friend). This resulted in the ContentProvider APIs, which Jeff then used as he started working on the Contacts application. "Obviously, we should have an address book and a call log, so I started building the Contacts ContentProvider to have an address book so you could dial the phone." Once that worked, he continued moving up the software stack to work on the UI of the Contacts application itself.

After Contacts, Jeff moved on to various other parts of the platform and the core applications. He helped out with the SMS app at one point, which was primarily being developed by Wei Huang. He also helped out on the telephony software that Mike Fleming was writing, and then assisted with the dialer app for the phone.

Dialer and Contacts, at that time, were both part of the same application. Jeff wanted to make some operations easier in the Dialer, so he created a controversial UI feature he called "Strequent." "In the dialer, there was one tab for your dialer, one tab for your call log, and one tab for your contacts. I created this other tab called Strequent. It was your starred contacts, followed by your frequently called people. Everyone thought it was really weird. I remember Steve Horowitz[26] didn't like it at all, but Rich Miner liked it." Rich convinced Steve to take it.

Jeff eventually worked on most of the core applications and ended up managing the apps team. He remembered a particular user issue with Calendar: "Sergey [Google's co-founder] came by. The Calendar app was crashing. His wife was sharing her calendar to him from Outlook. It turned out that Outlook had recurring events with exceptions that we had never seen before. Our event parser was crashing."

Jeff went to Sergey and explained the problem. "'We figured out the problem: your calendar has some data in it that we've never seen before and didn't expect, and it's causing our app to crash.' He said, 'My data isn't causing your app to crash! Your app is crashing on my data!'" Jeff remembered the

---

[26.] Steve was the Director of Engineering before 1.0.

situation clearly, many years later. It's hard to forget a Google founder and executive arguing with you.

The process that Jeff went through, starting at the lowest level of the system to get a native debugger working, then working on core framework internals and APIs, then data functionality and APIs, and ending up writing applications using some of the lower-level stuff he'd built,[27] is a good example of what people on the team did. Nothing, essentially, existed before Jeff got there, so he helped create the pieces one by one, building each one on top of the previous ones as more functionality came online. In a similar way, everyone on the team was building things up from the very basics and moving up to higher-level functionality as they were able to, eventually writing the applications that defined the user experience of Android.

JASON PARKS BROKE IT

Another Be/PalmSource alumnus who came to help out on Dianne's framework team was Jason Parks, who joined the Android team at Google in the Spring of 2006.

Jason Parks (known to the team as "jparks") had a catch phrase growing up: "I didn't break it, but I know how to fix it!" This slogan and concept stuck with him, eventually resulting in error codes in OSes he worked on with the label JPARKS_BROKE_IT.

Jason started programming early, learning BASIC in sixth grade. He continued programming through childhood and in college, but didn't graduate. "I wasn't really good with the words; I never finished the English courses. I had twenty-two credits to finish, but I applied to a job by accident." Jason had been playing with BeOS on his own, so when he saw a job posting for Be, he applied.

"But I applied for the wrong job; I applied for a manager/architect position. In their system, you could only apply for one position at a time. I thought, 'There goes that, I'll have to let it go until they reset it.' I got an email back for a phone interview for a job I was definitely not qualified for." He ended up

---

[27.] Jeff kept moving around the system as time went on. He worked with Near Field Communication (NFC is the close-proximity networking technology that allows you to pay for your coffee using your phone. I've heard that you can also pay for other things with it as well) and games, and eventually started and led what became Google Play services.

getting an interview and a job offer, but for a different position. He asked why they called him back when he'd clearly applied for the wrong job; he was told that his application caught their attention because he was so unqualified for the role.[28]

Jason worked with the other future Android people at Be, like Dianne, Jeff, and Joe, moved with them to Palm, and eventually left PalmSource to join the Android team.

Like Jeff and Joe, Jason also worked on many different areas of the platform. His first week, he worked on software to deal with time zones. Then he got telephony data working during his second week. He then moved on to various bits of the framework and apps over time.

Jason also played an important role in the overall organization—getting people to do stuff. One of the ways this happened was as a moderator between different groups. When people had disagreements (such as the various Danger-vs.-PalmSource-factions conflicts), Jason would try to mitigate those problems. "When the telephony guy was upset around APIs, he'd come to me and ask me to go talk to them [the framework team]. Same with Swetland. Horowitz would send me to talk to Swetland to calm him down. Between Mike [Cleron] and me and Dianne, we had a good working relationship. I'd explain to others the way things should be done.

"There were a lot of hotheads, a lot of conflict. Not only did you have the PalmSource/Danger thing, you had Googlers coming in saying 'This is the way you must do it.' But I think that conflict helped us."

Jason would also be tasked by Steve Horowitz to make sure that certain things happened. "Some people on the team called me the bulldog, because I was Steve's attack dog. When he needed something done, he would send me in."

FRAMEWORKING

The list of projects happening on the framework team goes on and on, because it really is the heart and soul of the Android platform. So much of

---

[28.] Getting hired at a company starts with getting noticed. With the number of resumes that any tech company constantly receives, it's important to just get someone's attention. I wouldn't normally recommend applying for the wrong job to achieve that goal, but it seems to have worked for Jason.

the rest of the system is reliant upon the fundamentals that were created on this team by Dianne, Jeff, Jason, and others. And it was all built from scratch, starting when these people began joining the team in late 2005. Meanwhile, the other pieces and apps of the platform were being built on top of the framework, like building the plane while it's flying with a cabin full of passengers, all hoping it reaches the destination before it reaches the ground.

14

UI TOOLKIT

The UI toolkit provides most of the visual elements on the screen. Buttons, text, animations, and the graphics that draw all of those things are all part of the UI toolkit on Android.

In late 2005, there was no UI toolkit (nor was there much of anything else, either). There was low-level graphics functionality that allowed some things to be drawn on the screen using the Skia library. And there were two conflicting ideas for how to build a UI toolkit on top of that graphics engine.

On one side, Mike Reed's Skia team had a working system which used XML to describe the UI and JavaScript code to provide the programming logic.

On the other side, the framework team preferred a more code-centric approach.

This decision, like so many in Android, happened through sheer effort. Andy Rubin had recently decided that Android would use Java as the main programming language. Joe Onorato decided it was time to dive in and implement the UI layer in Java. "It was basically a furious 'Let's get something done' time. Took about a day, 24-hour marathon.[1] I had Views [UI elements] up on screen."

---

1. Joe: "I had The Postal Service / *Give Up* CD playing on repeat for that coding binge. I still have weird delirious memories when I hear that album."

Mathias Agopian said of Joe, "He didn't tell anybody. One morning he showed up and said, 'Problem solved, it's in Java. Now we don't have to talk about it anymore because it's there.'"

Mike Reed remembered the decision to go with Joe's implementation: "Joe came in with very clear ideas. Especially because we were remote [the Skia team was in North Carolina], we just took a step back and let it work itself out."

Joe demoed his work to Andy, which didn't go as well as he'd hoped. "The first time I showed it to Rubin, he was less than impressed. The first thing I did was draw a red X on the screen from the UI. Apparently, that was the thing that something would draw on Danger when it kernel-panicked.[2] I showed him what I thought was a major achievement: 'Look, I got a View hierarchy done!'. But to him, it looked like the phone just crashed. He's like, 'Wow, you made the kernel panic.'"

But Joe's work was significant. It allowed developers on the team to start writing other pieces of the system that needed UI functionality.

Of course, many parts of the system were in flux during early development, and the UI toolkit was one of them. The system that Joe built was multi-threaded.[3] This approach is unusual in UI toolkits, as it requires very careful coding to correctly handle requests coming in willy-nilly without regard to threading concerns.

In March of 2006, three months after Joe wrote the initial View system, Mike Cleron joined Android. He saw complexities mounting in the growing code base that depended on Joe's multi-threaded UI toolkit.

MIKE CLERON AND THE UI TOOLKIT REWRITE

Mike Cleron never pictured himself going into computer science until he was in college. "I thought I was going to be an Econ major until I took Econ 1." His computer science classes worked out better: "I really enjoyed my

---

[2] A kernel panic is essentially a complete OS crash. A Linux kernel panic is the equivalent of the Blue Screen of Death on Windows.

[3] An explanation of multi-threaded programming is . . . way beyond the scope of this book. Suffice it to say that a multi-threaded architecture is much more complicated than a single-threaded one because the UI code is not as much in control of when it is being called from various parts of the application, potentially in parallel on different threads.

---

freshman year courses where we learned not about programming, but about data structures and algorithms. I thought binary tree traversal was the coolest thing ever. Big time nerd.

"It was the only thing I could possibly have gotten a degree in, because it was the only thing I could do still reasonably competently when the rest of my brain was shut down from exhaustion. I took a bunch of political science courses, close to being a major, but at one o'clock in the morning, 250 pages from finishing a 500 page reading assignment, I'm asleep. But when I'm 16 hours into a 16 hour programming assignment, my reptile brain is still letting me program in Emacs on my VT100.[4] I thought, 'I'd better major in this because I can graduate.'"

He continued on in computer science, eventually getting his master's degree, and stayed on at Stanford as a lecturer, developing some of the curriculum for undergraduates to make their on-ramp to computer science a little less severe than his had been (Mike's was the first year that Stanford even offered a computer science degree). "My mission as a lecturer there was to try to make the people who followed in my footsteps have less of a difficult time than I did. They [Stanford] had basically taken all their graduate level courses, subtracted a hundred, and said 'Now you have an undergraduate course.' They all assumed that you'd already had a computer science education and now you just needed to know a little more about compilers or automata."

Mike worked at Apple after he left academia, then moved to WebTV in 1996, where he worked with many future Android engineers. WebTV was acquired by Microsoft in 1997, and Mike continued working there for several more years.

In early 2006, Mike's manager at Microsoft, Steve Horowitz, left to join the Android team at Google. "It was really Steve leaving that made me think it was time for me to go. I wasn't having that much fun at Microsoft anymore, and Steve leaving wasn't going to make it better."

Steve said, "I remember having the talk with Mike Cleron, telling him before I had actually come to Google. I said, 'Mike, I have to let you know that I've just accepted an offer to go lead engineering on the Android acquisition

---

[4.] The VT100 was a video terminal connected to a larger computer in some back room, showing text characters. These terminals were common in the days before everyone had PCs, much less laptops, and pre-dated the graphical interfaces that became common after MacOS and Windows became pervasive.

at Google.' Before I could finish the sentence, he was like 'Here's my resume!' Mike was my first hire, and came on board fairly soon after I did."

Mike began life on Android by working on the UI toolkit, along with a host of other things, including the launcher[5] and the system UI. He eventually became the manager of what was called the "framework team," which comprised the UI toolkit, the framework team,[6] and various parts of the system UI, like the lock screen, launcher, and the notification system.[7]

One of Mike's first projects after joining Android in March of 2006 was to rewrite the UI toolkit code that Joe Onorato had written. There was growing disagreement over the toolkit's architecture; some people on the team felt that the multi-threaded nature of the system was causing undue complexity in both that code and in the apps that used it.

Mike figured there were three possible approaches for a UI toolkit. "The best outcome would be thread-safe, easy to use multi-threading. Second was single-threaded but at least you could wrap your head around it. Worst was multi-threaded but buggy, because you couldn't reason about it. We were headed for the last thing."

Mathias Agopian talked about writing code for the multi-threaded system. "When you wrote a View, you couldn't write it the traditional way, with member variables.[8] That led to a lot of multi-threaded bugs because app developers were not used to it. In particular, Chris DeSalvo[9] was a fierce opponent to this multi-threaded thing. Joe and Chris were going at it, fighting all

[5] Launcher is what the team calls the home app, which consists of the home screen and the *all apps* screen. Launcher is in charge of starting (launching) applications when users tap on their icons.

[6] Yes, there was a framework team in the framework team. Recursion is so important in software that it's used even in organizational structures. It all started out as a small group called the framework team, which did all of this stuff. But as the team grew and people focused on various aspects of it (like the system UI and UI toolkit), then the larger framework team comprised several sub-teams, including the actual "framework" team, which handled the non-UI portions of the APIs and OS.

[7] Mike continued to manage that overall framework team until 2018. He was my manager for several years when I worked on the UI toolkit team.

[8] The complexity of multi-threaded programming is that any thread can change values of things like member variables at any time. So if one thread assumes a certain value and then another thread changes it, it can lead to inconsistencies and unpredictable outcomes.

[9] Chris was an engineer on the framework team.

the time, Chris saying it was crap, didn't work. Mike was trying to weigh in, see what could be done."

Steve Horowitz got involved, as the director of the engineering team: "It was down to me deciding which one are we going to pick, because they could not convince one another. Honestly, I think we would've been okay with either direction, but I had to make a call."

Mathias continued: "Joe literally dropped it: 'Do whatever you want. It's not mine anymore.'"

Mike then rewrote the UI toolkit to its current single-threaded form. "That's the nastiest CL[10] that I worked on, trying to make all that stuff work in a different way." Mike's code formed the basis of the UI toolkit that the Android system had from that moment on.[11]

Along the way, Mike wrote, or at least inherited and enhanced, other fundamental pieces of Android's UI toolkit, like View (the basic building block of every UI class), ViewGroup (the parent and container of views), ListView (a list of data that could be scrolled and flung by the user), and various Layout classes (ViewGroups that define how their children are sized and positioned).

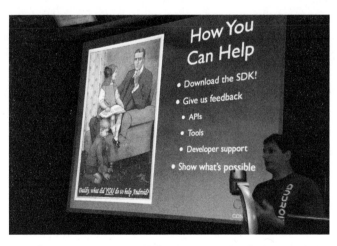

Mike Cleron, presenting at the first internal tech talk about Android at Google in August of 2007 (picture courtesy Brian Swetland)

[10.] CL = Changelist, discussed in the Jargon appendix.

[11.] And still has, to this day. It's much larger, of course, after a growing team of developers have worked on it, adding functionality and fixes over the last many years, but it's still the fundamental View system that Joe wrote overnight and then Mike rewrote to be single-threaded.

But Android's UI toolkit is more than just views and layout classes. For example, the UI toolkit is responsible for handling text.

ERIC FISCHER AND TEXTVIEW

Mike Cleron said that when he arrived at Android, "Eric Fischer, as far as I could tell, just found TextView in a stone cavern in a mountain somewhere. There was TextView in finished form. I never saw anyone creating TextView. It's just always been there."

A few years earlier, Eric had worked with Mike Fleming at Eazel, a startup founded by some members of the early Macintosh team. Both Eric and Mike went to Danger when Eazel fell apart in 2001.

One of the appeals of small companies like Danger is the ability to work on many different kinds of projects, compared to the opportunities available on a team that supports just part of a larger product. While at Danger, Eric worked on everything from text and internationalization to the build system to performance optimization. Working at Danger also gave Eric, years later, an appreciation for the faster development process at Android. "Android offered the promise of much faster and more flexible development by giving Google, and not the carriers, final responsibility for what went into the software."

Eric joined the Android team at Google in November of 2005. "My very first piece of code for Android was a C++ text storage class. For the first few weeks I was there, we thought we were going to write the user interface elements as C++ classes with JavaScript bindings." A few weeks later, Andy made the call to standardize on Java for Android.

"Once we decided to use Java instead, one of the first steps toward getting a working system was writing a new implementation of the core classes of the Java standard library, and I did some of that. All of that code except for the time zone handling was, I believe, replaced by the Apache Commons implementation before the first public release.

"I touched some other parts of the software, but most of my work went into the text display and editing system. The earliest development hardware was candybar[12] phones with only a 12-key numeric keypad, which is why

---

[12.] The "candybar" form factor, with the screen at the top and keyboard at the bottom, was named for its long, rectangular shape, which resembled a chocolate candy bar (maybe, if you squinted really hard and were really hungry for dessert).

there is a `MultiTapKeyListener` class for that style of agonizingly slow text entry. Fortunately, we quickly moved on to the Sooner development hardware with a tiny QWERTY keyboard instead.

On the left is the early candybar phone, nicknamed Tornado, which the team used until the later Sooner device. The phone on the right is an HTC Excalibur, which was the basis for Sooner after some industrial design modifications (and replacing the Windows Mobile OS with Android). (Picture courtesy Eric Fischer.)

"I made sure to handle bidirectional text layout from the beginning, which was sufficient for Hebrew, but not for Arabic."[13]

Software engineers tend to get emotionally attached to their code, and that was the case for Eric, who displayed his passion in the license plate for his car. "I had the California EBCDIC personalized license plate, for the 1960s IBM character code that competed with ASCII. Someone else in building 44 had UNICODE."[14]

---

[13] Arabic languages require bi-directional text support, which was finally implemented years later in 2011 for the Ice Cream Sandwich release (Android 4.0) by Fabrice DiMeglio and engineers on Google's internationalization team.

[14] ASCII and EBCDIC were competing standards for encoding text characters for computers. EBCDIC offered a larger character set (256 vs. 128), but was more complicated and non-intuitive for programmers. UNICODE is an international standard for text encoding, which incorporates ASCII (plus a lot more).

UNICODE battles EBCDIC as text standards in the Google parking lot (Eric Fischer's car is the one with EBCDIC). (Picture courtesy Eric Fischer.)

Text rendering (drawing the actual pixels for the text that is seen on the screen) was handled at a different layer, by Skia, discussed in Chapter 11 ("Graphics"). Skia rendered font characters into bitmaps (images) using an open source library called FreeType.[15]

One of the pervasive problems in the early days of Android was performance; the limited capabilities of the hardware at that time drove many of the decisions about the software design and implementation. These decisions bled over into how the code was written for the platform and the applications. As Eric said, "All my attempts at generality were undermined by the urgent performance concerns of running fast enough to be usable on the very slow early hardware. I had to put in all kinds of special fast paths to avoid memory allocation and floating point math when laying out and drawing plain ASCII strings with no style markup and no transformations like ellipsizing or password-hiding."

Eric observed an ongoing tension on the team, with disagreements on how things should be built. "Sometimes it felt like it shouldn't have succeeded. It was a classic 'second system effect' where a lot of us had done something similar before and thought we could do it again without all the mistakes from the first time. Those of us coming from Danger wanted to

---

15. Coincidentally, FreeType was created by David Turner, who joined Android in late 2006 to work on completely unrelated technology, the Android emulator.

make another user interface toolkit based on Java class inheritance, but get it right this time with a real operating system underneath and a robust service architecture on the other side of the network. The people coming from PalmSource wanted to do their activity lifecycle model and interprocess communication model again, but get it right this time. The people coming from Skia wanted to do QuickDraw GX again, but get it right this time. We were all wrong, and wrong in ways that clashed badly with each other. It took years of work to straighten out the consequences of all our bad early decisions and the interactions between them."

ROMAIN GUY AND UI TOOLKIT PERFORMANCE

More help for the budding UI toolkit came later, in 2007, in the form of an intern from France, Romain Guy.

Romain became a tech journalist in high school, writing articles on various programming languages, operating systems, and coding techniques. This freelance job gave him experience in, and access to, many of the popular platforms and languages of that era. He was introduced to operating systems like Linux, AmigaOS, and BeOS, and he became an expert in Java.

Romain went to a university in France and majored in computer science. But that school leaned more heavily on leadership and project management skills than pure programming, and Romain preferred the programming part of software development. So he came to Silicon Valley.[16]

Romain got an internship with Sun Microsystems,[17] where he spent a year working on Swing, the UI toolkit for the Java platform.

[16.] This dynamic of programming vs. managing continues to this day. I have friends in, and have talked to many developers in, various countries where simply being a programmer is not respected, or compensated, as much as being a manager of programmers. But being good as a programmer doesn't necessarily mean someone will be good at (or interested in) managing programmers. So developers that are passionate about programming and want to continue to do that job, while earning more money and respect than their society allows, end up either forming a consulting company (which bills companies for far more than the companies pay their full-time programmers) or giving up and moving to another place (like Silicon Valley) where the job of programming is more highly respected (and compensated).

[17.] Sun is where I first met Romain, in 2005. I was on the same team, working on graphics. We started writing a book together on Java UI technology, which we finished while he was back in France, finishing his degree. The book is called *Filthy Rich Clients* . . . but that's another story altogether.

The following year, in April of 2007, Romain came back to the US for an internship at Google. He landed on the Google Books team, where he was asked to work on a desktop application related to Gmail. It wasn't a topic that excited him, and he only lasted a week on that project. He knew people at Google like Bob Lee (who transferred to Android's core libraries team around the same time), Dick Wall (who worked on Android developer relations), and Cédric Beust (who was writing the Android Gmail app). They convinced Romain to come over to the Android team, and convinced management that the team needed him. Cédric asked Steve Horowitz to pull strings, and between Steve and Andy, they made it happen.[18] Romain transferred to the UI toolkit team, where he helped out Mike Cleron.

At the end of the summer, Romain flew back to France to pick up his degree and then returned to Google[19] to start a full-time job. He had gotten offers from both Sun and Google, but decided to join Google. "Sun had made me an offer that was much better than Google's. I joined the Android team because I loved the vision, the reason why we were doing this. There were a lot of reasons for Google, but it was also the idea: it was a space that could use a good open source operating system. At that time, there was no such thing that was viable for consumers at scale.

"Linux already had something. But to me this had a better chance because it was focused on a particular product. It was not a spec or just an idea of an operating system; it was also building the product. It was clearly a challenge, and chances are it would not succeed, but we had a shot at it. The best way to make it happen was to help.

"It was actually part of what made the job so fun in the early days. Until probably Gingerbread,[20] or maybe even ICS,[21] it wasn't clear it was successful

---

[18.] Dick Wall had that same conversation with Steve. Perhaps Romain wasn't transferred because of their glowing recommendations as much as Steve wanting to stop people asking him about it.

[19.] Meanwhile, I was still back at Sun, arguing that he should rejoin the Java client group there. But he decided to join Google and Android instead. In hindsight, he probably made the right career choice (one which I would make a few months later, leaving Sun in 2008 and eventually joining Android in 2010).

[20.] Android 2.3, released in late 2010

[21.] ICS = Ice Cream Sandwich, or Android 4.0, released in late 2011

enough to survive. Every release was not quite a 'do-or-die,' but it was 'do-or-maybe you should be careful about what's going to happen.'"

When Romain started as a full time employee, in October of 2007, the initial SDK was about to ship. There was still a lot of work to do on the platform to make it to 1.0. One of the first things he worked on was making touch input functional, which had become a hard requirement for that first release.

He also spent significant time and effort making the toolkit code faster. "Mike asked me to improve performance of invalidating[22] and re-layout.[23] Until then, invalidate()[24] was really dumb; it would just go up the hierarchy and mark everything invalid. If you did it again, it would go back up again. It was really slow. So I spent a lot of time adding all those dirty flags.[25] That made a huge difference."

But to do this work, he needed a tool that didn't exist.

There is a grand tradition on the Android team of having many small, single-purpose developer tools, each of which worked a bit differently than the others, and none of which worked together. This has changed over time, and most of these apps are now incorporated into the Android Studio IDE so that developers have consistent tools. But in the early days, the tools were written separately, one by one, by the developers who needed them.

For the view invalidation performance work, Romain needed a new tool. "I wrote 'hierarchyviewer' because it was really hard to know what was getting invalidated. So I wrote this viewer that would show me the tree of views and blink them a different color when they were marked dirty, when they would draw, and when there was a requestLayout().[26] As I was making optimizations, I could see what was happening. It would blink less!"

---

[22] "Invalidation" happens when UI objects have changed (like the text on a button changing) and may need to be redrawn.

[23] "Re-layout" happens when UI elements are added, removed, resized, or repositioned, causing other containers and elements to reposition and resize themselves accordingly.

[24] invalidate() is the method that is called to trigger invalidation.

[25] The UI drawing code tends to be very fragile because there are many "flags" that hold information about the drawn state of each UI element. That complex logic helped Android become fast enough to be usable on those early devices. But it created code that was somewhat brittle and difficult to maintain. Many times, someone would fix a bug or implement a new feature only to trip over these flags and unintentionally break some of the invalidation logic.

[26] requestLayout() is the method that is called to trigger the re-layout process mentioned earlier.

Another UI performance project that Romain took on was ListView.

ListView is a container that holds (wait for it . . .) a list of items. The trick with this element in particular is that it is, by its very nature, incredibly performance-sensitive. Its only purpose is to contain tons of data (images and text) and to be able to scroll through the items quickly. The key is "quickly." As items are coming onto the screen, the UI toolkit has to create, size, and place all of these new items, which then disappear as soon as they scroll off the other edge of the screen. It's a lot of effort to do all of this, and on that early hardware the toolkit couldn't keep up with it, so the user experience was . . . not great.

When Romain inherited this widget from Mike Cleron, it was able to contain, render, and scroll items. But its performance was far from acceptable, so Romain put a huge amount of effort into optimizing it. Avoiding object and UI element creation was a general pattern of Android development at the time for performance reasons, and ListView was an easy place to see why that pattern evolved.

LAUNCHER AND APPS

Like others on the team, Romain jumped into many other projects on Android in those early days (and beyond). Besides his core UI toolkit responsibilities, he took over the launcher application from Mike (who had started to lead the framework team and had other responsibilities beyond code), and also helped out on the Email[27] app when the contractor working on it left. Fortunately, Romain had relevant experience from his time as a tech journalist. "I had written articles on how to implement the IMAP protocol, so I was not completely out of my league. But that was on top of everything else that we were doing . . . which was a little much."

He also helped out with other apps. Since the platform was new, a lot of functionality was developed in response to application requirements. Applications needed new features from the platform, so they worked with the platform team to implement them.

[27.] Email was, at that time and for a few years after that, separate from Gmail. Gmail was the app used to retrieve mail for a Gmail account . . . and that's it. Email was used to connect to other mail services on the backend, like Microsoft Exchange.

One of the ongoing efforts for the apps teams at that time was performance. "Serving their needs was important, but also having them understand the cost of things. That's why hierarchyviewer came to be, because apps were creating way too many views. View hierarchies were way too expensive for our devices. That was a way to show them, 'You can see this monster tree that you've created, and this is very expensive for us.' Despite all of the optimizations we had, that was very expensive. So it was a way to help them figure out how to optimize their code. That's how I also came up with the merge tag, the include tag, and the viewstub,[28] to help them achieve what they need, but also reclaim some of that performance."

MANIFEST DENSITY

After 1.0 shipped, there was still plenty of work to do to get the platform to the state the team originally envisioned. One of the projects that had begun early on but which wasn't fully realized at 1.0 was support for different screen densities, which is described earlier in the Resources section of Chapter 13 ("Framework"). After 1.0, Romain took over the work begun earlier by Dianne and finished it off in time for the Eclair release,[29] in the Fall of 2009.

Screen density has a direct impact on the quality of the images on that screen; a screen with higher density can represent more information in the same space, leading to sharper, better images. Higher-density screens have resulted in higher-quality phone and laptop displays over the last several years. Higher-density camera sensors have also led to higher-quality photos, as the megapixel count of images produced from those sensors has soared.[30]

The initial G1 device, and all other Android devices until the Droid, had a density of 160 pixels per inch (PPI), which meant that there were 160 distinct color values (vertically and horizontally) in every inch of screen real

---

[28.] merge, include, and viewstub are all UI elements that essentially work like placeholders in the hierarchy and help minimize the number of views, and therefore the overhead for the toolkit.

[29.] Eclair was the release that Droid shipped with. The Droid had a higher screen density than the previous devices, so it was important that the density work was finished by then.

[30.] How fitting that Romain worked on pixel density; his hobby is landscape photography (you can see some of his work at *https://www.flickr.com/romainguy*, as well as on ChromeCast screensavers). So he benefited from advancements in hardware pixel density at the same time as he was enabling Android to take advantage of those improvements.

estate. The Droid had a density of 265 PPI. This higher density meant that more information could be represented, resulting in, say, smoother curved lines and text, or images with more detail. But developers needed a way to define their UIs to take advantage of these changes in density.

The system that Dianne, and then Romain, implemented allowed developers to define their UIs independent of the actual size of the pixels on a device, using the unit *dp* (*density-independent pixel*). The system would then scale these UIs appropriately based on the actual density of the device that the application was running on. This mechanism for handling screen density, along with related capabilities in the resource system for serving up different assets based on the density and the entire UI layout system for handling UI organization independent of screen sizes, were critical as Android matured. Android changed from a platform running on top of only one kind of device (the G1 and its follow-on devices at the same size and density) to a world full of all kinds of screen sizes and densities as manufacturers started to introduce vastly different formats for their customers.

TOOLKIT PERFORMANCE

Many pieces make up what the team calls the UI toolkit, since it's basically the visual side of the entire framework. What really defined the work for the team at that time (Joe, Mike, Eric, Romain, and others) was coming up with the toolkit APIs and core functionality, and then working on performance, performance, and performance.[31] The UI for Android is basically everything that the user sees, so performance for this front line of the platform is even more important, because problems there are so very noticeable. So the team kept optimizing things . . . and to some extent, still does.

---

[31] Performance was everyone's responsibility, but in late 2006 Jason Parks created the Turtle Team, a group of people who reviewed and worked on app performance on an ongoing basis.

15

SYSTEM UI
AND LAUNCHER

The system UI of Android is the set of all of the visual elements that the user interacts with on the screen outside of apps, including things like the navigation bar, the notification panel, the status bar, the lock screen, and the launcher.

In the early days on the team, all of this work happened in the overall framework team, which consisted of just a small handful of people. Functionality like the status bar, lock screen, and launcher were written by people who were also writing core framework and UI toolkit code.[1] This was an efficient way to handle the different pieces, because the same people who were writing these pieces were also writing the platform features that were needed, so they could implement everything they needed on both sides of the problem. On the other hand, it also meant that they were all incredibly busy.

LAUNCHER

In the run up to 1.0, in 2008, launcher (the home screen app responsible for viewing and launching applications) was just another implementation detail of the UI toolkit. Mike Cleron, the original developer on the UI toolkit team, worked on launcher before passing it on to Romain Guy. Romain

---

[1] In fact, there wasn't even a name for this collection of things. Dan Sandler said that when he arrived on the team in mid-2009 they were all just individual pieces. He and Joe Onorato gave this collection of pieces the name System UI, which seems to have stuck.

continued to own and improve the app for several releases,[2] in addition to the rest of the UI toolkit work he was responsible for.

One of the ongoing projects that Romain worked on for launcher (and for the rest of the system) was performance. Romain remembered the constraint that Steve Horowitz gave him: "Launcher needed to cold-start[3] in half a second. Launcher has to go peek at every apk[4] and load the icons and strings, so there was a lot of multi-threaded code and batching and deferring updates on the UI thread."

Romain was also constantly adding features to launcher, like folders for organizing application icons, and application widgets, and shortcuts (icons on the home screen), and a parallax effect between the wallpaper background and the pages of the home screen.

Later on, for the launch of the Nexus One, Andy Rubin wanted something visually exciting. Joe Onorato explained: "For Eclair, Rubin wanted something flashy." Andy was light on specifics; Joe remembered him saying, "Just do something cool." In the two months that they had, they wrote a new launcher using the 3D capabilities of the new device. "GL was just starting to work well enough, so we did that 3D launcher."

The 3D launcher was a special effect in the all apps screen that lasted for several releases. The user saw a normal 2D grid of applications, but as they scrolled the list up and down, the top and bottom edges faded away into the distance like a *Star Wars* intro-text effect. It was subtle but powerful, hinting at the 3D power behind the system (and the potentially large number of apps on the system), but without being too ostentatious or difficult to navigate.

---

[2] Finally, in mid-2010, the launcher was given a dedicated team, after Google acquired the company BumpTop and assigned most of those engineers to work on the launcher.

[3] *Cold-start* means that it is the first time the application is being launched since reboot. It is the worst-case scenario for an application, where it has to load in everything to start up. A *warm start*, on the other hand, benefits from the application still running in the background, so much of it is still in memory and startup is therefore much faster.

[4] Apk, or Android Package, is the file format of an Android app. It contains all of the code, images, text, and anything else the app needs to launch and run. Developers build their source code into an apk file, which is uploaded to the Play Store and then downloaded by users onto their devices.

The Nexus One all apps screen had a 3D effect that showed the top and bottom of the apps list scrolling away into the distance.

NOTIFICATIONS

Years ago, before the age of smartphones, I frequently missed or was late for various meetings. I used a calendar app on my PC, but it was better at telling me when I had missed an appointment than when I was about to miss one. I remember wishing for a way to be notified about these events in real time, so that I could stop missing them.[5]

This connection between the digital data in our lives and timely updates for that data was finally made through notifications on our smartphones. Of course, these updates go way beyond calendar events to email messages, texts, and a plethora of other updates from the various applications and services on our phones.

One of Android's unique and powerful features, since the very beginning, was its system of notifications, alerting the user to information from their installed applications, even if they weren't using those applications at the time.

[5.] Or so that I could at least choose the ones I wanted to miss.

Before smartphones, notifications were simpler (and less useful). Early data devices, like the Palm Pilot PDAs, had alert features in calendar and alarm apps. The user could configure these applications to play a noise, show a dialog, or illuminate an LED. Alerts of this sort were therefore limited to things the user thought to enter. All of the data on the device was created and synced by the user; there wasn't information coming out of the ether onto the device.

But once devices started connecting to the internet, new information, including email, messages, and even new calendar appointments, could land on the device asynchronously, and the user had to be told. Thus the need, and solution, for notifications was born. Dan Sandler, who joined Android in 2009 and led the system UI team, said, "The Danger Hip-top/Sidekick device took a tentative step forward in the state of the art on user alerts, with its rainbow notification light under the scroll wheel that could be used for SMS and new emails. Android would pick that ball up and run very, very far with it."

There has always been a tension between apps and the operating system. Every app assumes that it's the most important thing in a user's life, so obviously the user wants to know everything possible from that app at all times. The user, meanwhile, might be surprised and annoyed to receive a notification from a game they just installed informing them that there's a new level available. Part of the job of the system UI team over the years has been to provide limits for the applications to obey, as well as tools for the users to be able to mute overly chatty applications. In fact, part of the job of the operating system itself is, as Dan explained, "to provide limits for applications. Usually this is about shared resources on the device, like files, CPU time, and networking. With notifications, Android added the user's attention to the set of things that the operating system mediated."

Dianne Hackborn implemented the first notification system; icons appeared in the status bar at the top of the screen to alert users that there was information available in these other applications. Then Dianne and Joe Onorato worked on the Notification Panel, which the user pulled down from the top of the screen to display more information for the notifications. Users could tap on an item in the panel, which launched that application so that the user could see that new email, read the new text message, and so on.

Joe explained, "[Dianne] did the first pull-down. But I spent a bunch of time making its physics work."[6]

Ed Heyl said, "I remember Joe, over the weekend, worked and worked and worked, and he finally got it working. He's walking around the office showing everybody, 'Look, what do you think about this? Watch, you just go like this, and you pull down and it shows you stuff, and then just goes away.'"

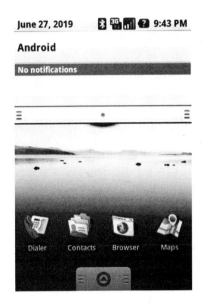

June 27, 2019   9:43 PM

Android

No notifications

Dialer   Contacts   Browser   Maps

This is what notifications looked like in early versions of Android. The notification shade pulls down from the top of the screen to show current alerts for the user from all of their applications.

Notifications were acknowledged to be something that distinguished Android from the other players in the smartphone market from day one. In the article "Android: A 10-Year Visual History"[7] *The Verge* had this to say: "It was almost universally acknowledged that Android nailed the notification system on day one. It would take iOS another three years before launching

---

[6.] One of the things that Joe had to figure out was how to make the panel move smoothly in and out, which was difficult on such limited hardware. The trick was to pre-allocate three entire windows in the system to the different pieces that the panel needed: the background, the items, and the status bar. Even when the panel wasn't showing, it was still taking up these precious resources just so that when it was needed, the user wasn't disappointed by its appearance.

[7.] *https://www.theverge.com/2011/12/7/2585779/android-10th-anniversary-google-history-pie-oreo -nougat-cupcake*

a design as effective at triaging messages and alerts coming from users' ever-growing collection of mobile apps. The secret was in the G1's unique status bar, which could be dragged downward to reveal every notification in a single list: text messages, voicemails, alarms, and so on. The fundamental concept lives on (in a refined form) to today's latest version of Android."

LIVE WALLPAPERS

Android 1.0 shipped with a feature called *Wallpapers*, which allowed users to choose a picture to serve as the background of the home screen in the launcher. Wallpapers were a great way to show off, and personalize, a smartphone's large display.

But Andy wanted something new and special for the Nexus One, which was launching with the Eclair 2.1 release in January of 2010. He asked for a feature called *Live Wallpapers*. Since smartphones offered not just a large screen, but also a powerful computer behind that screen, wouldn't it be nice to use the computer to enable rich graphical experiences that moved and entertained?

So Andy asked the framework team to make it happen. Dianne Hackborn and Joe Onorato worked on the underlying system and Romain and others worked on the actual wallpapers, coming up with the designs, the overall look, and the actual functionality for the first set of them.

They had five weeks to make it happen.

Andy had originally asked that the wallpapers be implemented in Processing, a graphics rendering system. This was a great idea in terms of functionality, but when Romain got it working on Android, he saw that it wasn't going to be fast enough for mobile phones. With an animation rate of only one frame per second, the wallpapers were more Dead than Live. So Romain found a different way to make them work.

Jason Sams (a graphics engineer on the team who had also worked at Be and PalmSource with Mathias, Dianne, Joe, and others) had been working on a low-level graphics system at the time called RenderScript, which allowed applications to take advantage of both the CPU and the GPU for drawing graphics quickly. Romain used RenderScript to achieve fluid animation for the wallpapers that needed it, and ended up writing these four wallpapers for the release:

- Grass, which showed blades of grass gently swaying against a backdrop of sky, whose color changed according to the time of day where the phone was located.

- Leaves, which showed leaves falling on water, creating ripples on the surface. This was a team effort, with Mike Cleron wrapping a ripple effect (originally written by Mathias Agopian ... or it might have been Jason Sams) into a wallpaper, adding pictures he took[8] of leaves from a Japanese maple in his yard.

- Galaxy, which showed a "3D"[9] view of the universe, with a massive star field rotating around the center.

- Polar Clock, which showed the time in a more visually interesting way.

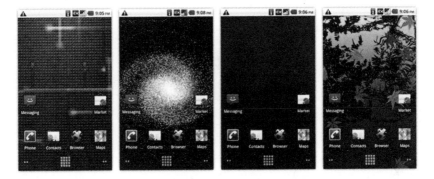

Four of the Live Wallpapers that launched with the Nexus One: Particles, Galaxy, Grass, and Leaves (picture courtesy the Android Developers Blog, February 5, 2010)

In addition to these wallpapers, Mike Cleron wrote one called Particles, and Marco Nelissen (who worked on audio for the platform) wrote three wallpapers including two sound visualizers.

---

[8] Mike, an accomplished photographer, said, "I needed some images quickly and did not want to go through a huge legal/copyright review." I believe that many photography hobbies are started, or at least encouraged, because someone needs to use a simple picture for an application or a presentation, and the overhead of getting permission to use someone else's work is too onerous or time-consuming for such a casual requirement.

[9] I put "3D" in quotes because the galaxy looked three-dimensional, but the graphics actually consisted of only 2D images. As Romain said, "That's graphics for you: if it looks good, it is good."

At the end of the five week period, the team had a fully functional Live Wallpaper system, including an API that external developers could use to write their own. Sadly, Romain was only able to invent, design, prototype, and implement four wallpapers in that five-week period, and the team launched the device with fewer than the ten wallpapers that Andy had requested.

THE FACE OF ANDROID

Android's system UI provides the graphical functionality that allows a user to control their device. From logging in, to timely notifications, to navigating around the UI, to launching apps, the system UI is the first app-like thing that the user interacts with on their device. It allows users to get to the functionality and information they need, which is what their smartphone is all about.

Dan Sandler sent me this drawing, saying, "After I described System UI as 'the face of Android' one too many times, I created this unofficial logo . . . which most of the team is horrified by."

16

DESIGN

Design is everything. Design is how people see a product, what they feel when they use a product. It's part of why something succeeds and something fails.

—IRINA BLOK

IRINA BLOK AND THE ANDROID MASCOT

One of the most recognizable aspects of the Android operating system is the green robot mascot, designed by Irina Blok:

Although this logo has come to represent Android worldwide, it was originally intended just for developers. Irina said, "The objective was to create excitement in the developer community and create something that was very much like a Linux penguin."

There were not many constraints on the design project. The Android team came to Irina's internal branding team and made a request. They said the name of the product was Android, and they wanted a compelling launch story. They suggested making it look human, and wanted something that would get developers excited.

Irina spent about a week coming up with various ideas before submitting the final design.

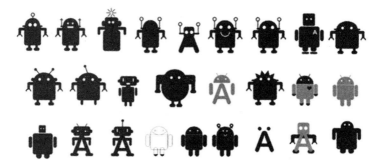

Series of sketches that Irina produced on her way to the final bugdroid image (pictured on the far right, in the second row; picture courtesy Irina Blok)

Note that the black logos seen in the sketch sheet are not "black" as much as they are colorless; black is just a neutral color she was using while she iterated on early shapes and ideas. You can see the A for Android incorporated into many of the ideas (though not the final one). You can also see that there is a black version of the final logo, in the center bottom of early designs. That's close to where the design ended up (with the addition of two antennae), but Irina remembers it as one of her first ideas.

One of the important elements in the final design was the shape itself. "The logo was inspired by an international symbol. There is a very simple symbol of a human. I tried to come up with the equivalent symbol for Android." Irina had worked with ideas of pictograms for other branding projects, which were powerful because of "how people see pictograms and signs and how they can communicate without words. They're so simple and they communicate across all cultures."

Irina also strove for simplicity: "Since the logo was meant to be a blueprint, the shape itself couldn't be too intricate."

Blueprint refers to another aspect of the final design: it was released into open source and developers were encouraged to use it and to create variations on that theme: "It could be decorated differently. That's what this logo system is."

There are a couple of elements about how the mascot was released that made her blueprint system work. One was that the bugdroid[1] is explicitly licensed for reuse, under a Creative Commons license. On the Android brand

---

[1] The robot has been called many names. For example, the original art files are simply called *robot*. But the only name used by the Android team for it is *Bugdroid*, which was coined by Fadden.

---

guidelines site, it says, "The green Android robot can be reproduced and/or modified as long as the following Creative Commons attribution line is included...."

This license gives anyone the right to use and modify the robot. But if it were just a small JPEG file, it wouldn't lead to very interesting variations. That's where the second part of the strategy kicks in: The logo was released in multiple file formats that lend themselves to redesign. First of all, there is a high-resolution version in the PNG format with a transparent background. But if you really want to modify the image, you'll want one of the other *vector* formats (EPS, SVG, and AI), which allow you to work directly with the robot's geometry.

Making the robot freely usable was revolutionary. Irina spoke about more traditional approaches of branding: "Identity comes in brand guidelines, which is a really giant book with restrictions: 'Here's a clear space around the logo. Here are the colors. . . . ' The logo is sacred. And this was just completely ripping that traditional notion apart." This aspect of the logo came not from the Android team itself, but from Irina's branding group, in response to Android being open sourced: "This was our creative idea to address that. Being a designer, your job is to communicate what the product stands for. That was a revolutionary creative idea at the time. This was not given to us as a constraint; this was our solution, which I think is the best thing about this logo."

Once the robot was released into the wild, it began to grow outside of Google and Android. "The logo was released as a system and it started to take on a life of its own. It started to be dimensional. You could see statues. It was almost like giving birth to a child and then watching the child grow. It started taking the first step, and then started to talk. Once it moved on, I watched it grow from a distance."

Once the external community got ahold of the robot, it took on a life way outside of its original target audience of developers: "It was just a developer release. It was never meant to be a consumer-facing logo. It was a small project, focused on developers. But it became so popular that it just grew bigger and bigger and bigger and spread to being consumer-facing."

It can be difficult to gauge the effectiveness of branding with any product. "Sometimes you can't really measure the impact of the brand. The brand gives a product personality. And it generates excitement. Because we're all human, and it's emotional, and it helps to tell the story, and relate to the brand. This also excites the developers to develop more stuff, and it also excites the consumer.

"Design is everything. Design is how people see a product, what they feel when they use a product. It's part of why something succeeds and something fails.

"At the time, you don't think about those things—you just get things done. So it's very intuitive. You don't do user research for the logo: you just get it done."

GIVEN THE GREEN LIGHT

And what about the iconic green color of the original logo? Variations on the robot come in all kinds of colors, but green is the original and the main color associated with it. Irina said, "Green is the original color of code."

As in, green text on black terminal screens, like the VT100, a callback to programming in the old days (and scenes from the movie *The Matrix*, which were visual callbacks to the same terminal-coding origin). The logo was always about software.

Along with the final design, Irina sent in some variations, to inspire people to play with it.

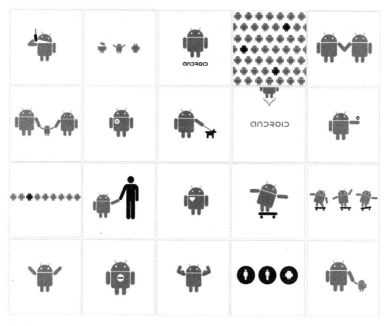

Variations on the robot that Irina submitted for inspiration, many of which ended up on t-shirts at the Google merchandise store (picture courtesy Irina Blok)

"My job was to inspire and try to come up with guidelines for how to use this mark. But not to iterate on what this means to me. Because it's not about me. It's about everybody."

JEFF YAKSICK AND UI DESIGN

The design of Android's user interface has gone through several contortions and generations over the years, getting progressively more polished and consistent with each effort. But in the beginning, there wasn't even a single designer, much less a design team or design concept.

Jeff Yaksick was the initial Android design team. He didn't start on Android until December of 2005, six months after the Android team started at Google, around the time that hiring started ramping up.

Jeff started his career at NeXT Inc., but later moved to WebTV (which was then acquired by Microsoft), where he worked with future Android people including Chris White, Andy Rubin, and Steve Horowitz. After co-founding Android, Chris reached out to Jeff to see if he was interested in joining their startup (which was then focused on a camera OS). But Chris couldn't promise that a future at Android would be as secure as Jeff's Microsoft job, so Jeff stayed where he was. Then Google acquired Android in July of 2005 and Jeff joined the Android team that December.

When Jeff started, there wasn't a lot to design for; the initial Android system was really just coming into being. So he worked on some of the basic visuals, like the look of buttons. And checkboxes. He also worked on color palettes, gradients, and fonts.

"One of the first things, was: What do we use as a font? I looked at all the open source font stuff at the time. The original font that I found wasn't broad enough for as global as Google intended to be.[2] So I worked with Ascender, a font studio. I helped art-direct the original font for 'Droid,' the system font."

---

[2] Another example of Android aiming high from the beginning, thinking more about the eventual platform for a large (and international) ecosystem, rather than just a point-product for the US.

Design sketches and final set of Droid fonts (picture courtesy Steve Matteson)

Jeff eventually got some help when German Bauer joined, in September of 2006. Jeff and German worked on a wide spectrum of design tasks, from the look of the UI controls to the launcher to the design of the mail and browser applications.

Eventually, since there was a lot of design work necessary for the first release, Andy contracted with The Astonishing Tribe (TAT), a UX design firm in Sweden. TAT designed the overall look of the system and the core experience that shipped with the G1.[3] Jeff and German continued to help out on various apps like Settings, and rounded out the widget set (buttons, checkboxes, and other UI elements) for the system. They also inherited all of TAT's work when their contract expired.

There was a mad rush in the run-up to 1.0 to re-implement the phone UI. There were some legal constraints about how it had to look and function which required a lot of redesign work without much time left in the schedule. "We scrambled, did a Herculean effort to redesign the phone experience so we could actually ship a phone. I had designed this kind of dark-themed UI with a gradient color: green for connected and red for hung-up. Toward the end, before we shipped, it got a review between Andy Rubin, myself, and Sergey Brin. Brin was notorious about speed, and said, 'Why do we need gradients?

---

[3] There's a subtle Easter egg from TAT: the analog clock face on the G1 shows the word "Malmo," which is the name of the town where TAT was located.

They take more processing power.' I think he'd be happy to have big buttons on the screen, nothing exciting. I had come into Google from Microsoft and I was still kind of new. I didn't really know that Sergey Brin and Larry Page were kind of running the show. So I was a little snarky to Sergey."

Bob Lee mentioned this founder-design dynamic as well: "When we were first starting, Larry and Sergey, probably Sergey, insisted on no animations,[4] because they were a waste of time. Which to look at phones now . . . That's kind of why Android was a little more spartan."

There was still plenty to do after 1.0, as the system kept evolving. Jeff worked on the early software keyboard experience, which was new after 1.0, since the G1 used only a hardware keyboard in 1.0. The design team also started to grow after 1.0, adding more designers and people to lead that team.

TOYS

One other thing that Jeff helped out with were Android toys.

Jeff was into *urban vinyl*[5] toys in those early days coming up to 1.0. He had the idea of producing a toy for Android. Dave Bort, an Android engineer, was friends with Andrew Bell,[6] who ran the artist studio Dead Zebra, Inc. Jeff sent Andrew some ideas of what he was thinking and they worked with Dave and Dan Morrill (on Android's developer relations team) and made it happen.

The original mockups that Jeff sent to Andy to propose doing a line of Android figurines (picture courtesy Jeff Yaksick)

[4.] Dianne remembered, "We had some arguments about this. I had started implementing animations in the window manager, but we were forced to turn them off. I would have been unhappy if we had to turn them off forever, but at least for 1.0 it did take some work off of us."

[5.] I didn't know urban vinyl was a thing until Jeff used that phrase. I think it's just a more complicated way of saying "action figures" to make it okay for adults, just like "graphic novel" is a more mature and intellectual way of saying "comic book."

[6.] They met years earlier at San Diego Comic-Con.

From that original toy grew an ongoing series of Android collectible toys. On a regular basis (nearly every year), another set of new designs come out (and then sell out quickly). Jeff contributed three of these designs: Noogler, Racer, and Mecha.

Jeff's Racer figurine (right), pictured with the classic Bugdroid (picture courtesy Andrew Bell)

The design sheet for the Racer figurine (picture courtesy Andrew Bell)

The Noogler figurine that Jeff designed. "Noogler" is the term used at Google for someone new to the company (as in "new Googler"). The cap on the figurine is similar to the one that all Nooglers are given in their first week at Google. (Picture courtesy Andrew Bell.)

The other figurine design that Jeff contributed to was on a slightly different scale: the first lawn statue. As 1.0 was approaching, Andy decided that the Android building on the Google campus needed a statue. Andy knew someone that created foam statues: Giovanni Calabrese, owner of the company Themendous. He connected Jeff with Giovanni, Jeff sent in some designs, and they made it happen. Andy originally asked for a larger statue than was possible, given the realities of transporting it from the studio, so they reduced its size to make it work.[7]

The original Android statue (nicknamed "bigdroid"), shown next to Andy McFadden for scale, in October of 2008. The statue stood for many years on the lawn in front of building 44, where most of the original team worked. (Picture courtesy Romain Guy.)

---

[7] Everything about early Android entailed making it work under size constraints.

Jeff reflected back on Android's and Google's design evolution: "When I joined Google, it was probably akin to Microsoft early on, when they started to do Windows 95, and then Vista. At that point, design started to matter. NeXT, Microsoft, Google—they're all engineering-based companies. It's always been a challenge to convince engineering that this stuff's important. I think Apple definitely helped move the needle: Design is important."

17

THE ANDROID BROWSER

To understand the Android Browser application, it's important to first understand the state of web browsing before Android.

Google has always cared deeply about web technology. From the beginning, Google's main mission has been supplying results to search queries. So investing more broadly in web technology like browsers made sense; the better the vehicles are that deliver those results, the better experience Google could offer for those results. This was especially important to Google back in the early 2000s, with the state of web browsing enabled by browser companies at that time.

THE GREAT BROWSER WARS

In the early days of the internet, the Netscape browser was king; desktop users would download and use Netscape because that was how you got to the web. But Microsoft came out with their own browser, Internet Explorer (IE), eventually bundling it with Windows. Bundling IE virtually guaranteed that Microsoft's browser would become the default for most users because it came installed as part of the OS and it was (at that time) good enough. Internet Explorer even became the default browser on MacOS until Apple came out with its own Safari browser in 2003.

The tension between Netscape and IE was at the heart of what Wikipedia amusingly (albeit correctly) calls the "First Browser War," which resulted in lawsuits and, ultimately, Netscape's demise as Internet Explorer[1] took over the planet.

---

[1] In 1997, I was talking to a Microsoft "evangelist" about the concern of writing web applications that could run cross-platform. The fear of developers at that time was that web apps written for IE would run only on Windows, since there was functionality for IE that differed from that on Netscape's browser. His response, somewhat tongue-in-cheek (but somewhat not) was that cross platform wouldn't be a concern when everyone ran IE and Windows.

During this time, Microsoft was essentially in the position of dictating how people could access the Web, since IE was increasingly the door through which they entered.

To ensure that all users had access to great web experiences, including new web technologies that were being introduced, Google started funding web browser development. At first, Google worked with the Mozilla foundation, helping out with the Firefox browser. In particular, Google contributed engineering resources by implementing or helping out with some of the improvements in that browser, including things like performance improvements, inline spell-checking, the software update system, and browser extensions. Google didn't have an operating system on which to bundle a browser, like Microsoft or Apple, but it could provide a better browser alternative and encourage people to switch to it.

Google decided to push this approach further when it created the Chrome browser in 2006. It started from scratch (using the open source WebKit code base) and built an entirely new browser to enable the kind of web experience that Google wanted users to have. Google focused on adding modern web functionality and on making browsing faster.[2] Google also bundled access to its search engine by default in Chrome; typing a search query in the browser's address bar showed search results on google.com as if the user had gone to Google's home page and typed into the search bar.

Chrome launched in September of 2008 and eventually got good traction. Users returned to the world of downloading a browser app instead of just using the one that came conveniently bundled with their desktop computer.

ANDROID NEEDS A BROWSER

Android's need for a mobile browser was different from Google's need for a desktop browser.

Unlike the situation with desktop browsers, the Android platform was being built from scratch. They didn't need a better browser; they needed *any* browser. Specifically, they needed an application through which users could

---

[2] There's a video on YouTube that the Chrome team posted in 2010, "Google Chrome Speed Tests" (*https://youtu.be/nCgQDjiotG0*) that proves the point by comparing website loading speed to a potato gun, sound waves, and lightning. It's not clear how websites or browsers relate to any of these things, but it's pretty funny and gets the point across.

view websites on their phones, just like they would on their desktops. They also needed a way to incorporate web content directly into other applications, because they realized that the line between mobile applications and web content was blurring.

For example, a mobile application may want to show content from a website to a user. Sometimes it's better to show that content directly in the app, rather than redirecting the user off to a browser app. This dynamic not only enables a more seamless experience, but also ensures that the user doesn't leave the app forever. Also, many developers were more familiar with HTML and JavaScript, the languages of the web, so giving them a way to create web content in mobile apps expanded the developer audience and made it possible for people to create basic Android applications more quickly.

The Android team created WebView to answer this need. WebView is a viewer for a web page that can be embedded inside a larger Android application. It was developed in conjunction with the Android browser because the browser is, essentially, a WebView surrounded by extra controls and UI.

But in the beginning, none of this existed and the platform needed all of it. So they needed a developer to pull it together. Fortunately, many of them had worked with such an engineer at Danger: Wei Huang.

WEI HUANG AND THE ANDROID BROWSER

Wei had years of experience developing web browsers and developing software. But that experience didn't start in childhood.

When Wei was twelve, he took a programming course. But the workings of binary math eluded him and he gave up. When his mother showed him an article about computers being the future, Wei was convinced that he'd just ruined his life.

Many years later, in high school, he tried programming again, this time with more success. He ended up getting a degree in electrical engineering and then fell in love with computer graphics programming in grad school.

After grad school, Wei got a job at Microsoft, working with other future Android people, including Steve Horowitz. Wei worked on the web browser for the WebTV and IPTV products, learning what it took to render web content on non-desktop screens. But eventually, he wanted to do something else. "Helping people watch more TV didn't seem like a really noble thing."

Steve put Wei in touch with Andy Rubin at Danger. Danger had not yet made the pivot to phones; they were still working on their "Nutter Butter" data exchange device, which didn't interest Wei. "I wasn't sure that was going to sell. The business model seemed a little weak. So I decided to go to AvantGo. I felt I had a more sure thing to succeed there.

"It was not a very bright decision."

AvantGo went through an IPO shortly after Wei got there, in September of 2000, right around the time the dot-com boom was starting to implode. AvantGo suffered along with a lot of other startups. "My timing was just horrible. I caught the end of that boom and then everything crashed." Also, the work and the culture were not quite what Wei wanted, so he looked elsewhere. "I reached out to Andy. After the VC funding, they decided to do a phone. That sounded more exciting, so I joined Danger in January of 2001."

At Danger, Wei was once again working on a web browser. Danger's phones were very limited, so the model was different from the way that browsers ran on desktop computers (or on Android phones later). Danger ran a *headless*[3] browser on the server. When a user navigated to a web page in the browser app on their Danger phone, that page would render on the server. The server would then reformat the page and send down a simplified version to the phone. This approach didn't give users complete web capability on their phones, because it lacked the dynamic capabilities of web pages. But they had a web browsing experience that was close to what they were familiar with on desktop computers and far richer than they were used to on other phones.

Wei spent four years at Danger, shipping browsers on a couple of Danger's Hiptop devices. Eventually, he was ready for something new, hopefully at another startup. A friend from Danger, Chris DeSalvo, suggested he talk to Andy Rubin, who had since left Danger and was running a startup in stealth mode called Android. Wei IM'd Andy that evening. Andy asked if he wanted to join.

"He said, 'Oh by the way, we're being acquired by Google.'

"I had this sinking feeling, because I was looking for a startup. This was not a startup. I had to think about it. I didn't know Google well at the time. I thought it was just a search company. I didn't really understand the full

---

[3] Headless essentially means a computer without a display. In this case, the server created content that was displayed elsewhere.

spectrum of Google's ambitions. But the excitement Andy conveyed still convinced me to join."

Wei started on the Android team at Google in September of 2005. He was the second post-acquisition employee, after his friend Chris.

Wei's first project was ... another browser. But there was a lot of work to do before he could write the browser application because Android, as a platform, didn't really exist yet. "I downloaded the code base. I was a little surprised. How did you sell this company to Google for just a bunch of JavaScript?"

The first task was to pick a starting point for the browser. By the time Android began, there were multiple open source browser engines to start from, so Wei didn't have to write the entire application from scratch. WebKit, which was based on another open source browser project, KHTML, was started by Apple and was the basis for Apple's Safari browser. "I really liked the code base, so it was a no-brainer for me."

Wei got to work building a browser based on the WebKit engine. Meanwhile, the browser team was growing, starting with management: Rich Miner.

RICH MINER BUILDS THE TEAM

Rich Miner, who went on to help establish many of Android's early corporate partnerships, knew business and he knew tech. He was introduced to programming in elementary school, when the class learned Fortran on punch cards. "All of that, to this day, has me amazed at how much memory we consume in our apps, and I think of what I was doing to squeeze modified code in place."

Rich first showed his crossover skills of business + engineering when he was a freshman in college. He'd written a game for his Commodore 64 computer and proceeded to sell it with the help of some friends. "My roommates and I had a cassette[4] duplication system in our dorm and made packages ourselves. I would go around and literally peddle them to local Commodore dealers. I took an ad out in one of the Commodore magazines and did email fulfillment."

[4.] Cassette tapes were commonly used for long-term storage in early personal computer devices. This was before floppy disks became the norm, and way before hard disks were affordable and prevalent (and larger). Users would load programs by "playing" the cassette in a player that was connected to the computer, essentially streaming the stored bits into the computer's memory. Early cassette devices for the C64 held about 100 kilobytes per side of the cassette and transferred data at a rate that could take up to 30 minutes to load from the cassette. Compare this size to 256MB on the original G1 in 2008 (2,500 times larger) and current gigabit internet streaming speeds (25 million times faster). Cassette storage wasn't large, but at least it was slow.

Rich had gone to the University of Massachusetts Lowell to study physics, but soon switched majors. "I lasted half a semester and realized I should be doing computer science. My grades were starting to reflect it too."

During his undergrad years, Rich became a lead for the Center for Productivity Enhancement at the school, bringing in grants for millions of dollars from companies like Digital, IBM, and Apollo. He continued working in the lab during grad school, becoming a co-director while pursuing his PhD. One of the projects incubated at the lab led to Rich starting a company called Wildfire Communications in December of 1990. Wildfire offered, among other things, a voice-based automated assistant that could route calls and take messages. Wildfire continued for nearly ten years, until it was acquired by Orange, the French telecom company. After the acquisition, Rich started Orange Labs in Cambridge, where he was the director of research and of a new venture fund.

While at Orange, Rich helped launch the first Windows Mobile phone on Orange's network. It wasn't a positive experience because of the measure of control that Microsoft wanted over the resulting device. Rich came away from that project with the desire for an open platform for the mobile ecosystem, instead of having choices limited by platform providers.

Rich Miner was a co-founder of Android, and part of the business team that helped get it acquired. But once at Google, he was looking for ways to help out the growing engineering team. He took on the job of managing the nascent browser effort.

Rich stayed in the Boston area after Android was acquired, far away from the rest of the team in Mountain View. Google only had a small sales office in downtown Boston, so Rich lobbied Google execs Eric Schmidt (CEO) and Alan Eustace (VP of engineering) to start an engineering site. It was a hard sell. "Eric had had a bad experience with the East Coast. Sun Microsystems, under his watch, had started an eng office here. But they put it way out in the periphery, outside of the city. I had to convince him that a place near the universities could attract the best talent. We could build a great office."

Rich convinced the execs, and Google started an office in downtown Cambridge down the street from MIT.[5] Rich hired the first handful of engineers there, including some for Android.

---

[5] Now that site is an office with multiple buildings, hundreds of engineers, and projects that go way beyond Google's mobile efforts.

Rich hired a former employee of his from Orange Labs, Alan Blount, to join the browser team. Meanwhile, in Mountain View, Wei found another engineer for the team: Grace Kloba. Years before, when he was working at Adobe, Wei had convinced Grace to drop out of her PhD program and join him. This time, he persuaded her to leave Adobe.

GRACE KLOBA, WEBVIEW, AND THE ANDROID BROWSER

Grace first learned programming from her mother, who was part of the first generation in China to receive computer education, in the late 1970s. Her mother moved quickly from student to teacher; after she took a three-month intensive programming course, she returned to university to run a computer lab and teach classes on programming languages. Along the way, Grace picked up elements of BASIC and Fortran programming.

Grace later chose her undergrad major based on the nice facilities that the image processing lab had. It worked out well, teaching her fundamentals of both computer science and electrical engineering. After college, she came to the US for a graduate program in computer graphics at Stanford. One of her classmates at Stanford was Wei, whom she'd gone to school with ten years earlier in China.

Grace had passed her PhD qualification test and was searching for a thesis topic when Wei reached out to her about an opportunity at Adobe. Grace left grad school and joined Adobe for several years. Then, in 2006, Wei (now at Google) reached out again, and Grace interviewed and got an offer from Google.

Wei wanted Grace to work with him on the browser team, but he had to convince Steve. Android hired domain experts that had worked on embedded systems, mobile devices, and OS platforms, and Grace didn't have that kind of experience. But Wei assured Steve that it would work out, and Grace joined the Android Browser team in March of 2006.[6]

One of the problems that Grace had to solve was making web content easier to view on the small screens that mobile phones had at the time. She

---

[6.] Grace learned what she needed to work on the browser team. So much so that she soon led the team, and continued leading it for many years as it grew to a much larger size.

had experience in laying out text content,[7] which came in handy when she enabled the browser to display text in a reasonable way on a small display, without the larger content area that web page authors envisioned when they wrote the original HTML content.

She worked on many other problems across the browser and the Web-View component during her time on the team. There were, after all, only a handful of people supporting that large swath of functionality for the first several years of Android's existence. Some of the things she implemented included multi-threaded support, improved network capabilities, and common browser UI elements like tabs.

There was also a last-minute project to get pinch-to-zoom[8] working for the Nexus One launch in early January of 2010. Grace returned from the holidays to find Andy Rubin asking how long it would take to implement that feature. He really wanted it for the upcoming launch, which was happening that month. Three weeks later, Grace delivered the feature, and the phone shipped with that new functionality.

CARY CLARK AND BROWSER GRAPHICS

The Android team was mostly located in a single place, in Mountain View. But the browser team was a striking exception to that rule: Grace was in Mountain View, Wei was in Seattle, and Rich and Alan were in Boston. Then the Skia team, in North Carolina, joined the browser effort after they'd finished getting their graphics engine working.

The browser had different drawing requirements than the rest of the Android system. Rendering graphics was something the Skia team did well, so they took on the job of rendering the browser content. For example, Cary Clark spent significant time getting web pages that were intended for desktop computers to look and react reasonably on this new, very constrained type of device.

---

[7] Text layout is a much harder problem than it might seem from the outside, given the complexities of fonts, character sizing, and language support. Text technology is one of the deep caverns of computer technology. Most engineers I know that are experts in text spend their entire careers in that single area, because it is infinitely complicated (and because everyone else avoids it, knowing that it might suck them in forever).

[8] Pinch-to-zoom is the name of the gesture used to zoom in and out on content by dragging your fingers apart (zooming in) or together (zooming out) on the screen.

Cary had a long history in 2D graphics, and browsers, before he arrived on the Android team. But his background in programming went back even further. In 1968, when he was eleven years old, he got a Digi-Comp I for Christmas. This device was not a computer as we know it today, but used plastic and metal parts to perform simple boolean and math operations, like counting from zero to seven.[9] Cary was so fascinated by this machine that he wore it out and asked for the same present the following Christmas.

He upgraded to a used Apple II in the late 70s while he was at college, spending so much time learning programming in his dorm room by taking apart Steve Wozniak's BASIC implementation on the Apple II that he flunked out of college. He eventually came back and finished his degree, but in the meantime had started working in sales at a hobbyist computer store. When customers had questions about their Apple computers, Cary would call up the regional Apple tech support office for answers, but realized that the staff had no idea how things actually worked. So he applied for and got a job there. As part of his job in regional support, he would occasionally call Cupertino headquarters, but realized that the support staff there also didn't know enough, so he complained loudly and eventually ended up moving to Cupertino and working in the main Apple tech support office.

During the development of the Lisa[10] and the Mac, Cary moved into management, while still programming on the side. But eventually he chose to do software engineering full time: "I was a terrible manager." He was at Apple until 1994, working on various things including leading the effort on QuickDraw GX,[11] which was a new 2D graphics library that was able to draw

---

[9] Seven seems like an arbitrary place to stop in a counting system. One of the limitations of this toy was that it had three bits of information. Three bits can be used to represent, in binary, numbers from 0 (with all three bits set to 0) to 7 (with all three bits set to 1).

[10] The Lisa was to some extent a forerunner of the Macintosh, launching a year before the Mac in January of 1983. Various factors led to its failure in the marketplace, including a high price tag, sluggish performance, and competition (both internal and external) with the Macintosh. But its use of a graphical user interface was a sign of things to come, from the Mac and, eventually, Windows.

[11] I remember seeing Cary Clark give a technical presentation about Mac graphics at WWDC (Apple's annual developer conference) way back in the early 90s. I had forgotten all about it until I ran into him on the Skia team at Google years later. Tech is a teeny, tiny, small town. A really crowded town with millions of inhabitants all over the world, but a small town nevertheless, where you keep bumping into people you've met elsewhere.

much faster than the Mac's original QuickDraw library. The code name for this project was Skia, which Cary chose from a Greek word which referred to drawing a shadow on a wall. QuickDraw GX's main functionality was drawing outlines and filling them in, so the code name fit.

Cary eventually left Apple for other tech companies including WebTV, and Microsoft after the acquisition, where he worked with various future Android engineers. Cary worked on the WebTV browser, trying to make content intended for desktop computers look and interact in a reasonable way on a TV with a completely different input mechanism. He eventually moved out of Silicon Valley to Chapel Hill, North Carolina, where he worked remotely for Microsoft. There he started talking with Mike Reed, whom he knew from his time at Apple. Mike pulled Cary into Openwave, where Cary again worked on browser technology. Then Mike, who had left Openwave by then, called Cary again, bringing him into his new graphics startup named Skia, in honor of Cary's code name for QuickDraw GX.

When Cary started to work on the Android browser, there were a few problems that he had to solve. For example, input was complicated, figuring out how to turn keyboard, D-pad, trackball, and eventually touch events into interactions on a web page. Mike said, "The first thing that had a touchscreen still had a trackball and arrow keys. So we had to live in both worlds. It was somewhat harder on the browser, because there were two ways to set the current item of interest and focus. You could fling with your finger, or you could hit the down arrow a bunch of times. So there was some complication."

One of those complications was how to navigate through the links on a web page. If the user was trying to navigate with the D-pad, there needed to be a way to go to the "next" link. So if they tapped the right button on the D-pad, the focus needed to shift to the next link to the right. But web pages don't have a concept of links being positioned relative to each other, so it wasn't obvious which link to focus on, based on that user input. Also, Cary had to devise a system for visually indicating that a particular link had focus, so the user knew which link would be clicked when they pressed the selection button.

Smooth scrolling was another hurdle. Mike said, "Apple set the expectation that everybody smooth-scrolls. We were not smooth-scrolling the very first version with trackballs and arrows. When we would scroll twenty pixels, we just popped, just like every desktop on the planet. And now suddenly, you gotta smooth-scroll everything, whether it's from a finger fling or not. That's when we really pushed hard. Cary invented[12] the Picture[13] object, which we didn't have in Skia until then, which is a display list. The browser could go through the display lists from all of the slow Java single-threadedness, hand it over to a different thread, and then we could fling the picture, draw as fast as we can draw, and not have to talk to the browser."

Another task was just getting real-world web pages to display reasonably on small devices with limited memory. Cary had worked through related issues on the WebTV product years earlier, getting web pages intended for desktop computers to show up reasonably on TV screens. But the problems he faced for the Android browser were new: there was just too much content on web pages, including "pages that were just insanely tall. Especially when they were fit to the width of the phone screen."

Cary's favorite example from that time was the Wikipedia page for *cheese*,[14] which for some reason is a really, really long entry. "It was many hundreds of thousands of pixels tall. You couldn't represent that number of pixels in our math system, so we had to figure out how to fix that."

When that problem was addressed, another arose; even if the user could eventually see all of the content in a very long page, it took a very long time to scroll through it. So Cary implemented a system in the browser that would detect when the user was trying to scroll repeatedly and would pop up a magnifier object on the page, with a zoomed-out view of the entire page, allowing the user to quickly go to a specific location on the page.

---

[12] Cary agreed that he *implemented* Picture for Skia, but not that he invented the concept. He gave that credit to Bill Atkinson, one of the engineers on the original Macintosh team at Apple who helped create the original QuickDraw 2D graphics engine for the Mac. "Bill Atkinson invented Pictures, and he probably stole it from somebody else. I was just standing on the shoulders of giants." Most software that is written is either re-implementing existing concepts or building upon and extending them in new ways.

[13] The Picture object in Skia is essentially a pre-processed list of the low-level information that the system needs to draw a particular scene. Rather than having to parse web content to draw things as the page scrolled around, Skia translated the page into a Picture object, which could be drawn much more efficiently.

[14] The cheese page (*https://en.wikipedia.org/wiki/Cheese*) has several thousand words, over one-third of the length of "Earth" and nearly one half of the length of "Universe." It's not clear why the cheese page is so long. Who knew that cheese was so complicated?

18

LONDON CALLING

Another boost to the browser team came from across the ocean.

Google's London engineering office was originally started to work on mobile projects . . . but not on Android. The engineers in London made Google apps and services work on the plethora of mobile platforms and devices available at the time. Prior to the iPhone and Android (and for the first couple of years after they launched), there were many phone platforms being used in the world, and Google wanted to make its apps available on them.

The mobile effort initially began in Mountain View, and attracted engineers such as Cédric Beust,[1] who led a team getting Gmail to work on mobile devices. But eventually, Google started a new office in London, with the charge of creating software for Symbian and Windows Mobile, two of the most prevalent mobile OSes at the time.

Andrei Popescu, who worked on that early team,[2] talked about why London was chosen for this work: "In 2007, the core mobile expertise was in Europe, not the US. Europe had 3G well before the US. If you look at the

---

[1] Cédric went on to make Gmail work on Android, as we'll see later.

[2] Andrei eventually became the director of engineering for Android in London.

mobile OSes developed at the time, the center of excellence was in Europe. Symbian[3] was developed in London, Series 60 and UIQ[4] were things developed on top of Symbian by Nokia and Ericsson. So Google made a conscious decision to create a mobile center of excellence in London.

"We also did a good job at hiring—London is an excellent place to hire. We can attract talent from all over the world, and there are excellent computer science schools across Europe. And geographically it makes sense," since London is one of the closest major European cities to California (where Google's headquarters are located) and there are direct flights between the two.

But the site needed a lead for the mobile effort, so in early 2007 Google hired Dave Burke.

DAVE BURKE AND THE LONDON MOBILE TEAM

Dave Burke was into computers at a young age. He combined a joystick, a photoelectric cell, the magnifying glass from a family projector, a tape recorder, a speech synthesizer, and some code he wrote and created a device that would fire a rubber band at anyone who entered his room. "I was hooked. My poor sister."

He studied electrical engineering through undergrad and a PhD, after which he ran the engineering team at a startup. By 2007, he decided he wanted more experience than he could get at that small company, so he took a job at Google leading the new mobile team. He wanted to move to Silicon Valley at the time, but London was where the opportunity was.[5]

In 2007, there were two distinct mobile efforts happening in London: Mobile search and browser-related work. The team made Google's software in these areas work on a variety of non-Android devices. On the side, Dave started playing around with Android, learning the APIs and how to program Android apps.

[3.] Symbian was used heavily by Nokia, which had engineering offices throughout Europe and headquarters in Finland.

[4.] UIQ was a user interface software platform based on Symbian and used by Nokia.

[5.] Later, in 2010, he moved over to Mountain View to lead the Android graphics and media teams, and eventually the entire Android engineering team.

Nine months after Dave joined, the Android SDK went live. There was going to be a large event in London, and Rich Miner asked Dave to give a talk about Android, introducing the SDK to that audience. So Dave did some live coding[6] in front of the crowd, creating a simple web browser application in eight minutes.

The talk went well and Dave was feeling pretty good about it until the next day. "I got an email from Andy Rubin, going 'Who the hell is this guy and why is he talking about my project publicly?'" Apparently, Rich hadn't gotten around to telling Andy that he'd asked Dave to do this.

Dave said, "My relationship with Andy started at a low level. I figured it could only get better from there."

Over time, the London team started doing more projects for Android. Meanwhile, the apps that Dave's team was working on were eventually subsumed by the product teams directly (like YouTube). The mobile team was dissolved and Dave's organization moved into Android.

ANDREI POPESCU AND THE LONDON BROWSER TEAM

Andrei Popescu's team was responsible for London's mobile browser efforts. He was a natural choice for that project, since that's what Andrei had worked on at Nokia.

After getting his undergraduate degree in computer science in Bucharest, Romania, Andrei left his home country to get a master's degree in Helsinki, Finland. He figured he would return to Romania after he got his degree. That was over twenty years ago: "I'm still on that journey."

After he finished graduate school, in 2002, Andrei landed a job at Nokia, in Helsinki. He was working on an MMS[7] editor. "I was very depressed: I'd done all this studying in two countries, gotten a master's degree, and here I

---

[6] Writing code live, in real time, is not the typical way people present. It's much easier to just paste code onto slides and explain it, rather than writing the code and either boring the audience (if there is a lot of it to write) or failing (because the author forgets something simple and ends up with compiler errors that have to be tediously fixed in front of an increasingly frustrated and restless audience). But it can be a great way to demonstrate how simple something is, which was Dave's goal with that presentation.

[7] MMS = Multimedia Messaging Service: this is the protocol used whenever pictures are sent in text messages.

was programming this shitty little thing, couldn't do much, in a really weird variant of C++ on an operating system that seemed already, for those times, very arcane and bizarre. At the time, I didn't have the foresight to appreciate that I was working on a technology (mobile) that was going to change the world and also shape my career for the next decades."

Fortunately, he met Antti Koivisto at Nokia, who was working on something more interesting. "He was working under the radar on a full web browser for Nokia phones, for Symbian, based on a library called WebKit." They got this working and shipped a full browser application to a very large audience of Nokia users.

After that project, Andrei wanted to move to London. He didn't care what the job was, he just wanted to relocate. "Google was kind of a dream. But for me, the one motivation at the time was to move to London. I sent hundreds of applications and got one reply: Google."

Andrei started at Google on the Mobile team in January of 2007. Initially, he worked on a project to get Google Maps working on Nokia phones. But soon he started a project called Lithium, which was meant to be a full web browser for Windows Mobile.

On Andrei's team were Ben Murdoch (then an intern[8]), Steve Block, and Nicolas Roard.

NICOLAS ROARD, GEARING UP

After going to university and working at a startup in France, Nicolas began a PhD program in Wales. Eventually the money ran out on the research grant, and "I still needed to feed myself." So, PhD in hand, Nicolas applied to Google in London and started there in April of 2007, working on Andrei's Lithium project.

Lithium was an application built on top of the WebKit browser engine. Imagine if the browser you use on your phone didn't come with the phone, but had to be downloaded as a separate application. The prototype was promising, but ... huge. Lithium required users to download what was a very large (especially for that time) binary for their phones. The project was killed and Andrei's team started working on Google Gears instead.

[8.] Ben was eventually hired full time and has worked in the London office on Android-related projects ever since.

Google Gears was an effort at Google to provide richer capabilities for browsers at that time, such as local storage and geolocation.[9] Gears was eventually discontinued when these capabilities became standard in browsers with HTML5. Gears launched for desktops in 2007, and Andrei's team made it work on mobile browsers.

At first, the team ported Gears to Windows Mobile. By this time, when the Android SDK launched, it was clear that the Android platform and product would exist at least to some extent. So the team worked on porting Gears to the Android browser. Gears continued to ship as part of the browser until it was finally deprecated in the Donut release, in late 2009; it made more sense to integrate those features directly into the browser instead.

In the early days of Android, Google engineers outside the Android team didn't just casually contribute code to Android. In fact, they couldn't; nobody outside of the Android team even had the rights or permission to do so.[10] But the work on Andrei's team was important enough to the Android platform to include them. Andy granted Andrei's team full source code access, making them the only team outside of Android with access at that time.

The more that the team worked with the Android browser, the more they just became part of the overall browser team. Andrei's team focused primarily on forward-looking browser features. For example, they worked on creating and implementing the web standard for geolocation. They also made the video element[11] (another feature in HTML5) work in the browser.

---

[9] Geolocation allows the browser to use the user's location, if the user grants that permission. It's useful for things like navigation in mapping apps (if you want to know how to get somewhere, it's good to know where to start).

[10] It's important to realize that this walled-off situation of Android code was sharply different from code in the rest of Google. For the most part, software at Google is in a single, shared repository, and engineers can easily see, and even contribute to, code in other projects. But the Android code existed elsewhere and was not even viewable, much less changeable, by people who were not on the team.

[11] The video element allows video content (such as that on YouTube) to play in a browser. This feature was an important change for web browsers, as the main way of playing video in browsers prior to this was through the Adobe Flash plugin. Having video capability built directly into the browser meant that users wouldn't have to have a plugin installed to watch video content. This was particularly important in mobile devices, where browser plugins like Flash would not necessarily work.

In 2008, during the run-up to Android 1.0, the VP of the mobile team (Vic Gundotra) disbanded the mobile effort, including Dave Burke's London team. Mobile projects were absorbed into the individual product teams instead. The landscape of mobile computing and devices had changed radically since the time that the mobile effort was first begun. The iPhone had been out (and popular) since mid-2007, and Android was launching soon. Smartphones were ushering in a new world where mobile apps were going to be increasingly important for the company, and the company was incorporating mobile capabilities more directly into its products.

Dave's team had proven to be successful and useful to Android, so with the help of Hiroshi Lockheimer, they convinced Andy to bring them all into Android. They dropped the work that they were doing for other platforms and focused entirely on Android engineering efforts.

ANDROID AND WEB APPS

Android's browser and web technology continued to improve, and the team continued to dedicate increasing effort and people to the project. In 2013, the Android browser (and WebView) was replaced by Chrome on Android, when the company decided that having multiple teams and projects focused on similar technology goals probably didn't make sense. WebView and the browser are still an important part of the mobile technology stack, allowing users to browse rich websites and allowing developers to write applications using web technologies.

19

APPLICATIONS

THE MOBILE APPLICATION ECOSYSTEM

The millions of applications available to Android users are critical in maintaining the platform's relevance. Apps are, after all, where users spend most of their time on their smartphones.

If someone came out with a new device or platform now without having any kind of application store to go along with it (much less a densely populated store), it simply wouldn't work. When RIM introduced BlackBerry 10, their final operating system for smartphones,[1] they added a compatibility mode that allowed users to install and run Android applications. They did this in recognition of the fact that the BlackBerry application ecosystem (even though the company and its phones had been around for many years) could not offer the breadth and variety of applications available on the app stores for Android and iOS.

But even with a vast market of apps available, there still has to be some core set of apps that come with the platform, especially from companies like Google and Apple, that allow users to access the services and functionality they expect from those companies.

When Android was new, there *was* no ecosystem of other apps. So the Android team built the core set of apps that would ship with the device and provide compelling functionality for users.

Today, these Google apps (Gmail, Maps, Search, YouTube, and many others) are developed by the teams that own those products. So rather than a team in Android writing the YouTube app, the YouTube division writes the core YouTube services and infrastructure, and the web app, and the Android app, and any other client applications that tie into the larger product.

---

[1] RIM is no longer developing the BlackBerry 10 operating system or releasing devices built with that OS. Now they build phones running Android.

But in the early days, none of the other product teams were able to do this work. These other groups all had enough work to do and didn't have time to work on developing an application for this new and unproven platform. Also, Android's platform and APIs were changing constantly, all the way up to the 1.0 launch. Why would an established product take on the work and headache of writing an app[2] when they'd just have to keep re-tooling it as the APIs changed out from under it?

So engineers on the Android team took on the job of writing these initial versions of the core applications. These were individuals, not teams, because it was rarely the case that more than one to two people worked on any of these initial applications (the same applications which are now maintained and developed by much larger teams). For example, the initial Gmail client for Android was written primarily by Cédric Beust, with some performance assistance from Mike Cleron.

CÉDRIC BEUST AND GMAIL

I knew we were onto something the very first time we were able to get a push notification.

—CÉDRIC BEUST

Gmail for Android had its roots in versions for other platforms because of its main author: Cédric Beust.

In 2004, Cédric joined Google and ended up (as many new engineers with server-side experience did) working in the ads group. After a year, he was looking for something new to do and found a small team working on mobile technology. This group worked on making Google apps and services functional on the various mobile devices of that era. Cédric joined the team and started the Gmail effort. He eventually grew and led a team of about twenty people who developed the J2ME Gmail application.

In those days, there was no pervasive mobile "platform" like the two that exist today (iOS and Android). Instead, there were many vendor-specific platforms that covered specific segments of the market, like Microsoft's Windows CE and RIM's BlackBerry OS. There was also J2ME, which purported to

---

[2] Fadden: "They also weren't interested in fixing service bugs that only impacted the Android app (like Calendar). Or even investigating them. I may have some repressed anger here."

run across a wide variety of devices, using the same language (Java) and some variation of the J2ME libraries. So a company trying to target a wide variety of devices across the ecosystem found the concept of J2ME very enticing. But the realities of J2ME were . . . difficult.

Cédric said, "We started looking at how we could do Gmail on J2ME. It was quickly obvious to us that it was a terrible idea. It was everywhere . . . but every single vendor, and even the same model, had different versions of J2ME. They all had different restrictions. They didn't all implement the same profiles. Some had Bluetooth, others did not. There was no constraint, no compliance or anything like that. Any phone could claim to be J2ME-compliant and didn't support half of the things we needed. So we were in a world of hurt."

But Cédric's team was eventually able to ship a version of Gmail that was true to the core experience of Gmail on the web, running on these much smaller and more limited devices. "We shipped Gmail on J2ME on about 300 different devices, with a pretty good UI. Some devices caused a lot more trouble than others, but overall we pulled it off."[3]

Some time after Android was acquired by Google, Andy Rubin contacted Cédric. As the lead of the mobile Gmail team, Cédric was a likely person to help write Gmail for the nascent Android platform. He was already interested, but when Andy described the dynamics of the project, he was sold. Andy's team was a collection of low-level kernel experts, many of whom had experience shipping constrained mobile devices.[4] They were creating a platform based on the Java programming language (of which Cédric was a fan and an expert), and they needed expertise for writing applications. "Hearing that these guys were open-minded and that we need to write it in Java was even more interesting and appealing to me."

Cédric, like many of the early engineers on Android, came with related experience and opinions, and a strong desire to do it right on Android. "I knew the pain and knew exactly what I didn't want to happen again. Debugging J2ME meant that you couldn't connect a debugger, you had to

---

[3] On November 2, 2006, Cédric posted a blog announcing the availability of Gmail for J2ME (*https://googleblog.blogspot.com/2006/11/gmail-mobile-client-is-live.html*). By then, he had been on the Android team for two months.

[4] Particularly those folks who had worked at Danger.

`println()`[5] on the status bar to find out where you were in the code. It was an absolute nightmare. So I knew exactly what I wanted to fix."

When he started, there were two apps being developed for Android: Gmail and Calendar.

It makes sense for applications to be developed closer to their product groups now. But it was very useful at that time, for the apps and for the Android platform itself, for them to be developed by engineers on the Android team. For one thing, the platform and all of the APIs were changing constantly, and the applications had to react to these changes. Also, in many cases, the application developers required platform changes in order to support their requirements. App developers like Cédric were primarily responsible for the applications, but they would also help out when necessary on the core platform and the Android APIs, especially for app-driven platform changes.

"I worked with Mike [Cleron] on the layout system, the View system, how to do all the original APIs for layout and the algorithms, the two-pass algorithms. I worked with Dianne [Hackborn], and all the others also, with Intents.[6] I remember hours in rooms trying to find out how we would name these things which we call *Intents* now. We spent hours painting that bike shed,[7] trying to figure out what was the best word. And eventually we came up with 'Intent.'"[8]

---

[5] `println()` is the mechanism in Java to output text to a console window. Debugging J2ME essentially meant printing text directly to the screen. Debugging tools have come a long way since the early days of software, but the `println()` approach ignored all of those advancements and went right back to the painful start.

[6] Intents are Android's system of launching other applications based on actions requested by an application, like "take a picture" bringing up the camera app, or "send a message" launching a messaging app.

[7] *Bike shedding* is a phrase often used in software engineering to describe the process of spending way too much time working on something that probably doesn't matter that much. Wikipedia equates it with Parkinson's Law of Triviality, exemplified by a committee formed to discuss plans for a nuclear power plant instead spending most of its time discussing the color to paint the staff's bike shed. In this case, it really was bikeshedding, because besides spending a lot of time discussing it, they actually decided in the end to use the initial proposal (Intents), which came from an earlier incarnation of the idea at PalmSource.

[8] The amount of time and effort spent on API names seems ridiculous from the outside, but to API developers it makes sense. A good name should be both descriptive and concise. And never forget that that name, which will be part of the public contract between the platform and the developers of applications, is something that everyone will have to live with for as long as the platform stays around, so you should spend some time on it and try to get it right.

"We were all excited by the general idea behind it: How do we get an app to be able to call into another app without knowing whether that other app is installed or not? We're going to say, 'Can someone handle this?' And if they do, they can. We were pretty excited."

All of this work was happening while the platform was evolving and the team was growing. "I was also involved in staffing up. We needed Java people. We needed a hundred Java people right now. So staffing up and hiring and interviewing like crazy at that time, and also writing a lot of code. And throwing away a lot of code, because a lot of the code I was writing was calling into APIs that were, a week later, changed or removed or modified."

Application developers must perform a tricky dance when writing their code on top of a platform that is being developed in parallel. Many capabilities and APIs of that platform are in flux, and many of the capabilities that applications need simply don't exist yet.[9] Someone has to implement these features in order for the applications to be able to do what they need to do. On Android, that happened by having small teams of people doing a lot of work all over the place, across various parts of the platform and in the applications. Said Romain Guy, "The team was small. Making those changes was pretty fast; we all had access to the entire source tree. I remember leading up to 1.0, I was making large changes to the View system to clean up the APIs. You make a CL that touches 800 files and you touch all the apps and fix them as you go. So it was not necessarily the apps having to do this, though it was also that. Everybody was pitching in."

One of the hard constraints that Gmail had to deal with was performance. Originally, the Gmail app was written such that every message was its own WebView.[10] Essentially, each message was a separate web page, which has a lot of overhead that's not obvious in the text that the user sees on the screen. Romain said, "But that was way too hard on that device. So Mike rewrote all of that."

---

[9] Dianne talked about this dynamic: "There is a turning point in platform development where you can tell you are on the downward slope, when you find that as you try to build your apps and stuff on top of it, you are no longer having to stop and implement something in the platform to get some feature you need." The platform was a long way from the downward slope when Gmail was being developed.

[10] WebView is a UI element that can display web content (HTML). See Chapter 17 ("The Android Browser") for more on WebView.

Steve Horowitz, director of Android's engineering team at the time, talked about the Gmail performance problems. "Cédric took an approach to the architecture that was good up to a certain point. Part of that, honestly, was maybe just the capabilities of the View system at the time. How many Views could you stack to create those threads?

"So Mike had to come unravel a bunch of that stuff and redo it so the entire thread was not an independent View, but there was one View you rendered into. There was a fundamental re-architecture of Gmail just to make it work."

Meanwhile, the requirement to use WebView put additional demands on the team. It made sense to use WebView because email messages require web capabilities. While many email messages display plain text, there are enough variations in what that text can contain, and how it can be formatted, that the ability to display an HTML (web) version of that message is necessary.

So the team depended on the WebView component, which was being developed by the browser team. But the HTML embedded in Gmail messages wasn't plain HTML. It was a subset of content types and expectations about how that content would be displayed. Making it work for Gmail on Android required understanding what Gmail did on the backend and getting the browser (and WebView) team to be able to display this odd variant of HTML.

There were good things about working on Gmail as well. One of the motivating things about developing Android applications at that time was that the platform had capabilities that simply didn't exist anywhere else. Engineers were able to create much more powerful application experiences than had existed before.

"I knew we were onto something the very first time we were able to get a push notification. We weren't quite sure we could do it, that we could keep a connection open and to have the server tell us, 'You have new mail.' For J2ME, we did not have that; you needed to refresh constantly. But at some point, I was able to send an email and I saw my phone react. The first thing I did was to run to Steve Horowitz's office and show him. His jaw dropped. He knew we were working on it, but he didn't know if we could do it."

Romain Guy said, "What I loved about the first Android phone, about 1.0, is that we had push notifications for email and chat, which was huge back then, because the iPhone didn't have any of that. I remember that my phone would get the emails faster than my desktop. My phone would beep, and then a few seconds or minutes later my desktop would finally show the new email."

While Cédric was responsible for the Android side of Gmail, a substantial portion of the overall application depended on the mechanism that talked to the Gmail backend. That work happened on the Android services team.

20

ANDROID SERVICES

One mouse click away from a disaster of unprecedented[1] proportion in the mobile industry.

—ANDROID SERVICES TEAM SLOGAN

For the most part, the Android team operated separately from the rest of Google. Google funded the project and checked in with the leadership team, but otherwise left them alone. The Android team kept their heads down, writing the operating system, the tools, the apps, and everything else they needed, without interacting with the larger engineering organization in Google.

Except for the services team.

If you're writing a single-player game, which only needs to deal with the local device and storage, you can do that independently of any back-end infrastructure or mechanisms. But for most other applications, which deal with information outside of that application, or data that you want to store off-device, you are probably going to need to interact with systems on the backend. The application running locally on a device is really just a window into data and services that are all managed on external servers. Maps, Search, Gmail, Calendar, Contacts, Talk, YouTube: all of these applications rely on data and functionality that is stored on Google servers.

Google wanted to make its applications and services available to mobile users through the Android operating system. So the need for figuring out how to connect Android devices to the Google services running on the backend was paramount.

---

[1] Dan Egnor pointed out that this later became "*not* of unprecedented proportion" after Danger (years after the Microsoft acquisition) ended up losing massive amounts of user data due to a server outage. Whoops.

To make sure that this work happened, Android started the services team, which was initially three people: Fred Quintana, Malcolm Handley, and Debajit Ghosh.

DEBAJIT GHOSH AND CALENDAR

Debajit always assumed he would study science in college, while programming on the side to support his primary academic interests. But in high school, he realized he could just do programming as his *main* focus. So he changed direction and went to college in computer science, getting his master's degree in 1998.

Debajit spent a few years working on speech recognition, which combined a growing interest in mobile with the ability for users to get information on the go. In 2005, a colleague went to Google to form a speech recognition group. He reached out to Debajit to see if he was interested in coming to Google to work on mobile technology.

At first, Debajit wasn't interested, thinking, "Google? I don't want to work at Google—it's way too big of a company." But when he thought about some of the mobile possibilities, he was swayed, thinking, "I'm not sure about this Google thing, but it'd be really interesting to learn about mobile."

Debajit started on Google's small mobile team (not the Android team) in early 2005. The mobile team was created to make the company's services available on existing mobile devices, and brought in Debajit to lead the server-side team. "The first project I was working on was trans-coding traditional web pages into what could be viewed on the really cruddy browsers you'd have on cell phones at that time." The browser application on the phone would make a request to view a website. The content from that site would come down to the Google servers, get translated into something that that very limited phone device could handle, and that simpler version of the site would be sent down to the phone. This was similar to the approach that Danger used for its Hiptop phone browser years earlier, and WebTV for its TV browser years before that, with a server translating between what web pages actually looked like and what was possible to display on an actual device.

In the Spring of 2005, Debajit returned from a vacation to find a stack of resumes on his desk, along with a request to interview the members of a startup named "Android" that Google was interested in acquiring. "I'm in this vacation haze, trying to figure out, 'Android? What's this Android thing?'"

He interviewed the engineers on the team, including Brian Swetland and Ficus Kirkpatrick. "Ficus spent a bunch of the time talking about Brian. So I got to know some of the personalities very early on."

Debajit continued working on the mobile team, checking in with Andy Rubin and his team occasionally. Then, in late 2006 he reached out to Cédric Beust, a former colleague on the mobile team. He also chatted with Steve Horowitz, the engineering director for Android, and learned more about what they needed. The team was starting to think about Google services. For example, Android needed to figure out a story for the Calendar app, and how to sync with Google's calendar services.

Meanwhile, Debajit had been working on a side project, synchronizing calendar information to J2ME devices. He was still interested in how to get information to people on the go, and calendar data was an important part of that problem. In talking to the Android team, he realized that, by joining them, he could make his side project his full time job. So he transferred to Android, joining the now three-person team working on Google services.

Each engineer on the team worked on services for specific applications. Fred Quintana worked with Jeff Hamilton, who was writing the Contacts app for Android. Malcolm Handley worked with Cédric on Gmail. And Debajit worked with Jack Veenstra on Calendar.[2] All of these applications had the same requirement for sending data to and from Google servers, so the team collaborated on a centralized sync mechanism.

Soon after that initial services engineering team got rolling, Andy Rubin brought in someone he knew from Danger to lead the project: Michael Morrissey.

MICHAEL MORRISSEY AND THE SERVICES TEAM

Michael Morrissey went to college and grad school in math, but realized he'd rather do programming.[3] He started playing around with a BeBox and eventually ended up getting a job at Be.

---

[2] The Calendar app had begun earlier with some work by Joe Onorato.

[3] Mike Reed on the Skia team had a similar background of math in school transitioning to programming as a career. Same for me. Maybe all math people are programmers who just don't realize it yet.

One of the things that Michael found most interesting was printing—he enjoyed the interaction of the OS, the drivers, and the graphics code. This was a good thing, because the state of printing on BeOS was terrible at the time. Michael remembered, "Jean-Louis Gassée, the founder and CEO of Be, was really angry one day that he couldn't print. He always had to switch to a Mac to print something. He was really, really mad."

Michael encouraged external developers to write printer drivers for Be. That's how he first met Mathias Agopian (who later started Android's graphics team). "He had written all these amazing Epson drivers. He was really into the color side of it. He kept sending these drivers in." Mathias was doing this work as a hobby, but he eventually joined Be.

Michael left Be after an uninspiring IPO and an ensuing and doomed pivot to an Internet Appliance device. On a suggestion from Hiroshi Lockheimer, he ended up at Danger in March of 2000. At first, the company was working on a small device that made it possible to carry around your contacts and email, and then sync to other devices by connecting them. But the dot-com implosion, which started soon after Michael arrived, forced them to start looking into other product directions, ending up with Danger's Hiptop phone.

During his time at Danger, Michael worked on back-end services, connecting applications on the phone to data on Danger servers and to the internet in general. "I loved server-side stuff, so I started building out the backend, and the protocol between the device and the server." For example, Danger phone users had many different kinds of email services they needed to connect to. Rather than handle all of those services locally on the device, the Danger servers would connect to those various email services and translate the results into a single protocol that Danger devices understood. Similarly, the browser worked by having the servers translate full web pages into simplified representations that were sent down to the phone.

One of the innovations at Danger was a persistent connection between a device and the servers. Through this connection, a device would get new email or messages immediately. This was huge back in 2002. Even if you had one of the few phones at that time with email capability, those devices typically required you to synchronize them manually with your computer. So you would get that message about the meeting you needed to attend an hour after it ended. But on Danger phones, you would know that you were missing the meeting as it was happening.

In 2005, Michael moved on from Danger to Microsoft, enticed by a nascent project to create Microsoft phones. At the time, Microsoft licensed their OS to manufacturers like HTC. But someone at Microsoft envisioned a future where the company would also make its own phones. This is basically the model that Apple pursued, but with the addition of having a licensable OS (like Android, except that Android is free).

But the project had a hard time getting traction in the company, since it was running counter to Microsoft's traditional software business. In one frustrating meeting, Michael recounted that an executive wouldn't sign off on their phone being a Windows device because it wouldn't run PowerPoint, even though that use case was not the point of the phone and the very limited device was ill-equipped to take on that additional burden. Through meetings like this and various other obstacles, the project had a hard time making forward progress.

Meanwhile, Andy Rubin kept checking in with Michael every quarter to see if he wanted to come help out on Android. Eventually, Michael ran out of patience with the project at Microsoft and joined Android to lead the services team in the Spring of 2007. He looked at where the team was at and told Andy and Steve what they needed to do. "They were like, 'Great! Go. Run. Do this.'"

Michael helped organize the team to get all of the right things happening. "I had had the luxury of working on this stuff at Danger, so I knew a pattern that would work for these things. I saw the bigger picture, in terms of how the services had to be architected: how you would build a persistent connection, what the transport layer should look like, and all the landmines you would have to watch out for."

Michael also worked on growing the team. He needed people who knew how to deal with Google infrastructure. "One of the things I realized pretty early on was that we wouldn't get anywhere unless we had people who came from inside of Google, because Google had such a weird way of doing things. If we brought in people who had the kind of domain knowledge of the mobile industry, but not the Google knowledge, that wouldn't be good because it would take them forever to get through the Google machinery. I thought it would be faster if we took people who were at Google and transferred them onto Android and instructed them about the domain of mobile along the way."

One of the early problems to solve was push functionality: when something changed on the server side (for example, an email arriving in the user's inbox, or a calendar event being updated), the server needed to update the device so that the data on the phone and the server would match. Debajit coined the term "tickle." "We wanted to 'tickle' the device. We came up with terms like Light Tickle, letting the device know that something's changed, please sync. Heavy tickle: including the payload. We favored a Light Tickle approach, but it depended on the use case."

The team came up with an approach where the phone would have a single, dedicated connection to Google servers on the backend. The connection, called the Mobile Connection Server (MCS), would be persistent, so that messages could always be sent or received, ensuring that the phone would be notified whenever there was new information on the server. Each application had its own specific requirements for data, but they all shared this single connection through which the server would alert the device that something changed. The connection was also used for the initial Google Talk functionality, to send and receive messages.

Establishing that persistent connection back to Google servers wasn't just a technical problem; it was also one of constrained resources.

Michael Morrissey, October 21, 2008—the day before the G1 launch (picture courtesy Brian Swetland)

The networking ops team controlled the persistent connection mechanism that Android needed. At that time, Google worked on the assumption that everything needing a network connection was web-based; data transfer requests used standard web HTTP request mechanisms. But Android needed to use a completely different protocol, so they required a dedicated network resource called a Virtual IP (VIP). The problem was, the network team didn't want to give them one. "The way that Google was built, for a whole bunch of boring reasons that I won't go into, these were extremely rare. There was literally only capacity for only about 200 of them. A bunch of them were used, and the network team would not give them out at all."

Debajit and Michael met often with the networking team to persuade them to give a VIP to Android. These kind of discussions were not new to Michael: "A lot of my job was running around trying to convince people on Gmail, and Calendar, and Contacts, and all these other teams that this was a big thing for Google, and they should be helping us with engineering on their side and SRE[4] support."

Finally, networking ops relented and gave them the VIP they needed on a provisional basis, along with a friendly wager. They said that if Android didn't reach a million users in the first six months, they would take back the VIP, and Michael and Debajit would owe them a case of whisky. Debajit remembered, "Whisky was definitely part of this discussion. That was the currency."

They were able to set up the persistent connection and get MCS up and running, on port number 5228.[5]

Android won the bet, though Michael said it depended on when you defined the timeframe. The networking ops team said that it was from the moment they gave them the VIP, whereas Michael defined it from the moment 1.0 launched. In any case, it was obvious at that time that Android was successful enough to warrant not losing the connection to all of those Android devices.

---

[4] Site Reliability Engineer: SREs keep the servers and network working.

[5] *28* was chosen based on the number on Debajit's hockey jersey.

LAUNCH FIRE DRILL

Android's unique requirements for persistent connections meant that Android needed dedicated servers in specific data centers. Anyone dealing with data knows that you always need a backup in case something goes wrong with the main system. It's why we have redundant disk arrays and backup storage, and it's why many households have two parents so that the children can ask the other parent if they don't get the answer they want the first time around.

But Android wasn't just about serving a single user, or a small number of them; they needed a system that would scale to many, many more users. One backup site wouldn't be enough. It was entirely possible for one system to go down. And it was possible, albeit unlikely, that a second system would also have problems. So they enabled a third data center just in case; three would surely be enough to cover all of these situations.

Launch day: October 22, 2008. One of Android's servers had already gone down earlier in the week, but was fortunately working again in time for the launch. On launch day, a second server went down due to "unplanned maintenance." Google wanted to work on it, so they just took it out of the system. So immediately, on launch day, Android was down to two servers. Fortunately, two was still enough for a robust, fail-safe system.

Then one of those servers caught fire.

There was an overheating issue in the data center that day, so they had to shut down the system to work on it. Michael said, "We were really sweating bullets—we were down to a single data center! We just lost two; if that third one went down, none of the sync stuff would work properly—there would be no chat or whatever. We were really panicked."

That last server stayed up, so there was no outage. But the team had come a lot closer to failure than they thought they would.

DAN EGNOR AND OTAS

If you're not careful, your OTA download can brick[6] the world.

—MICHAEL MORRISSEY (AS REMEMBERED BY DAN EGNOR)

[6.] Brick (verb): To turn a useful computing device into a rectangular object as useful as a brick, except not quite as heavy. Bricking is a common term in the mobile space to indicate the problems of taking a software update that can render a phone useless (unless you need an expensive brick).

Since the beginning, one of the impressive things about the Android operating system is its Over-the-Air (OTA) update system. Occasionally (or too frequently, if you're running internal, pre-release builds), you get a notification on your phone that the system would like to update itself. Eventually you get tired of its incessant nagging, tell it to go ahead, and then it does its thing. It downloads the update, reboots, configures itself, and shows the login screen; it's ready to go.

It may not be obvious as a user, but you've just had your phone completely replace the fundamental pieces of itself on the fly, and it all just worked. It's like having your brain swapped out while you're standing in line at the coffee shop, and then continuing to order that coffee, as if nothing happened.

And it all just works. Every time. Well, okay, there was that one time.... More about that later.

Early on, the team recognized the importance of being able to update the phones remotely. Updates might be needed for something as major as the next release of the platform (like upgrading from, say, Android 8.1 Oreo to Android 9 Pie) or something smaller, like a monthly security/bug-fix release. Or maybe there would even be the need for an emergency fix if something went horribly wrong with a release. In any case, there needed to be a mechanism for devices to get these updates without having to go through partners, carriers, and anything else that might stand in the way of Android updates getting out to users.

In August of 2007, Michael Morrissey brought in Dan Egnor to work on the update system.

Dan was programming in childhood, hanging out in the computer lab at the college where his mother taught. Eventually, the college cracked down and wouldn't allow faculty kids in the lab, at which point his mother got him an Atari 400. "I used it intensively. All of the grownups were impressed at how fast I could type on this ridiculous membrane keyboard."

After college, he ended up at Microsoft, then a startup, then as a quant[7] on Wall Street. In 2002, Google held a programming contest, which Dan entered for fun, and won. "They gave a corpus of documents and said to do something fun with it. I made a little geographical search app. They flew me to Mountain View, had me talk to a bunch of people and asked if I was interested in a job."

---

[7] Quantitative analyst. Quants use math, computer, and finance skills to price securities and determine trading prices and strategies.

Dan turned them down. He wanted to stay in New York and Google did not have an office there at that time. His rejection confused the team at Google, since the contest was meant as a recruiting ploy. A year later, Google opened a New York office and Dan signed on as the second employee. He worked on search and maps-related projects, eventually moving out to Mountain View.

Meanwhile, Dan heard rumors, along with the rest of Google, about what was happening in that skunkworks project of Andy Rubin's. "It was all very secretive. 'Are they making Cameras? Andy Rubin—he was the guy at Danger, right?'"

Dan had always been a mobile enthusiast. "I had been carrying a [Danger] Hiptop, for as long as there had been Hiptops and was a big fan. And I was a fan of mobile computing. I was that guy with the weird little mini-PC and radio system that could get on the internet from anywhere, back when it was super crazy to do that. I was an enthusiast in early Wi-Fi and related technologies, back when that was so novel there were user groups that you would go to and talk with other Wi-Fi enthusiasts about how this was going to change everything." So he was intrigued about what was happening in the Android group.

At the same time, Michael Morrissey was looking for people like Dan for the services team; he needed engineers familiar with Google's backend, because Android devices needed to talk to those servers so they needed experts to create the software to do it. The timing was right and Dan joined the team in August of 2007, three months before the SDK was released and a year before the 1.0 launch.

Dan joined the small services team, which at that time consisted of the manager, Michael Morrissey, plus engineers Debajit Ghosh, Malcolm Handley, and Fred Quintana. The other three engineers were focused on data synchronization plus the specific details of the applications that they were working with (Calendar, Gmail, and Contacts, respectively). Dan helped out with some of that stuff, and core infrastructure for services overall, but he mainly took responsibility for what they called Device Management. This work included Over the Air updates as well as the check-in service. There was already a basic update mechanism, but Dan rewrote it into the system that Android used when it launched.

Dan had help and advice from his manager. "Michael Morrissey was very much the grizzled old hand—I mean, he's no older than I am—with the voice of wisdom. He had managed similar things at Danger, he had seen a lot of shit go down, and definitely had wise wisdom, in terms of what to pay attention to, what to focus on, what architectures were likely to work, what could be a pain point. He remembered many times when the ability to just push an OTA to fix some problem saved that company's bacon. So this was going to be really important: if you've got something out there not behaving well, you can quickly ship a fix. Or if there's some security issue, it's important to have a very quick turnaround OTA thing. We do not want to leave this in the hands of carriers if we can avoid it."

Meanwhile, the OTA system itself had to be carefully designed to anticipate all of the things that could go wrong, from running out of space on the device, to restarting in the middle of an update, to security vulnerability. The team thought hard about all of these issues and came up with an architecture that seems to have worked so far.

First of all, the team divided the bits on the device into *system* and *data*. The system partition contained the Android platform itself as well as preinstalled apps, which was read-only (except for the OTA updates). The rest of the information on the device, including downloaded applications, application data, user preferences, and account information, was stored in the data partition. This segmentation meant that if there was ever some catastrophic problem, the device could do a factory reset, blow away the entire data partition, and the phone would at least work. The user would have to set up their accounts again and reinstall applications. And they might have lost some application-specific data.[8] But much of the data was safe anyway, because it was either on external SD-card storage or up in the cloud.

During updates, the read-only system partition would have to be perturbed, because that's where the new bits from the update had to go. The question was: how would the update system guarantee that there was enough space available, the right bits were being modified, and the updates were able to proceed even in extreme circumstances of the phone restarting during update or running out of battery?

The solution was to have a series of incremental updates. So rather than treating the entire Android system as a single amorphous blob, updates separated the system into individual portions that would be

---

[8]   Oh, no—Candy Crush put me back at level one!

dealt with on their own. For example, an update might have new bits for the framework, the media stack, and the SMS driver. These, then, might reside in different modules which could be handled independently. The update system packaged updates for each of these modules, downloading all of them prior to starting the update process. The update rebooted and launched into the update app, which walked through each of these modules one by one, installing each one, verifying that the results were as expected, swapping it in on top of the old one, and then proceeding to the next one. If the phone ever died or restarted in the middle of the update process, it could pick up where it left off, without leaving the system in some unfinished, indeterminate state. "Our goal was, even though it said on the screen 'Do not power off your phone,' if any number of power cycles, battery pulls, whatever happened, it would still eventually arrive at a completed, updated state."

One of the problems that can occur is running out of space. What happens if there is not enough free memory on the device to download the update? Or what if the update results in a system size that is too large for the available memory and runs out of room mid-update? This was especially a concern on early Android devices, where space was at a premium and it was entirely possible for a user to have used up most of the available storage space.

Fortunately, the team anticipated this problem. The main strategy to ensure that there was enough room for updates was to use the cache. "We had this cache partition, set aside for that purpose. It was shared. Applications could put temporary data there that was allowed to be deleted. But it mainly existed so the OTA system could download into it." While the cache was ostensibly available for applications to use for temporary files, its real purpose was to enable the update system to function, so that there was always enough room for updates to download and install.

Of course, there was always the theoretical possibility that the system might run out of room anyway. After all, Android was created to be used by manufacturers for all kinds of unpredictable configurations. In that case, maybe an OTA wouldn't be possible; but it still wouldn't leave the phone in an unusable state. "There was some weird thing where the device was full, the cache was full, and nobody was deleting that data, then the OTA download might fail. So you might not get your OTA, which was bad if it's critical. But it's not as bad as an update leaving you with a brick."

The final area to nail down for updates was security. Updates were allowed to write to an otherwise read-only partition, so that they could update the core operating system on the device. So what's to stop some malicious software from pretending that it is an update and similarly changing the system software?

The approach that Dan and the team used, with the help of Android's security team, was to only allow trusted files to replace those on the system. Update modules would each be signed with keys that could be verified by the system as trusted by Android. The Security team added another level of protection so that each entire update had one more layer of key encryption in addition to that used by each of the individual modules. With all of those layers, the system was deemed secure and was allowed to ship (and to update).

After launch, Dan searched the web to see if anyone was poking at the security aspects of updates, to make sure that there were no problems. He found a discussion about it on a hacking forum. "People were interested in hacking their way into this phone. One person who was pretty well regarded on the forum said, 'Give it up. Code's solid. I can read how it works. You're not going to get past it. Game over—look somewhere else.'"

Dan quoted that discussion in his annual performance review that year, when talking about his work on the OTA system, concluding: "The internet has reviewed my code."

One of the impressive things about Android OTAs is how reliable they have been since the beginning. Engineers on the team have taken hundreds of updates, both for internal pre-release builds and for official releases without problems.

But there was this one time . . .

Originally, the update mechanism provided a single, huge binary file for the entire system. So even if there was just a small update to one specific area of the platform, updates would still require downloading and installing the entire system. That wasn't a great experience (for users or carriers), due to the size, bandwidth, and time required for such large updates.

Sometime soon after 1.0, the OTA team (which now included Doug Zongker as well as Dan Egnor) implemented delta updates. The system figured out what had changed between the previous system and the new one and would only download and install the bits that had changed. The system worked and the team was ready to release it into the wild.

At the time, Michael was moving to Mountain View from Seattle. He thought, "Everything seems pretty good, I'm going to take a week off and move my family. A couple days into that, it was ten o'clock on a Tuesday night, my phone rings. It's Dan Egnor. I answer the phone, and I'm like 'Dan, what's up?' He said, 'First, I want you to know, everything's perfectly fine.' That immediately tells me—this is not fine. 'But . . . we bricked a bunch of devices.'"

The problem was that the image used to create the delta for that update was slightly different from the one that HTC (the manufacturer of the G1) had put onto the phones. The update mechanism using deltas only worked if the systems matched exactly. So when the update was applied on those phones, the system was corrupted and the devices were bricked.

The good news was that there were only 129 devices affected by the problem. It was still horrible for those users, and there was a bunch of customer service work that had to happen to replace those phones. But 129 out of the fleet of all G1s was pretty good for this kind of catastrophic failure. The reason the problem was so contained was that the phased-rollout and check-in service mechanisms that the team used worked as intended; Dan and Doug were monitoring the updates as they rolled out. They detected the problem immediately and put a stop to the update until they diagnosed and fixed the problem.

This failure also resulted in new policies and processes to ensure that it didn't happen again. And so far, it hasn't.

When the team was developing the OTA system, updates were not a common thing for mobile devices (other than Danger's, of course). The iPhone, when it first launched, didn't have updates like this. To update an iPhone, you needed to plug it into your Mac, the same as syncing music on an iPod. Nowadays, Over the Air updates are just an expectation of our wireless mobile reality. Your phone downloads and reconfigures its entire operating system wirelessly and reboots into the new OS, and of course it's all going to be okay. What could possibly go wrong?

The other necessary piece that made the OTA updates work reliably was the check-in service, which provided the ability for Android servers to monitor devices in the field. Dan wrote the basics of the system, but received some help when Chiu-Ki Chan joined the team in early 2008.

CHIU-KI CHAN AND THE CHECK-IN SERVICE

Chiu-Ki got her start in software development at age eight, when her mother enrolled her in a summer programming course. They had thought she'd just learn computer usage skills, but the course also covered programming in BASIC, and Chiu-Ki enjoyed it, especially the sense of power she got from it. "As an 8 year old, I really enjoyed bossing the computer around. In real life, people bossed *me*. But as a kid, you can actually tell the computer to do something."

Many years later, after getting her master's degree in computer science, she joined Google in 2003 to work on search quality. That project made sense, since she'd specialized in text processing during her graduate program.

After working on search for a few years, she wanted to try something new. She had friends on the Android team, including Dan Egnor whom she'd known on the search team, so she joined the services team in February of 2008. The Android team had launched the public SDK the previous Fall, but was still months away from shipping 1.0.

Like Dan, Chiu-Ki had experience with the Google back-end infrastructure, so the services team was a logical place for her to start on Android. Eventually, she would work on the Android Market team, as well as the Maps team. But when she first joined the team, she helped out with the check-in service, getting things ready for the 1.0 launch.

The check-in service worked hand-in-hand with OTAs as updates rolled out to the fleet of devices. From his experience at Danger, Michael believed in rolling out an update slowly, in a way that could be tracked and reverted. Dan remembered Michael telling him, "'If you're not careful, your OTA download can brick the world.' He insisted, quite correctly, on having a staged rollout canary[9] process, where we'll roll out to internal users first. We'll have a way to monitor that they actually booted back up with their new OS and are still checking in with that. We'll have those plots [real-time graphs of check-in results] so we can

---

[9] *Canary* is a term that is used regularly on Android to mean the bleeding edge of whatever piece of software you're talking about. Much like canaries in a coal mine (proverbial and actual), canary builds of software will be the first to experience problems, and the team uses a small set of canary users to test the waters before rolling out a release to a larger set of users.

deliver to internal users, watch it bounce down as they all reboot. Then we'll deliver it to .01 percent of external users, watch the same plot in case there's something weird. Then we'd go from .01 percent to .1 percent to 1 percent to 10 percent to a rolling ramp, always watching those charts and looking for signals."

DISTINGUISHED SERVICE

The underlying capabilities that the services team provided for Android can't be underestimated; they are fundamental to making the Android platform so powerful for users. Pieces of the platform like the kernel and the framework are necessary just for making the device boot and run. But without services that allow users to get instantaneous messages and email, or to synchronize calendar or contact information, or to get necessary release updates, Android wouldn't have been nearly as compelling as a smartphone platform.

21

LOCATION, LOCATION, LOCATION

CHARLES MENDIS AND BOUNCE

One of the most compelling mobile apps is Maps. The ability to see where you are and navigate to where you'd rather be is one of the true killer apps for mobile phones in general. But once upon a time, before Android 1.0, this app didn't exist. Android had to staff a team to make it happen.

Meanwhile, another engineer at Google, Charles Mendis, had an idea for a different app that needed mapping technology.

Charles Mendis worked in the banking industry in Australia, but was encouraged to apply to Google by a friend of his. The friend ended up at Amazon, while Charles joined Google in 2006. "I joined as an opportunity to see the USA. I'd never been. My wife and I had gotten married and we wanted to travel around and see the world. This seemed like a great way to live in the USA and see the country. The plan was to move back to Sydney after four years to start a family." That was many years ago, and Charles still lives in California and still works at Google.

Charles started on the Ads team. "When you first started, you had a choice of two things: you choose Search or Ads.[1] Did you want to do the Search thing, or did you want to make money? I was allocated to AdSense."

Charles wasn't particularly interested in mobile technology at the time. "I didn't have a mobile phone at the time. I never liked mobile phones; they were a pain. People could just hassle you whenever they wanted. Who wanted that?"

But the following year, Charles's wife became pregnant with their first child, which gave Charles an idea for an app. "I wanted to know where she was. If I had to go pick her up to take her to the hospital, I wanted to be able to see the location." He wanted to build an app that would give him this information.

In the Spring of 2007, he managed to get some hardware from the Android team. "I harassed Ryan Gibson and Brian Jones, and they gave me a couple of Android devices.

"I wanted to get familiar with Android development, so I convinced the team I was working with, the AdSense front end, to join as a developer program. Ryan had this challenge, where they wanted people to write apps and the winners would get more Sooner devices. I wanted a few more devices,[2] because I wanted my wife to have one and for me to have one. So we built a game called *Spades*.[3] It was a network multiplayer game so four people could join and play a Spades game. I used to play with the same group at my house on Fridays."

The team wrote the Spades app in a couple of months.

"After we built the app, we never ever played the game again. I'd be harassing them to test the app, and they were just like, 'I hate this game, I never want to play it. Don't want to play this game again, in any shape or form.'

---

[1] There were various other projects happening at Google at the time, including Google Maps. But a lot of engineering effort (and people) were going into search and ads at the time he was hired.

[2] This wasn't just Charles and his team being cheap and trying to get something for free; this was the only way they had of getting these devices. The only phones that were physically capable of running Android before 1.0 were the limited number of prototypes used by the Android team. So when Charles wanted more phones for development and testing, he had to prove to the Android team that they would go to a good home where they would be used for active development.

[3] Like the card game of the same name.

"But the good thing is that we got third place, and we got a bunch of devices as part of participating."

It was early August of 2007. Charles had the devices he needed for his team, and he also had experience in writing Android apps. Now he could write the location app he originally had in mind, to track friends' locations. He called it *Bounce*.

"We imagined people bouncing around. At any time, I could see where you were. The problem is, how do I get the location? Back then [on the Sooner device], we didn't have GPS. So I bought these Bluetooth GPS pucks from Amazon. Bluetooth didn't really work in Android. It was there, but there were no APIs." That is, the system had Bluetooth capability, but there was no way to access the functionality from an application, so Bounce couldn't use Bluetooth to communicate with the GPS pucks.

However, an application could issue a command to the system, just like a command that you might type into the DOS shell on Windows or the Terminal console on a Mac.

"There was one really long complex command that would effectively set up a Bluetooth connection to your GPS puck, all to work around the fact that we didn't have GPS. Then I could read the continuous stream of the GPS data written out to Bluetooth."

So now Charles had the location data from the GPS puck through Bluetooth. But what to do with the stream of data? He didn't want to write a server and log the location; he just wanted to use it to send real-time locations back and forth with friends.

"We started using SMS as our transfer protocol and our server. You would have a device with a GPS puck and I would have one. When I opened the app, I could say 'request [friend's] location.' It would send an SMS to your device and the Bounce app would intercept that SMS and say, 'Is Charles one of my friends? If he is, let me send my GPS location back.'

"So we had a basic version, where my wife could see my location."

On September 15th, there was going to be an executive review for a go/no-go decision for launching the Android SDK. Eric Schmidt, Larry Page, and Sergey Brin would all be there. Andy Rubin was presenting, along with Steve Horowitz, and they asked Charles to bring his Bounce demo.

That morning, the demo still wasn't complete. Charles and team had added a feature to Bounce they called *Memory Lane*, which would show your location history. But the feature had come online only recently, and since then he had only been at work and (occasionally) home. He needed to add some actual location history to demonstrate that feature, so he got in his car and drove around the area to add some data points on the way into the office.

At 9:00 AM, he was ready to go. "I'm just making sure Bluetooth stuff's paired and then I walk into the meeting. Eric's at the head of the table, Larry and Sergey are sitting in their usual chairs. Jonathan Rosenberg. It was pretty packed. The whole team is there. I was sitting in the back, and then Andy Rubin started. 'We're going to talk about what Android is, and at the end we're going to have some demos.'

"Eric's like, 'Let's just skip to the demos.'

"They turned to me: 'Okay, Charles, you're up.'"

Charles showed them Bounce and then spent the rest of the meeting answering their questions about what it was like developing for Android at that time.

At the end, Eric told Andy that they were approved to launch.[4] Which, two months later, they did.

"After the meeting, Andy turned to Steve and said 'That guy's joining my team. Make it happen.' Then Steve told me, 'Hey you're joining the Android team!'

"I was like, 'Actually, I'm pretty happy working on AdSense.'" Charles had just become the Technical Lead for his team and things were good. "But Steve talked to me and was pretty good at selling me on it. A few weeks later, I joined the Android team."

There was originally a plan to show off Bounce at the launch event in November. By then, Bounce was using the Google Talk connection that other Google services were using, which was better than the SMS hack it had been using. But Google Talk was not very stable at that time, so it would often drop the connection and the apps on either side couldn't do anything about it. In the end, Steve decided not to demo Bounce to avoid the possibility of failure in front of the press.

[4.] Meanwhile, Charles's first child was also approved to launch. Around this same time, while he was at work, his wife called him; it was time to go to the hospital. Charles drove with her and, several hours later, their son was born. They didn't end up needing Bounce to locate each other, but she did call him on her Sooner phone.

Eventually, Charles needed to turn Bounce from a demo into a product. The first thing he did was to sort out that Google Talk connection. Charles worked with Wei Huang, and they eventually got it working for Bounce and for the rest of the Google services apps.

Another piece that Bounce needed to improve was location services. The GPS pucks that Charles used for the demo were just a workaround for the early Sooner device that didn't have GPS. At that executive meeting in September, Sergey suggested that he pick up location from cell tower and Wi-Fi data. This approach was already in the works: Charles had started working with another team in the same building that was implementing the Maps feature *My Location* (also called the "blue dot"). That technology uses data on cell towers and Wi-Fi routers to place the blue dot, with the size of the surrounding circle indicating the uncertainty radius (since cell and Wi-Fi location is not as exact as GPS).

But Charles also needed to plan for other devices with more built-in location capabilities. The G1 device actually had GPS hardware, so Bounce could use that data directly when it was available.

Charles worked with Mike Lockwood, who was writing support for GPS and other hardware sensors. But Charles had a problem when using GPS on the device: "It was really power hungry. And really slow." The solution was for location services to use the lighter-weight and more approximate cell/Wi-Fi data in general, but it would spin up GPS when the user was directly using a mapping application to get more accurate location data. This approach avoided the power drain of having the GPS hardware constantly running, with the advantage of getting more accurate location information when the user clearly wanted it.

The final thing that Bounce needed was a name. Bounce was a code name, but products need real, trademarkable, non-infringing names when they launch, so the team, er, bounced around some ideas.

"We had a team at Google: all they do is name things. We went to them; they had a bunch of names. A lot of them were copyrighted. We said, 'Let's just go for a descriptive thing called Friend Finder.' And then someone pointed us at this adult dating site that was called Adult Friend Finder. So we weren't going to go anywhere near that."

The team was stuck without a name. Then they talked to Larry Page, just a couple of weeks before they launched. "Larry said 'What about Latitude?

You know, freedom, movement ... and it's tied to location.' So Larry came up with the name."

Apparently being a Google founder and executive wasn't enough work for Larry; he also named products.

By this point, Latitude was integrated as a feature in Maps, as opposed to a separate app. It didn't make the 1.0 release, because there was higher-priority work to be done for the initial release. But it launched a few months later, in February of 2009, simultaneously on Android, BlackBerry, Windows, Symbian, and on the web.

MAPS

"Apps were a little bit controversial because of the ownership," said Steve Horowitz. "For example: Maps. Maps was like the star mobile app for Google. Actually, all Google really *had* in mobile was Maps. So we wanted to write Maps, or bring Maps over [from the mobile team], but the mobile team weren't really big believers [in Android]. Eventually we convinced them to assign an engineer to help port Maps to the Android OS. He [Adam Bliss] came over from the Maps team and was instrumental in getting the Maps app running under Android."

Bob Lee shared an office with Adam. "He was creating the first version of Maps on Android. We had a prototype of a G1 screen. He made this demo; it was like the first time it was a full screen map. You could pan around on the big screen. Andy [Rubin] gave him the first G1 prototype within the team because of that."

In late 2007, Adam was joined by Charles, who set aside his Bounce app to focus on shipping Maps. "I joined Android to work on [Bounce], but then pretty soon that got killed because we had far higher priority things to do. We needed the Maps app before we had the shiny feature of location tracking."

Maps wasn't all that Charles worked on. Like the rest of the Android team, he did whatever needed doing. "I did a lot of the Dialog APIs, and worked on ListView, TextView, and basics in the system server. Whenever Dianne was overloaded, whatever few bugs of hers I could fix, or Jason Parks, or Jeff Hamilton, or Mike Cleron. I ended up being a kind of a firefighter, wherever was needed. The SMS app, MMS app, Gmail app, did a bunch of stuff. But mainly on the Maps app with Adam. But I also wanted the MapView API and the Location API, because we needed the Location APIs [for Bounce]."

About a year after he joined Android (around the time Android 1.0 shipped), Charles switched to the Maps team and became the lead. "There was a Maps team I was working with on the My Location stuff. I wanted to say 'Hey, we should take the Maps app and we should merge with that team and actually expand the features of the Maps app.' Because if you look back then, Maps ran on Windows Mobile, Symbian, and BlackBerry. BlackBerry was kind of the king back then. That was most of the volume. It had far more features there, like transit features. Because they had like 30–80 people across the world working on that app, while it was just myself and Adam working on this [on Android]. But we were building on the same APIs, we were using their server APIs. So at the end, after a lot of discussions, I moved from the Android team to the Maps team [along with Adam Bliss]. I stayed in building 44. I just moved my desk a few cubicles over."

Part of moving to that team was becoming the overall lead of mobile maps (for Android and the other platforms). But leading that team didn't mean getting his way. "Back then, I was trying to convince everyone, 'Let's stop working on Symbian, Windows Mobile, and BlackBerry and let's move to Android because I think it's going to be the future.' And everyone's like, 'You're crazy! We have no users of Android. Look at how many BlackBerries are shipping every month! It's more than you're going to ship in a year.'

"In the end, we decided to move from the code base we built for Android into what we called the 'unified code base.' So we dumbed down and didn't use all of the Android APIs. You couldn't use HashMap, you could only use a Vector. You couldn't use a LinkedList, you could only use a Vector. Basically, Vector was the only data structure you had.

"We moved to that code base, which gave us a lot of features on Android, so the Android users suddenly had more of a full-featured Maps app. But I couldn't use all of the features of Android."

Finally, after the Droid launched in late 2009 and Android started to get a large user base, the conversation on the Maps team changed. "That's when I could finally go back to the team, with the growth of Android, and start shifting us from Symbian, Windows Mobile, and BlackBerry onto Android.

"I remember when I took over the team. It was two years later I convinced them to be all in on Android. Till then, it was like 'No, we have to support all the platforms.' But after Droid in particular, our user base started to grow so much. We started to be able to do Wi-Fi scans, cell scans. When

I started, I remember the blue circle, which shows the uncertainty radius, would be at 800 meters. Within a year or two, we managed to get just the cell one to under 300 meters and the Wi-Fi from about 300 to 75 meters. So just the data collection[5] from Android driving that really helped get the blue dot much much tighter."

NAVIGATION

"At the same time I joined the Maps team," said Charles, "I started working on turn-by-turn navigation. Back then, you would buy Garmin and you would pay money. Or even on an iPhone you would pay $30/month for that. We felt like we could do this amazing experience."

But another problem had to be solved first: the data format that the Maps app was using. The maps that were displayed in the app at that time were basically just static pictures, which were problematic both in terms of usability and size. "We were using raster maps, which were PNGs.[6] If you rotated the map, the text was upside down. If you wanted to tilt the map, you couldn't." Also, the images used for the maps were large and required large bandwidth to download.

Keith Ito, then in the Seattle office, was working on turn-by-turn navigation. To address the data problem, he worked on a new way of displaying maps, using vectors.[7] Vectors are a way of describing the graphics of an image (like a map) with geometry instead of a picture. Rather than sending down map images (with text embedded in that picture), the server sent down a geometric description that would be drawn by the device at the appropriate resolution and rotation. And it would do so with far less data than the PNG image maps required.

[5.] Android collects anonymized data on Wi-Fi and cell tower locations from the phones that use those services (this is an option that users can opt into when they set up their phone). The more phones that are in those areas, the more data there is about where those towers and routers are, and the more accurate the information becomes for other phones that are using that information to track their own location.

[6.] PNG is a file format for images, like JPEG and GIF.

[7.] A vector is a line segment, with a location and a direction. Mapping information is essentially a collection of line segments, so a vector representation works well for encapsulating map data.

Keith built a demo of these new vector-based maps and sent it to Charles, in Mountain View, who took it to Andy's office: "Larry was in the office. I showed them the vector maps. You could tilt and zoom. Before, we had discrete zoom levels. Now you could zoom in a little or a lot, and the text wouldn't distort."

But there was a trade-off: performance. "To do it on a G1 was so hard because we were rendering it." That is, it requires more effort and time to draw a map's geometry, vector by vector, than it does to display an image. But it was a thousand times less data.

Andy knew that it would be important for the upcoming Verizon device. "Turn-by-turn navigation, on Droid, became one of the marquee features." Keith continued working with Charles on both productizing vector maps and on the turn-by-turn navigation feature.

There were still hurdles to cross in launching the feature on the Droid. For one thing, Verizon already had an existing application, VZ Navigator, that they charged money for and wanted to continue offering. But the feature did make it onto the Droid[8] and out into the world. Turn-by-turn helped drive not only navigation and Maps usage overall, but also Droid sales. People realized that they could use their phones, with their existing data plans, to get to where they needed to go.

---

[8] *http://googlemobile.blogspot.com/2009/10/announcing-google-maps-navigation-for.html*

22

ANDROID MARKET

Today, we take it for granted that there's a place we go to buy our apps. You have a phone, you want an app—you go to the application store to get it. Obviously.

But back before Android and the iPhone, that simple ecosystem didn't exist.

It's not that companies didn't want it to exist; they kept trying to create something like it. You could buy services from carriers (mostly ringtones and simple utilities), and there were various repositories for games. But the market for apps wasn't there (since there wasn't a lot that apps could do on those limited devices, at that time), so users weren't missing much. But once there were devices powerful enough to run real applications, users needed an easy way to get them.

But carriers had created *walled gardens*[1] where they controlled access to the earlier app stores. They wanted to ensure that malicious or bad apps couldn't take down their network, so they didn't want random applications running on their network that they could not control. They created curated places, like the app store on the Danger phones. But that extra layer of process and hassle dissuaded many developers from uploading apps, and prevented larger app store ecosystems from coming into being.

---

[1] See "Danger, Inc." in Chapter 2 on page 11.

Android wanted to fix this problem with Android Market. They wanted a store that anyone could upload apps to. Michael Morrissey, who was leading the services team on Android, told Nick Sears his goal: "I want a fourteen-year-old kid sitting in Kansas to be able to write an app in the morning and upload it in the afternoon to Android Market and have it go out to sell to all the customers."

This concept concerned T-Mobile (Android's launch partner for the 1.0 device, the G1). How could they verify that that kid in Kansas couldn't upload something that would take down their network?

And so began a long discussion between Android and T-Mobile to iron out the details that would make this work. There were two things that the Android team had to do to get T-Mobile to agree. First was assuring T-Mobile that their network would be safe. Second was allowing them to have their own curated app store, alongside Android's.

The first item, safety, began with having a secure platform. Given the kernel-level sandboxing of apps, the team was able to convince the carrier that Linux security standards would be sufficient. Next, the team required that developers actually sign in, and used existing infrastructure and policies vetted on YouTube to validate that the individual did not present an unreasonable risk for the company. Also, they used the power of crowd-sourcing, putting in place a system whereby users could report bad apps and the team would take them down. Finally, they convinced the carrier that, as much as T-Mobile would suffer if they had network problems, so would Google. Android's, and Google's, reputation was on the line. So Android had all the right incentives to make this system work and for the apps and network to be secure and safe.

For the second item, a custom store for T-Mobile, Google created what Nick called, "a store within a store." The actual application store was on Google's infrastructure, but T-Mobile was offered primary placement within the store for a limited set of apps that they curated. This placated T-Mobile enough to get them to that first release. But eventually this just went away; other carriers didn't demand this as part of their deals, and everyone realized that there was no particular reason for this requirement. All of the work was on Google to manage that infrastructure, and the open application store system seemed to be working.

The garden walls came down, and Android got T-Mobile to agree to let them have an application store on the platform. Now they just had to build it.

The application store for Android was developed in the services team, which was responsible for Google services and device management. But the team hired other people to figure out how to host and sell applications. The project was called *vending machine* internally. When it launched, it was called Android Market.[2]

Having an application store was always part of the plan. But the project started late, since the top priority was shipping the 1.0 release and the G1. When the G1 launched, Market was there, but it was clearly not a finished product. For one thing, it was called Market Beta.[3] More significant, users couldn't actually purchase applications. Instead, all apps could be downloaded for a cost of . . . $0. While the mechanisms of developers uploading their apps to Market and users downloading apps to their phones worked, the additional step of charging users (and paying developers) took more time and effort. The initial version of Market was great for users who want free stuff, but it wasn't as good for developers, who usually want to be paid for their efforts.[4]

The team brought in some much-needed expertise from the Google payments team. Arturo Crespo helped pull together the necessary infrastructure that allowed Market to process payments for applications. By the time Android 1.1 launched, in February of 2009, Market had the ability to sell applications (and developers had the ability to make money from their Android apps).

Market was one of the attractions of Android in the early days. It was easy to upload an application to the store and make it available to the growing set of Android users. Dan Lew, an external Android developer working on travel apps at the time, said, "I worked on a bunch of silly side project apps. Android was a good place for that because putting up a nearly pointless app on the Play Store is relatively painless."

But Market was more than a convenience for developers and for users; it helped create a world of apps that made Android a powerful ecosystem that went way beyond the phones people bought and the operating system

---

[2.] Android Market was renamed in 2012 to the Google Play Store.

[3.] Beta in a product name is not known for generating a feeling of polish and doneness.

[4.] As a software developer, I can testify to that.

running on those phones. Users were able to benefit from not just the basic phone and built-in capabilities, but also from the almost limitless potential of apps that they could install. It was Android Market that helped create this powerful dynamic for the Android platform overall.

23

COMMUNICATIONS

MIKE FLEMING AND TELEPHONY

It has been said that mobile phones are not just for browsing content, play-ing games, and checking email and messages; some people have been known to also use them for phone calls.[1] Or at least that was the theory behind the communications software that Android built for 1.0.

There are two important aspects of communication on a device: phone calls and messaging. Android had different teams for these features. And by "teams," I mean there was a different person working on each.

To make the actual telephone part of Android's phone platform work, the team brought in Mike Fleming. Mike knew that space already since he wrote the telephony software back at Danger.

Mike Fleming came to Silicon Valley in early 2000 to work for a company called Eazel, where he met Eric Fischer (who would later work on text func-tionality for Android). Within a year, Eazel ran out of funding and laid off nearly everyone. Andy Hertzfeld,[2] one of Eazel's founders and an engineer on the original Macintosh team, helped many of the employees find positions at either Apple or Danger.[3] Mike and Eric went to Danger.

Danger had recently shifted its product focus to target mobile phones. Mike was brought in to make the phone application work, which the engi-neering manager thought would take a couple of weeks. Mike said, "We

---

[1] It's true; you can look it up. On your phone.

[2] Andy later joined Google and was involved in some meetings with the Android team early on.

[3] Andy Hertzfeld knew Andy Rubin; Hertzfeld was a co-founder of the company General Magic, where Andy Rubin worked in the early 90s.

discovered that it was really the entry point to a large set of industry standards and certification. So it was quite a bit more complex than expected."

Mike stuck around Danger for about four years, before interviewing at Android, where he knew former Danger people. He started in November of 2005 and was given the task of making Android telephony work. At least he had a better idea of how complicated that job would be the second time around.

Mike had mixed feelings in taking the job. "I joined Android because I really wanted it to exist. But honestly, I didn't really want to work on it. I had done telephony and I was kind of burnt out on it. But somebody had to bring that domain expertise. I joined Google to work on Android, but I had no intention of staying past Android 1.0. So my headspace going into the project was a little bit odd."

Dan Bornstein, on a work-from-home day, sent an email to the Android engineering team with the subject, "Logcat preventing me from using my keyboard." (Picture courtesy Dan Bornstein.)

With the state of Android at that time, there was no shortage of other work to do in addition to telephony, so Mike took on other tasks as well. For example, he worked with Swetland to make debug logging more efficient and accessible to developers. On Android, this system is known as *logcat*, which stands for cat-ing[4] a logfile.

Mike also helped out with the Java runtime. Dan Bornstein was working on making the new Dalvik runtime work, but the team needed a placeholder to use in the meantime. Mike pulled in JamVM, an open source runtime for

---

[4.] The Unix cat command is short for "concatenate" and is used to output file content.

Java. This gave the team something to write Java code against and gave him enough functionality to start working on the code for the telephony software, which he finished up once Dalvik was working.

One of the tricky parts in the telephony work was that the G1 phone was launching with 3G connectivity, which was new for T-Mobile. Since T-Mobile was getting it to work on their network at the same time, the Android team needed a way to test it, so T-Mobile parked a dedicated 3G COW[5] on the Google campus to allow G1 users to test the new network.

COW #1: This was one of the mobile cell towers T-Mobile set up near the Android building. (Picture courtesy Eric Fischer.)

Although Mike made telephony work on Android, he did not work on the telephone application (also known as Dialer), although he had wanted to do just that. There were deep, architectural disagreements between the different factions of people who had worked at Danger, Be/PalmSource, and WebTV/Microsoft. Eventually, Steve Horowitz, who was running engineering, stepped in and worked out a deal that got the teams past this period of conflict and indecision. Mike remembered, "At some point there was a decision made that the Danger people would work on the lower parts of the system and the Palm and Microsoft people would work on the upper layers. I

[5.] COW = Cell On Wheels, a mobile cell site that exists for this exact kind of situation.

think that Steve Horowitz brokered that compromise with Brian [Swetland]. I remember being unhappy with it at the time. I wasn't bought into that. But that was the deal that was made."

COW #2: Another cell tower set up on campus for testing (picture courtesy Eric Fischer)

This segmenting of the Danger and Be/PalmSource/Microsoft teams brought up other tensions and philosophical differences. For example, Dianne proposed a model of *Intents*, Android's mechanism for allowing applications to launch other apps to handle specific actions, like "take a picture" bringing up a camera app, or "send an email" launching an email app. An application could register the Intents it could handle in its *manifest* (a file that is bundled along with an application that contains summary information about the app). Having the information available in the manifest file instead of just in the code of the application itself meant that the system could identify which apps handled which Intents quickly, without having to launch the apps to find out.

But others on the team weren't convinced. Wei Huang said, "At the time, we're like, 'Why are we making this so complicated?' I remember Chris DeSalvo and Mike Fleming were advocating making it simple: just do it when an app is running. There were a few things where I think Dianne had a much more of an in-depth idea how things would scale on the platform. But at the same time, I think that the activity lifecycle[6] was kind of complicated. And Swetland was very frustrated with how complicated things were."

Mike Fleming added, "I think that there was never really a forum for discussing an alternative to Activities and Intents. I think that that was probably the thing that I was the most upset with. As someone who's working on the lower layer, because I happened to have the domain expertise, but also had participated on doing the upper layer at previous companies, I was really upset that I wasn't able to be a part of the whole vision."

Wei Huang observed, "These people had a lot of experience in building mobile OSes. It was not without challenges; we had to figure out how to work with each other, because we had different opinions. And strong opinions. Overall, I think we managed to work through these differences. Not all of them, because Mike Fleming left."

In the Spring of 2008, six months before 1.0, Mike left Android. He said, "The product was struggling to come together. I felt that it was entirely possible that it would not make it out the door. It didn't work very well on devices. It was slow and crashed a lot. It worked well enough to use, but I found it to be a very frustrating and disappointing product.

"The telephony stuff was in good hands. The Dalvik stuff was in good hands. And I felt that I didn't have anything else that I could do to help it ship. I didn't expect to stay beyond completion. I didn't see what I could do to really help complete it. So I left for a startup."

Despite Mike's feelings about Android at the time, he had gotten telephony working before he left, and the product continued on its long journey toward 1.0.

WEI HUANG AND MESSAGING

Users of recent Android releases may wonder at the many messaging applications Google has provided recently, but Android has always had many of

---

[6.] Android's activity lifecycle is the system that controls the state of applications. You might think that applications are either running or not, but the reality is much more complex. For example, applications can be running in the foreground (with the user interacting with them) or running in the background (when another application is in the foreground). As applications are started, brought into the foreground, sent to the background, and eventually killed, they go through several stages of their lifecycle. The distinction between these lifecycle phases is one of the things that Android developers need to understand about their applications . . . and it's always been one of the more complicated bits of Android to fully understand.

these apps. To some extent, this dynamic is a product of there being so many different kinds of messaging: SMS (text messaging through the carrier), MMS (texting pictures or groups of friends), Instant Messaging (of various flavors), video chat, and so on. Even in the early days, there were multiple ways of messaging people, most using different underlying protocols and requiring different apps, but there was only one engineer working on all of them: Wei Huang.

In the Spring of 2006, Wei was on the Android Browser team, but after many years of working on browsers (at Microsoft, then AvantGo, then Danger, then Android), he was ready for something new. Steve Horowitz suggested that he take on messaging, since Android needed it and nobody else was on it. So Wei worked on the Google Talk application as well as SMS.

Owning both of these apps seems like a lot of work for a single engineer (and, indeed, multiple teams of multiple people are working on equivalent apps now). In fact, the underlying mechanisms for these apps to work was quite different, especially with the carrier requirements necessary for SMS messaging. But back in the early days of Android, this was a typical workload. Wei said, "At the time, we didn't have the luxury of even one engineer per feature. Other people were owning one or two apps."

Wei dove into Google Talk first and was able to get a demo working quickly. One of the things that helped get it going was that Google Talk (which already existed as a desktop app, with a complete backend on Google servers) used a very full-featured protocol for sending messages (XMPP[7]), so it was relatively straightforward for Wei to write an app to set up a connection to the server and send messages back and forth.

One of the hard parts with turning his app from a demo into a product was maintaining that connection between the server and the client. The connection would frequently drop, but the client wouldn't find out and would continue sending messages without realizing that the messages weren't going through. Much of the time that Wei spent on the project went into making the connection more reliable, with logic to handle the inevitable drops and retries.

Once the rudiments of the system were working, Michael Morrissey, who was leading the services team, suggested using this connection for all the Google apps (including Gmail, Contacts, and Calendar). Instead of each

[7] Extensible Messaging and Presence Protocol

of those apps having to maintain its own connection to the backend, they could all share this single, persistent connection. Software on the device would combine app data to send to the server through this single pipe and would receive responses from the server and deliver them to the appropriate applications. This was a similar architecture to the one at Danger that Michael had helped set up.

This connection was available not only to the existing apps; it was potentially available for pushing messages from other apps as well. Charles Mendis, for his Bounce application, wanted to be able to notify the Maps app when friends' locations changed. With push messaging enabled over this persistent connection, the Maps server could find out when a location changed and send that to the device, which would send it to the Maps app to update locations on the screen.

Wei worked with Debajit on the implementation, piggy-backing all this infrastructure onto the existing Google Talk connection. They wanted to release it in 1.0 as a connection not only for Google apps, but also for any apps that wanted to use push messaging. But then they talked to the security team, who told them, "There's no way you're going to launch this thing." It wasn't secure enough.

So even though the functionality and API for pushing messages was available to developers in pre-1.0 releases, it was removed in the .9 release. There's an item about it in the Android 0.9 SDK Beta release notes:[8]

> *Due to the security risks inherent in accepting arbitrary data from "outside" the device, the data messaging facility of the GTalkService will not be present in Android 1.0. The GTalkService will provide connectivity to Google's servers for Google Talk instant messaging, but the API has been removed from this release while we improve the service. Note that this will be a Google-specific service and is not part of the core of Android.*

This functionality made it into Android later (after the team fixed the security issues), eventually showing up in the Google Play Services library as something called Google Cloud Messaging.[9]

---

[8] *https://developer.android.com/sdk/OLD_RELEASENOTES#0.9_beta*

[9] Which was later rebranded as Firebase Cloud Messaging.

SMS

Meanwhile, Wei was also working on getting SMS working. Most of the effort for the project was in implementing and perfecting all the complex features and requirements needed for carrier certification. He said, "It was a pain because of carriers."

For a long time, Wei was working alone. But as 1.0 got closer, Android worked with engineers from Esmertec in China, especially to help with the integration of SMS and MMS and making them work correctly for carrier compliance.

Ficus, who had been working on camera and then audio drivers, also joined the effort to help make it work more reliably. He had a personal passion to have better messaging on Android. "I was trying to be a good Android dogfooder[10] and was texting... and it just didn't work. I felt like being younger had some perspective for me that was lacking elsewhere; it was a big part of social life in the mid 2000s. I just started fixing bugs, committing code. I didn't get any blessing to stop working on my other stuff or start on SMS, I just did it. I just felt that someone should fix it."

Another person helping out was Peisun Wu,[11] who was managing the project (in addition to other projects on Android). With everything from external contractors to carrier testing, there were many details to be managed.

Carrier testing complicated communications projects like these. Ficus explained: "There was a lot of carrier compliance certification stuff, which made me crazy. The MMS standard in particular is really complex. There are all these things you can do with it, making slideshows and images doing animations and playing sounds. And even though everyone knew that the only thing anyone ever actually wanted to do was send one and only one picture, you had to implement the whole thing because you had to go through carrier certification."

In June of 2008, Ficus, Wei, and Peisun flew over to China to work with the contractors. Sichuan had just had a major earthquake, so they met in Beijing and worked out of the Google office for two weeks.

[10.] *Dogfooding* (short for "eating our own dogfood") means testing our own stuff.

[11.] See Chapter 27 for more about Peisun.

Wei and Ficus, during the Beijing trip in June of 2008 (picture courtesy Peisun Wu)

Ficus remembered a later trip to work with the same team: "Summer of 2008, trying to ship. None of the prototype devices could leave the supervision of a Google employee. All of the contractors were in Chengdu, China. We'd previously met in Beijing, but this was during the Olympics and we couldn't get a place to meet. We had to find a place that had a GSM network, and a Google office so that we could have these test devices, and that the engineers could get a visa to. So we met in Zurich for two weeks."

Both Google Talk and SMS (with MMS) made it in time for the 1.0 launch.

24

DEVELOPER TOOLS

Developers, developers, developers, developers, developers, developers, developers, developers, developers, developers, developers, developers, developers, developers.

—STEVE BALLMER, MICROSOFT[1]

One of the reasons behind Android's growth is the developer ecosystem that was created along the way, enabling thousands (now millions) of applications for people to find, download, and use.

But this kind of ecosystem doesn't just happen automatically, especially for a new platform with no market share. In order to lower the barrier to entry for application developers, to make it easier for them to write and publish their applications, Android needed to provide tools for developers.

A determined developer could write code and use some obscure commands in a terminal to compile that code into an application. If that developer just wanted to write a "Hello, World!"[2] app, that's probably all they'd need.

But any real application involves a large amount of code and other materials, including multiple files, resources for images, text strings, and so on.

---

[1] There is a famous video you can find online of Steve Ballmer (then Microsoft CEO) saying "Developers!" over and over while pacing energetically back and forth across the stage at a Microsoft conference many years ago. On one hand, the video is a quirky piece of tech history (and a meme in the industry). On the other hand, he wasn't wrong. For companies like Microsoft, and projects like Android, it really is all about the developers that write applications for your platform.

[2] "Hello World!" is the canonical first application that a developer writes. It's an application that does pretty much nothing except print "Hello, World!" to the user, announcing its presence.

Sure, programmers could have come up with something more interesting as an initial proof of existence. Maybe it could compute digits of pi or draw a picture. But apparently saying Hello is the pinnacle of achievement for developers. Maybe it's based on a life growing up in dark computer science labs, where the opportunity to say "hello" to actual humans is limited, and therefore exciting.

That level of complexity is overwhelming if you're coding it all by hand in a text editor with just a command-line compiler for a friend.

That's why Xavier Ducrohet was brought onto the team, in April of 2007.

XAVIER DUCROHET AND THE SDK

Xavier (who goes by "Xav") had been working on tools for years. Most recently, he was building drawing tools at Beatware. It wasn't the most stable of jobs: "We were not always quite paid." But Xav's green card, which allowed him to stay and work in the US, was still being processed, and leaving a company can put that process in jeopardy. Also, he felt some responsibility for not causing a crisis for the small company. "If I left, the company would go under."

Beatware was eventually acquired by Hyperion Software in late 2006. Xav decided to stick it out a bit longer because of the stock he was still vesting. But in March of 2007, Oracle acquired Hyperion, and that was it; Xav didn't want to join Oracle. He called his old friend Mathias Agopian at Google.

Xav already had a good idea of what Android was about, even though the project was secret. Beatware had been in conversations with Android early on about providing some graphics technology. Beatware offered a vector-based image editing tool, which Android could have used for UI graphics. Vector images offer the advantage that they look better when scaled than pure bitmap images, which become blocky or distorted when they are scaled. But Android eventually developed its own kind of image for that purpose, called a *NinePatch*.[3]

Xav had known Mathias for years, from the Be community. Xav had played around with BeOS back when he was in college in France. He'd gotten to know the Be community in Paris at the time, which included Mathias as well as future Android engineer Jean-Baptiste Quéru. So when Xav wanted a new job, he reached out to Mathias. He had already interviewed with the team earlier when he was at Beatware, so his interview this time just consisted of having lunch with Steve Horowitz. He started three weeks later, in April of 2007.

[3.] NinePatch images allow for better-looking scaled images by defining areas of the image that should and should not be scaled when the image changes size. For example, the rounded corners of a button should generally retain their absolute size regardless of the size of the button, whereas the interior background of that button should scale to the new size. Android eventually offered vector image formats years later, which have mostly supplanted NinePatch.

On his first day, Xav sat down with Steve and Mike Cleron, who suggested he work on tools. To begin with, Xav dove into DDMS.[4] DDMS was a tool running on a developer's desktop system that was a container for many different tools. For example, DDMS provided a list of the current applications running on an Android device connected to the host computer. Selecting one of these would cause that application to connect to port 8700 on the host computer, at which point you could debug that application by connecting to that port from a debugging tool.

Xav's starter project[5] was to enable DDMS to visualize native memory. This isn't a particularly critical need for most Android developers, but it was very important at the time for the Android platform team itself. After that project, he refactored the monolithic DDMS tool into separate pieces consisting of the core functionality, the user interface layer, and the glue that tied the other two together into a standalone tool.

By refactoring DDMS, Xav was able to connect the pieces with an existing open source development IDE called Eclipse. By June, he was able to demonstrate, to the larger Android team, the entire workflow of opening up an application project within this IDE, compiling it, deploying it to the emulator, running it on the emulator, stopping at a breakpoint[6] in the code, and then stepping through the code, instruction by instruction.

This project was a good example of what things were like on Android. Someone identified a problem and would then just go hammer out a solution. Quickly. Xav joined in late April. By June, two months after he started, he demoed the entire, new, functional tools flow to the team. That set of tools shipped to external developers when the SDK launched a few months later and served as the basis for Android's developer toolchain for many years. He

---

[4] DDMS = Dalvik Debug Monitor Server. DDMS talked to the Dalvik runtime to get a connection to other services on the device.

[5] A starter project at Google is something that a new employee is generally given that allows them to ease into development in their area. It's usually a small-ish project that won't make them dive in so deeply that they'll get lost, and which they can finish up soon to have a sense of accomplishment. Starter projects weren't really a thing on Android. There was too much to do, so new people basically dove in deep and kept getting deeper.

[6] A breakpoint is a marker set in a debugger at a particular line in the code. When the application gets to that line during execution, it pauses and allows the developer to use the debugger to see current values of variables and the state of the program overall.

went from joining the company and team, knowing nothing about Android, to offering a tool that would form foundational support for all Android developers (platform and application, internal and external) in just a couple of months.

Xav on November 12, 2007—launch day for the first SDK (picture courtesy Brian Swetland)

Once Xav finished that IDE project, he created the SDK for Android. The SDK was an installable bundle of tools and other pieces for application developers that included the Android Eclipse plugin (and all the subtools like DDMS, ADB, and Traceview) and Android itself. The Android bits included the library of code that developers wrote their programs against, the system image of Android that ran in the emulator, and documentation so that developers could figure out what it was they were supposed to be doing. Again, Xav identified the need and put things together. And it's a good thing he did. This work was coming together around August of 2007. Meanwhile, the SDK for Android was set to ship that November, so it's nice that they had something to ship.

DAVID TURNER AND THE EMULATOR

One of the critical tools that developers need early on in a platform's development is a device to run that platform on; if you can't run your application, how can you verify that it does what it's supposed to?

But when Android was first being developed, devices that ran the platform were effectively unavailable,[7] so the team brought in someone to write a virtual device: David Turner (known to the team as "digit").

Before he wrote the original Android emulator, David was famous in programming circles as the original author of FreeType, a font-rendering library. One of the fascinating things about Google is that there are so many people at the company that are famous for doing a particular thing . . . which is completely unrelated to what they end up doing at Google. I've known famous classic game developers, inventors of fundamental graphics algorithms, and 3D graphics experts, none of whom worked on software at Google remotely related to the software achievements that made them famous.

Other companies hire people for what they've done, then ask them to do more of it. Google hires people for who they are and asks them to do whatever needs to be done. What these people have done in the past is a great example of what they can do, but does not limit them, in Google's eyes, to what they are capable of. That's how Google found itself with one of the world's great font rendering experts, working on the Android emulator.

David learned about coding for performance when he was a kid, programming in BASIC and assembly language on an Apple II+, and learning the importance of performance coding along the way. "The machines were so underpowered that every detail counted to get anything satisfying from them."

Years later, he was using a computer running OS/2, but disliked the fonts it used, so he posed himself a challenge: he wrote a renderer for TrueType[8] fonts directly from the specification, using as little memory and code as possible. The result was the FreeType renderer. He released it as open source. It caught on, and was used widely in limited, embedded systems from TVs to cameras to . . . Android. FreeType was (and is) the font renderer for Skia, Android's graphics engine.

---

[7] Later, as the team got closer to shipping 1.0, devices were still hard to come by, since the platform and the device hardware were being developed simultaneously.

[8] TrueType was a font format created by Apple in the late 1980s.

In 2006, an engineer on the Android team (which was always looking for embedded programmers) saw David's name in the source code for FreeType and reached out. "Of course, nobody told me why I was contacted by Google, so I prepared my interviews by reading a ton of stuff on HTML, SQL, web servers, and databases. To my surprise, all interview questions were about fundamental data structures, algorithms, and embedded systems, so they went a lot better than I initially expected."

David started on the Android team in September of 2006.

David's first project was getting a utility library up and running for C programming.[9] Android was using a very small and basic C library at the time, but it lacked some necessary features and had a more restrictive license than was desired for the eventual open sourcing of the platform. David assembled Android's "Bionic" library from various license-compatible BSD[10] Unix libraries, combined with new code to integrate with the Linux kernel and to support Linux or Android-specific features not present in the BSD codebase.

After this library work was done, David moved on to the emulator.

Initially, Android had a *simulator*, a program that ran on the developer's desktop computer that imitated the behavior of an Android device. But simulators fake many of the details; they mimic the behavior of the system on the outside but ignore many of the details on the inside, which means that the behavior of the overall system is not true to the actual device (and thus cannot be relied on for real testing).

Fadden wrote the original simulator but was getting tired of maintaining it when Android was in constant flux. David remembered, "It was maintained by one sole engineer who was fed up with fixing it every time we had an advanced feature. The plan was: the simulator is essentially dead, and we need a good emulator."

Android had the beginnings of an emulator already, based on an open source project called QEMU, which was created by Fabrice Bellard, a friend of David's. David overhauled this implementation: "We were using a very old version of the QEMU upstream at the time that had been modified pretty

---

[9.] Although Java is the main programming language for Android applications, there is also quite a bit of code inside of Android itself that is written in C++, C, and even assembly.

[10.] BSD = Berkeley Software Distribution, an early Unix OS with permissive licensing.

---

aggressively. Nobody understood exactly what was going on." David started by pulling in a more recent version of QEMU, which had problems of its own. "QEMU development at the time (around 2006 to 2010) was pretty bad. No unit tests at all, global variables[11] everywhere."

He eventually got things working better, but still had a lot of work to do, like making the Linux-based QEMU project work on Windows and Mac, and separating the Android-specific portions of the emulator to enable better testing.

The emulator was hugely important at the time. Hardware devices were very difficult to come by. Having an emulator that mimicked a real device made it possible (for developers on the Android team and eventually external developers) to write and test their Android code.

The emulator was like a real device because it emulated everything that happened on a real device. Not only did it look like an Android phone (in a window on your desktop computer), but the bits running inside of it, down to the chip level, were exactly the same as those that ran on an actual hardware device.

Another advantage of the emulator was speed, compared to actual hardware devices (for the developers that had them). Communicating to an emulator on the host machine was much faster than communicating through a USB cable to a real device. Pushing applications, or the entire Android platform, across a USB cable could take minutes. Pushing code to the emulator, which was running on the same desktop computer where the code was being pushed from, was much faster, so an engineer could be more productive with a virtual device instead of a real one.

On the other hand, the emulator has always been criticized for being incredibly slow. In particular, it took a long time to boot. Starting up an emulator mimicked booting a phone, since it emulated exactly what a phone would go through. You could leave the emulator running in most situations, especially for pure application development. But startup and runtime

---

[11.] Global variables are ones that can be accessed from anywhere in the code (as opposed to variables that are more "tightly scoped" and can be used only in more limited areas). Globals provide an easy way to share information across an entire source base, but can cause problems, especially as the code grows and multiple developers contribute to it, because it is difficult to reason about who is accessing what when. So global variables tend to be frowned on for real-world code, especially for large, multi-person projects.

performance of the emulator continued to be a common source of complaint until more recent releases.[12]

The emulator project was also a great demonstration of the, er, *scrappiness* of Android in those early days. It's not that the team was small . . . there wasn't even a team. There was just one person responsible for this monumental effort, and the emulator was just one of several projects that he worked on.

David continued developing and maintaining the emulator on his own, as just one of his jobs, for many years.

DIRK DOUGHERTY'S DOCS: RTFM[13]

All the tools in the world won't help developers write code if they can't figure out what they're supposed to write. At some point, the developers need to learn about the system and how to put things together in order to create applications. They need documentation.

"Reference documentation" for Android (as for many other platforms) tends to be written by the engineers that write the APIs and underlying functionality. That is, if an engineer adds a class called Thingie, then they will (or should[14]) write some kind of overview docs for Thingie that describe what the class is for and why developers should care. The functions inside of the Thingie class will (or should) also have docs describing when and how to call those functions.

But reference docs get you only so far. It's great to be able to go to the docs for, say, the Activity class and learn how to use it. But how did you learn enough to even know to look for Activity? What developers really need, especially for a new platform like Android, is some higher-level documentation,

---

[12] More recently, the emulator has taken advantage of the CPU and GPU on the host computer to improve both boot and runtime performance.

[13] A common developer acronym for "Read the F-ing Manual," RTFM is typically used when an engineer is asked a question that could easily have been answered by the questioner had they bothered to read the documentation.

Have I mentioned that engineers don't get into computers because of their people skills?

[14] Of course, there were many exceptions to that rule, especially for early-Android APIs. There were many classes in Android that lived for years in the public API with no documentation at all.

giving an overview and teaching the fundamentals. What is this platform? How do we write apps for it? Where is sample code that we can look at to see how it is done?

The Android SDK was going to launch in November of 2007. Three months before that, the team decided that they needed a tech writer and brought in Dirk Dougherty.

Dirk had been working at Openwave, a company that made a browser for mobile phones. A former colleague forwarded his resume to the Android team. Dirk interviewed and started a few weeks later.

"I came by building 44. I found my desk. It was in a conference room by the lobby, the one that later would become the arcade.[15] There were a bunch of tables stashed in there that were all empty. I didn't know what was going on, or if I was in the right place. Eventually, in came Jason, Dan, Dick, David, and Quang, who were starting up what would become the DevRel[16] team. We all moved in there and started learning about the platform. Someone drew a countdown calendar on our whiteboard with the number of days until the SDK launch, and right from then we started pushing toward the launch."

Dirk and the DevRel team pulled together the pieces that the SDK needed. "The first year was just constantly sprinting to get the website up, to get the basic documentation in place. It was mostly reference docs and tooling, combined with a few guides and API tutorials. We had ongoing preview releases and SDK updates as the platform stabilized. With the Developer Challenge and the intense developer interest, we needed to expand the docs. I got help from an external writer I'd worked with,[17] who partnered with me to write the Android fundamentals docs, explaining how all this

---

15. At one point, building 44 had a video game arcade, which held machines that some of the engineers owned, plus a few that Android bought to fill out the set. It was kind of amazing to have classic arcade games sitting there waiting for people to play them. But they spent more time waiting than being played; there was work to do.

16. *DevRel* is short for *Developer Relations*, which is the team that does most of the outreach to (and from) external developers, with materials like documentation, samples, videos, conference talks, and articles. At the time, the Android DevRel team was Jason Chen, Dan Morrill, Dick Wall, David McLaughlin, and Quang Nguyen.

17. Don Larkin, who had worked at NeXT Computer, Be, and (with Dirk) Openwave.

stuff worked. A few months later, we got more reinforcements as another internal writer joined the effort, Scott Main. We spent all of our time creating the fundamentals to go around the reference docs, and then bringing up the website. The engineering team gave us tons of support along the way. Getting things off the ground was a total team effort."[18]

[18.] The website was *code.google.com/android* at the time (now defunct). The developer documentation now lives at *https://developer.android.com*.

25

LEAN CODE

Once you've written it all, you can't go back and re-optimize.

—BOB LEE

One of the aspects that defined Android from the very early days was that it was incredibly optimized so that it would work on the very limited mobile devices of that time. The performance mindset of the team affected everything from the APIs (many of which were written in a specific way so as to avoid allocating memory) to the coding recommendations given to external developers. It was all about writing optimal code because every cycle, every kilobyte, takes away resources or spends battery life that is needed elsewhere.

At least part of this performance-first focus can be attributed to the background of the early team members. The engineers that had previously worked at Danger had made their operating system work on devices that were even more limited than Android's G1. And engineers from PalmSource were also familiar with mobile constraints and realities.

Bob Lee observed, "They [former PalmSource engineers] would say that one of the reasons it failed was that they were just trying to do more than the hardware could handle. Once you've written it, you can't go back and optimize. I just think they were avoiding that same mistake on Android. This was one of the reasons why Dianne [Hackborn] and everyone else were so anal about performance, and micro-optimized a lot of stuff. The phones were so slow back then.

"I remember everybody—me, Dianne, Dan [Bornstein]—would be in this war room, because over the course of a release there'd be all these places where people were using too much memory. We didn't have swap,[1] because it didn't make sense to have swap. Things would run out of memory and crash. It was this kind of heroic session in a war room where we'd just go on for days sometimes, and you would never know when the end was going to be, just trying to stamp out memory problems.

"It was all about allocating memory pages. Dianne, or Brian Swetland, had written these tools to see dirty pages, and which pages were getting touched. We just had to stamp it out. It was a lot of grinding to see which apps were causing the problems and try to pinpoint them."

Ficus reflected on how his time at Be and Danger impacted his work on Android: "A lot of us came from these embedded systems, this philosophy of extreme frugality when it comes to CPU cycles or memory. I think that's an interesting lens to look at a lot of the early Android decisions from. I look at a lot of these engineers like they were raised during the Depression and they learned to scrape the bottom of the pot."

The mindset of the entire platform team was performance-first. This came from a combination of the limited memory on those early devices, along with slower CPUs, the lack of GPU rendering (Android didn't use a GPU for UI graphics until the Honeycomb release), and Dalvik's garbage collector (which took time allocating and collecting memory). This attitude continues internally even to this day, even though every device is much bigger and faster. Everything the phone does spends battery power, so optimizing the platform code is still worthwhile. Recommendations for external developers have been relaxed since those early days, but the Android APIs and implementation still reflect the original performance constraints.

[1.] *Swap* space enables applications to allocate more memory than is physically present. The operating system will "swap" out chunks of memory to disk to handle this larger overall amount, allowing the application to access a much larger memory heap, by handling it through a combination of physical RAM plus disk storage.

26

OPEN SOURCE

I don't think the open source thing mattered.

Open source is many things to many people.

It can be a way to "crowdsource" work, getting a larger community to help out. Linux is a great example of this. While the original system was written by a single developer, Linus Torvalds, a large community of individuals and companies in the decades since has contributed everything from fixes to drivers to core system functionality.

Open source can be a way to advertise and share work. GitHub is a great place to do this and hosts many active (and cobwebbed) projects that show off the work of people who took enough time and care to finish and upload the code instead of just letting it fester on their local system. Open sourcing your own pet projects can be a great way to get your name out there as someone that does this kind of work; the ability to point to an available and transparent site is a good way to show potential employers your capabilities.

Open source can be a recruiting tool for companies. Similar to individuals advertising their own capabilities, companies often open source projects (applications or libraries for other developers) as a way to get the company's name out there to other developers. Square is, essentially, a credit card company. They might find it difficult to convince developers to join based on the excitement of their business alone. But they are well-known in the developer community as a provider of interesting and powerful open source libraries. Developers who are not excited about financial transaction software go

---

[1] The worst thing an interviewer can do to someone is to take their quote out of context. But I thought Iliyan would understand. At least I hope he will. Because I just like the quote to start off the chapter.

The full context was that we were discussing the factors that led to Android's success, and he . . . well, let's just save this for now. The complete quote is at the end of the chapter.

there because they want to help the open source community (including getting their own name out there as a developer on these projects).

Open source can be a way for big companies to quietly and gently euthanize a product. Sometimes a company decides to shut down a project and move those engineers onto a project with a brighter future. The company could, and often does, simply kill the product. But they could also release the old code into open source, as a gift to the developer community. The company does not see direct benefits by giving it away (in fact, it usually costs some effort and time to migrate projects to open source), but they can earn goodwill from developers by doing this, and reduce the pain of killing something that those developers were using and depending on.

Open source can also be a way to simply let other people get and use your software transparently. This is the open source model of Android.

All of Android's platform software has been available as the Android Open Source Project (AOSP), on *https://source.android.com/*, since November of 2008. The code for each release is open sourced at the same time[2] as the release is made available for devices. As soon as the release is available to users (on new devices or as updates for existing devices), developers can look at the code that was used to create that version.

Android accepts external contributions; developers can create accounts on *https://source.android.com/* and submit patches.[3] Those patches get reviewed by people on the Android team and can then be submitted into the Android source base, to be used on future releases.

In reality, external contributions are not frequent . . . and not expected. Android does get regular contributions from some partner companies. For example, partners tend to fix bugs to make things work the way they need them to for their devices. Maybe they noticed a corner case that they could

---

[2] The one exception to this was the Honeycomb release. The team focused exclusively on getting tablets to work in that release, with the result that it wasn't clear how things would behave on phones, because nobody was paying attention to that side of things. The decision was made to delay open sourcing the release to avoid manufacturers building phones using a release that really wasn't set up for it.

This caused a stir in the community at the time, upsetting people who thought Android was backing away from open source. The issue was resolved a few months later when the next release, Ice Cream Sandwich, which added proper phone support, was released to open source.

[3] Patches are source code deltas that fix a problem or implement a feature in the existing code.

improve, or a form factor that Android did not yet account for, or maybe they just found and fixed a bug. It makes sense for them to integrate it directly into Android itself so that they don't have to re-apply that fix every time a new version of Android is released. And Android does get some individuals contributing fixes occasionally. But external contributions are rare; most of what is there has come from the internal engineering team.

There are a few reasons for this dynamic. For one thing, the Android source base is huge, and contributing even a simple fix takes significant effort just to understand the context of the original code and implications of that change. But a more significant reason is Android's "eventual open source"[4] model itself. An external developer wouldn't have any way of knowing, when they found and fixed a bug, whether that bug had been fixed in the meantime in the internal/future version of the code, or even whether that block of code they've been spending all of their time working with even existed anymore. Code has a tendency to move around or get rewritten when future requirements or changes dictate.

But even though Android doesn't benefit from substantial external contributions, Android's open source model still provides significant advantages. First, application developers love it. A platform of the size and complexity of Android could never be documented so completely that a programmer could understand every nuance of it and how everything interacted internally. The ability to look at the actual code to determine what's really going on is invaluable; developers don't need to guess at what the platform is doing if they can look at the code itself. This transparency has always helped Android developers in writing their apps and represents a fundamental difference between Android and many other operating system platforms.[5]

Dan Lew, a developer who was working on Android apps in a small startup when Android was new, said that the code availability simplified development: "There were plenty of early platform bugs to deal with. I remember there being lots of hacks. But since Android was open source, usually those

---

[4] *Eventual open source* is my term for Android's open source model at the time. It was open sourced, but it was not *developed* in open source. Rather, the team worked on it internally for many months before the code was released in public. Today, many parts of the system, like the ART runtime and the AndroidX libraries, are actually developed in the open.

[5] One notable exception is Linux, which has always been open source and which was chosen early on, perhaps not coincidentally, as the OS kernel for Android.

hacks were at least discoverable. Without it being open source it would've been much harder to work around some of the problems."

The second, and arguably more important, element of Android's open source model is that Android's partners have free and easy access to all of it. This was actually the original reason for Android open sourcing the platform; it was a mechanism to make Android available for any prospective device manufacturer to get everything they need. There is no licensing and there are no protracted contract negotiations; partners can simply go to the website and get the bits they need to ship an Android-based device. And in so doing, they help to enable a consistent ecosystem of compatible Android implementations, because everyone is starting from the same common implementation. If they want to get Google services like the Play Store and Maps and Gmail, then there's more to it, but the core code for building a phone platform is available for anyone to download and use as is. Romain Guy explained: "That's what we all think when we think 'open source' for Android. Partners don't necessarily care about contributing, but they have everything they need."

Brian Swetland agreed: "One of the goals of Android, before they ever had contact with Google, was to give people an alternative to that dire future of a single company owning the mobile computing platform. The thinking was, how do you get people to adopt it? It's gotta be open. Otherwise, how can they trust that they have any level of control?"

Dianne Hackborn agreed, comparing Android's open source model to the licensing model she'd seen fail in previous experiences: "One of the things we struggled with at PalmSource in getting others to use our platform was that they were deathly afraid of someone doing to the mobile space the same thing that Microsoft did to PCs. For example, Motorola had a really hard time thinking about licensing Rome [PalmSource's UI toolkit built for Palm OS 6] but were all-in on buying the company and owning it. Being able to make Android open source made it a lot more comfortable for OEMs to adopt, since they could share some ownership of it, as well as making it extremely flexible for the rapid evolution of mobile devices."

It is this second element, opening up the platform for device makers, that distinguished Android from other platform offerings out there. Not only was the platform available to use, but the code was available to understand and play with as companies got it working on their devices. And, in the meantime, this open source platform was also a complete, production-quality implementation, verified on actual hardware products and ready for manufacturers to take and use.

In contrast, if you wanted to ship a Windows phone at that time, you'd have to license (and pay for) Windows from Microsoft. Also, the process of getting it to work on a new device was non-trivial. Michael Morrissey was working at Microsoft prior to Android and got to see that process first-hand. "When you were trying to bring up a new OS, whether it was Win CE or Pocket PC or whatever on a new phone, trying to integrate those things and debug bringing that up was incredibly painful. You had this thing called the 'Board Support Package,' which was all the low-level code that came from the OEM. And then you had all the higher-level Windows code. So if phone calls were failing, or the network was bad, or whatever, where did the problem lie? Nobody could figure out where that was.

"This was my favorite running gag at Microsoft: There was a team whose job it was to work with these OEMs to bring up new hardware. Except neither side was allowed to see each other's code, because it was secret. Samsung or HTC or whoever would send somebody over to Seattle, and they would sit next to somebody in this team. They would try to debug it without really letting each other see each other's code. They would just lean over and say, 'Here's what I think I'm sending you in this call. What are you seeing?' It was this long kind of ridiculous dance."

Of course, the fact that Android was open source meant that it was free for manufacturers to use, which was an added bonus. Michael said, "These OEMs would operate on pretty thin margins. So if you have a company like HTC and they're getting charged $10/unit by Microsoft, and they have to do a whole crazy bunch of integration work with Microsoft in order to get it to work, the idea of free and open source is magic. If you have Android, which is open source, then your OEMs can bring up new devices super, super fast, because they have access to all the code. On top of that, it's free."

On the other hand, if you wanted to ship an iOS-based device . . . you couldn't. Apple is the only manufacturer of the iPhone; they don't make their platform available at all. Similarly, RIM was the only supplier of BlackBerry devices. Meanwhile, Android was not only free, but freely and easily available for anyone to download, play with, customize, and build upon.

The fact that this model also made the software easy for application developers to look at the internal code and made it possible to accept any external (albeit infrequent) contributions was simply a happy coincidence that worked out in Android's favor.

Of course, there's more to being open source than simply saying that the code is open source. The team had to put the project together in such a way that external developers and companies could get to it, download it, build it, and understand how to do all of that. It took effort to pull it together in the time leading up to the initial release.

First, the source code itself had to be organized into a state that was ready for ongoing distribution to open source, which was the product of Dave Bort's efforts on Ed Heyl's team.

Chris DiBona, the director of open source programs at Google, also worked on part of the problem. Some of the tools that Android was using at the time were not suitable for external use. Google uses tools that are either licensed or built in-house and proprietary. Android's code needed to be buildable by external developers without proprietary or licensed tools, so the team adopted tools internally that could also be used (for free) externally.

Chris helped to make the decision to switch source code control[6] to a system called Git, which was unpopular with most of the engineers. Chris told them, "The kernel and systems teams [who were using Git already] were never going to leave Git. Git is the right answer for our development model. They needed an external person to hate. I offered to be that person."

The team made the change to Git, the code was organized for public consumption, and the project was open sourced in November of 2008, with the 1.0 release. And it's been open source ever since, providing transparency to developers and platform code to manufacturers.

Jeff Sharkey, who joined the Android team after 1.0, summed up the appeal of open source, for both partners and users: "I'm a firm believer in open source software because of the power it gives people to build things you never imagined or had the resources to build yourself. If you were an OEM in the early days of Android, you couldn't license iOS, and Microsoft offered a pretty homogeneous experience. In contrast, Android gave OEMs a chance to rapidly bolt-on features to differentiate themselves on store shelves.

---

[6] Source code control is a system for storing and managing the code. These systems typically have functionality that's useful to teams like code review tools, tools for merging multiple changes in the same files, and history for all of the changes that have been made.

"The ethos of the open source world also resonated with end users. Instead of a dictatorial mandate of exactly one home screen app, one software keyboard, one set of quick settings tiles, etc., Android lets users radically customize them. Phones are incredibly personal devices, and these deeper customizations (beyond just the outer case) give users a stronger sense of connection and ownership."

This chapter started with a quote from Iliyan Malchev, cruelly taken out of context. Here's the complete version:

"I don't think the open source thing mattered. We could have made it free to them without open sourcing it. I am an open source advocate. I think we should do even more open source than we do. But I just don't think that the strength of Android is predicated on it being open source. If we made it free without open sourcing it, it would have been just as successful."

That is, having the source code available in *open source* wasn't the important part; simply making the source code *available* would have been enough. Open source was just a natural and transparent way to achieve that goal.

27

MANAGING
ALL THE THINGS

Most of the other chapters of this book are meant to tell the story of how Android was built, piece by piece, and of the people who put together those pieces. But some of the people helping to pull things together weren't responsible for individual pieces; they were responsible for the overall effort. Welcome to the "business" side of Android.

ANDY RUBIN AND MANAGING ANDROID

Andy Rubin's interest in robots was there from the start of his career when he worked at Carl Zeiss AG on robotics. He later took a job with Apple, where he acquired the nickname "Android." Later, he was at WebTV with other future Android people, where Mike Cleron remembered him as "the crazy guy down the hall who played with robots."

After WebTV, Andy founded Danger and then, eventually, a startup that he named "Android."

Although Andy was running Android, both before and after the acquisition by Google, he generally let others manage the people. Chris White led engineering for the first six months, in addition to working on system architecture and design, but eventually Steve Horowitz was brought in to manage the growing team. After Steve left, around 1.0, Hiroshi Lockheimer took over. Andy depended on this management layer to deal with the people on the team while he focused on the business aspects of the project, like partner meetings.

Andy left the team while he was at Mobile World Congress in Barcelona in early 2013. Hiroshi told how he and Tracey were with Andy in a series of partner meetings: "That's when he decided to tell us he was leaving. It was after the LG meeting and before the Samsung meeting. We had a 15-minute break. He had told [Tracey] already, at some break or something. I was blissfully unaware. Kicked everyone out. It was just Andy and me. He was like, 'I've been doing this for 10 years. I'm tired. I'm going to leave.'"

TRACEY COLE AND ADMINISTRATING ANDROID

One of the people responsible for a smooth transition after Andy Rubin left was Tracey Cole. Tracey had been Andy's administrative assistant for 14 years and was the lead admin for Android when he left. She knew how to get things done in Android, and at Google, and she wasn't going anywhere.

In August of 2000, Tracey Cole was working as an admin at a biotech firm and wanted out. A friend suggested she talk to his friend Andy at Danger. She interviewed with Andy and Danger's other founders (Joe Britt and Matt Hershenson, both of whom joined the Android team years later) and became the admin for that team. When Andy left Danger in 2003 Tracey stayed behind but continued helping him on the side. Then, in the Fall of 2004, she joined Andy's startup, Android, starting work on the same day as Brian Swetland.

When Google acquired Android, Tracey moved over with the rest of the team. She was aware they were talking to Google, but not how far things had gotten, "I remember him meeting Larry and they hit it off. I went on vacation and came back and all of a sudden we were going to be working at Google."

Tracey continued to be Andy's assistant at Google, as well as leading the admin group in Android, until he left Android in 2013. At that point, she continued in her role administering the overall Android team and leading the other admins on the project, and also became Hiroshi's assistant.

HIROSHI LOCKHEIMER AND PARTNERS

When Hiroshi Lockheimer first got to Google, he managed partner companies, working with OEMs and carriers to get Android working on their devices and networks.

Hiroshi always wanted to be an architect: "Of buildings. Not a software architect. Actual building architecture." He wasn't interested in computers and didn't encounter programming until his first (and only) term at college. School didn't agree with him, and he went back home to Japan. But he'd caught the software bug. Back at home, he taught himself programming and started picking up consulting jobs. He also worked on hobby projects, including a text engine[1] for the Be operating system, which he open sourced. This work got noticed by people at Be, and Hiroshi landed a job there, moving to California in December of 1996.

Hiroshi joined Be right after an episode where Apple nearly acquired Be to provide the next MacOS. But Apple acquired NeXT Computer instead. Hiroshi recalled, "We were the company that wasn't bought."

Three years later, Hiroshi was ready for something new. Hiroshi's colleague at Be, Steve Horowitz, introduced Hiroshi to Andy Rubin, and Hiroshi joined Danger. "I ended up being the first employee at Danger Research. There were three founders, and I was the first lackey they hired."

Hiroshi brought other Be (and future Android) engineers into Danger: Brian Swetland and Ficus Kirkpatrick. But Hiroshi himself didn't last long there, leaving after just eight months.

After Danger, Hiroshi worked briefly at Palm, the same company that many Be engineers joined when Palm acquired Be a year later. After leaving Palm, he managed an engineering team at Good Technology (which was working on mobile communications software), and then joined Steve Horowitz again in early 2005. Steve was then leading the IPTV team at Microsoft.

By the end of 2005, Hiroshi was again ready for a change. "I was on vacation in Japan and Andy emailed me out of the blue. Hadn't talked to the guy since whenever I left him back in whenever it was [at Danger]. He's like, 'Hey I'm at Google now doing some stuff that I think you'll like.' He knew that I liked wireless devices. 'I think you should come talk to us.'

"I was at Microsoft, working on set top boxes at the time. It just wasn't for me; I really missed working on mobile devices. So I called him back in January."

The interview and hiring process at Google has never been known for its swiftness or simplicity, but Hiroshi's case is especially unique.

Despite Hiroshi's relevant experience and long track record in related tech companies, Hiroshi wasn't a shoo-in for Google interviews, especially since he didn't have a college degree. Steve Horowitz said, "Google at the time was very focused on pedigree. Google was like, 'He has no degree, I'm not sure we can hire him.' They were putting up a big fight."

Hiroshi said, "Twenty-some interviews, because they couldn't figure out how to hire me. They made me write an essay. Literally. I don't know if they

---

[1] When Hiroshi told me this story of his history writing text software, I told him that our text team on Android was looking for engineers and that he should apply. He politely declined.

fully grokked[2] the irony. They gave me homework to write an essay on why I didn't finish college.

"I was this close to saying 'Screw it.'"

Finally, the team was able to convince the Google hiring committee to hire Hiroshi. But even with that agreement, plus the results of 20+ interviews, and what must have been a stellar "Why I Dropped Out" essay, the hiring committee still refused to hire Hiroshi as an engineer. Hiroshi said, "They hired me under sort-of 'Misc,' and decided I should have the title of 'Technical Program Manager.'"

Through 1.0, Hiroshi was involved in the initial meetings with partner companies and worked with them to make sure that things happened. "It was the technology side of business, or the business side of technology, depending on how you look at it. We build software. But without partnerships, without hardware from someone else, especially back then when we didn't have Nexus or Pixel. . . . It was all reliant on OEM partners and operators who were going to ship these things. It was my job to program-manage that."

Brian Swetland commented on Hiroshi's role in managing partners: "No one wrangled partners the way he did, partially because a) he's really focused, but b) he's really technical. So he always understood the underlying technical issues, which was really helpful when we were trying to extract information we needed from partners, or to get them to do something that needed to be explained."

Hiroshi worked closely with the systems team because that was where Android software interfaced with partner hardware. "Swetland and I would go to Taipei. He would stay there for three weeks. I would go for a week, and then he'd be solo for the remainder of the trip. Making sure bring-up was happening. Bringing up the kernel, bringing up peripherals—he would be working with their engineers to do that, hardware and software. And then the prototypes would arrive here, and then the higher-level folks would run their stuff on it."

Around the time that 1.0 shipped, Steve Horowitz left Google. Andy was still in charge of Android but having someone else as engineering director had worked well with Steve, so Hiroshi took on that role. Tracey Cole said,

---

[2] To grok is to understand. Grok is a word coined by Robert Heinlein in *Stranger in a Strange Land*. It is commonly used by engineers, for reasons that have never been clear to me. Science fiction is a popular genre among engineers but quoting sci-fi books from the early 60s isn't very common. Yet we use this specific word all the time. I can't grok why.

"Andy leaned on Hiroshi very much, let him manage the team. He didn't like to manage people. He let Hiroshi take the reins on that."

Wei Huang credits Hiroshi with the engineering culture of Android: "Hiroshi was willing to dive into the details with me, to understand how things were working. Even when he became a VP, still running Android, he still reached out to us, to figure out 'Hey, SMS is not working, Hangouts is not working.' I think he was able to connect with the rest of the team, not just people who reported to him. Also, he cared about the product and that showed. And I think the way he communicated was down to earth. I really liked having Hiroshi in between us and Andy.

"I don't know how he could do it. How do you do it in a way that was genuine, and also having enough technical knowledge to ask the right questions? That's why he's where he is."

Hiroshi continued managing the engineering team through the Droid release and after, instituting traditions like Bacon Sundays[3] to pull everything together at the end to ship each release.[4]

Hiroshi in his tiny closet of an office in building 44, September 2008 (picture courtesy Brian Swetland)

---

[3] Described in Chapter 35 (appropriately titled "Bacon Sundays").

[4] Hiroshi is now the Senior Vice President in charge of Android, Chrome, Chrome OS, Photos, and more, managing thousands of people on some of the most important projects in tech today. Gosh, just imagine what he could have accomplished if only he'd gotten a college degree.

STEVE HOROWITZ AND ENGINEERING

If you look at the history of where we are and who "got" mobile and who didn't, it all goes back to the leaders and whether they had faith or vision at the time.

—STEVE HOROWITZ

Steve Horowitz was the engineering director for the Android team up to 1.0. He started on Android in February of 2006, after the team had started growing. There were around 20 engineers on the team when he began and almost 100 by the time they hit 1.0 nearly three years later.

Steve Horowitz learned BASIC and assembly on an Apple II in elementary school. In high school, he split his time between tech journalism and programming. He ended up getting an internship at Apple[5] straight out of high school and worked there every summer after that through college. After graduating, he joined Apple full time to work on Pink, a project to develop the next MacOS, and then Jaguar, which was developing next-generation hardware.

After two years at Apple, Steve went to Be, Inc., where he worked on UI toolkit functionality for BeOS, like the Tracker (the equivalent of Finder on the Mac). After several years at Be, Steve moved to Microsoft, joining the WebTV division just after it was acquired by Microsoft. There, he worked with future Android people like Mike Cleron, Andy Rubin, and Wei Huang. He also eventually hired Hiroshi to run the system software group for the Microsoft IPTV platform. Steve transitioned into management while he was at Microsoft, which led to his future role on Android.

While at Microsoft, Steve got an interesting offer from Tony Fadell[6] at Apple to run a systems software group for the iPod, at the time when that team was starting to think about the iPhone. "It was a good offer. But I had a lot of Microsoft stock, and they gave me an offer with a little bit of Apple stock. At the time, I liked what I was doing at Microsoft. The Apple offer looked interesting, but Apple [stock] would have had to go up a hundred

---

[5] Steve's hiring manager at Apple was Cary Clark. Years after hiring Steve into Apple, he worked for Steve at Microsoft. Later, he co-founded Skia with Mike Reed (another Apple colleague), which was acquired by Android, and Cary again found himself working for Steve.

Be nice to your colleagues—you will work with them again someday. And maybe even several somedays.

[6] Tony Fadell ran the iPod group at Apple for many years and later co-founded Nest.

---

times for it to be even close. Of course, sure enough, they did—more than a hundred times.

"Some parts of Tony's team, and this other guy Scott Forstall, were competing for what the architecture of the iPhone OS was going to be. In the end, I think Forstall's version won, but people from Tony's team moved over and became part of that effort. So in some weird alternate universe, I could have been working on iOS instead of Android."

Over the years that Steve was at Microsoft, Andy Rubin tried to get him to join Danger, but Steve wasn't convinced that they had what it would take, so he stayed where he was.

Then in the Fall of 2005, a couple of months after Android was acquired by Google, Andy tried again. "He said, 'I'd like you to come over and run engineering for Android—we just got acquired by Google.' When I talked to him and realized it was Google that was going to try this thing, I thought all the ingredients are now in place to actually disrupt mobile. I told Andy I'd do it."

Steve started on Android in February of 2006, as the Director of Engineering for Android.

Part of Steve's job on Android was to recruit talent. One of the people he brought in almost immediately was Mike Cleron, from his team at Microsoft.

Engineers on the team remember Steve's strong management skills, bringing calm to the team, and a discipline about cutting features so that they could hit their aggressive 1.0 schedule. Steve's priority was always getting the product to ship.

Michael Morrissey also remembered Steve's effectiveness in dealing with Google: "Steve was really, really good at managing the bureaucracy of Google. He knew how to navigate and work around process and procedure that didn't benefit Android."

One of the responsibilities of managers is helping the careers of the people on the team. But career wasn't the burning issue at that time; there would be plenty of time to talk about that after 1.0. There was work to do. Romain remembered hearing from Steve on weekends during that crunchtime period, where he'd get a single IM: "yt?,"[7] which would start a conversation, usually about a bug that needed fixing.

---

[7] "you there?"

MOBILE WORLD CONGRESS

Steve was part of the leadership team on Android, so he was both managing engineering and assisting on the business side. "Right after I joined, Andy, Rich Miner, and I went to MWC[8] with this idea of Android. It was basically a Flash demo; there really wasn't much there.

"We were meeting with and pitching as many people as we could on this idea of Android. We had this little room off to the side we'd bring people in. For the most part, they scoffed at us: 'Come back when you've grown up.' But we had a meeting with Paul Jacobs and Sanjay Jha [Qualcomm executives] and they got excited. They were enthusiastic and wanted to explore more. The other guys were dismissive.

"If you look at the history of where we are and who 'got' mobile, who won mobile and who didn't, it all goes back to the leaders and whether they had faith or vision at the time.

"The funny thing about MWC: contrast. If you look back at what it was back then, it was nothing other than this idea we were pitching, to where it is today, and it's just like . . . it is *all* Android." That is, Android went from having a hard time getting anyone's attention at MWC back then to today's reality, with Android having such a large presence at the show.

MANAGING CONFLICT

One of Steve's big jobs was navigating the differences between the various sub-teams. There were very strong divisions between the engineers that came from Danger and those that came from Be/PalmSource and WebTV/Microsoft.

"That's the thing about Android—like any team, it's stitching together personalities. It's certainly a lesson to anybody that small teams of incredibly talented people will win the day over big teams. There's no question. And that's obviously what we had in Android. But with that talent and that energy comes opportunity for conflict, interpersonally, architecturally. That's what I helped steer."

LEAVING ANDROID

Shortly after 1.0, Steve left Android (and Google). He was interested in a larger role, where he'd get to do more than engineering management. After he left,

---

[8.] Mobile World Congress is a huge annual trade show for the mobile industry.

Hiroshi took over the team. There's always that wonder, when we choose a certain path in our careers, or our lives: What if we'd taken the other road? Steve reflected, "The interesting question, which nobody could really answer including myself: If I knew then that Android would be what it is today, would I have made the same decision or not? Honestly, I don't know."[9]

RYAN PC GIBSON GETS HIS JUST DESSERTS

Android was "under the radar" at the time, but I heard whispers. Cool whispers.

—RYAN PC GIBSON

The larger a project is, and the larger the team is, the harder it is for things to stay on track or to hit a particular schedule. It's everyone's job to make sure that it does, but it is the particular skill set of what Google calls Technical Program Managers (TPMs) to see to the details. Hiroshi was doing this (as part of his job) on the partner side. Ryan PC Gibson was doing it for the platform.

Ryan's introduction to programming came from watching his mother meticulously copy BASIC programs from magazines into their Atari 800XL. "I learned that programming was mostly typing. To this day, I don't understand why software development takes so long."

Ryan joined Google in July of 2005. He arrived the same month that Android was acquired, but worked elsewhere in Google, on a software project for an internal sales tool. He was always interested in mobile technology, so he started looking around to see if there was anything closer to his interests. "Android was 'under the radar' at the time, but I heard whispers. Cool whispers."

He got an introduction to Andy and Hiroshi, and he interviewed with Mike Cleron. "He showed me Sooner, which had a keyboard and small D-pad. Compared to those old Nokias it was awesome, although navigating a 2D matrix of apps seemed clunky. Touch was right around the corner and changed

---

9. Years later, Steve ended up back at Google, running the software division of Motorola. "My biggest contribution was to abandon years of accumulated cruft and modifications and put Motorola on a pure 'vanilla' software path. I had deep admiration for, and faith in, the core Android team and wanted to use as much of their code as possible that would facilitate much faster upgrades and a better user experience." The strategy worked: the Moto X was upgraded to the KitKat release faster than any other OEM's devices, including Google's Nexus phones.

everything. I joined [the Android team] in January of 2007 and it felt like being back at one of my previous startups (with better food and solid financials)."

Being a TPM at that time was tricky, because many teams were unfamiliar with that role. As was Ryan himself. "I was a software developer for most of my career but had started to gravitate towards management. I never officially did the program or project managing thing before, so really had to figure it out as we went along. What added to the challenge was there were very few TPMs at Google at the time and most Googlers had never had a TPM on their team."

Fortunately, Android provided ample opportunity for good program management, and the early team recognized the benefits. "Hiroshi, Mike Cleron, Dianne, and Brian Swetland had all had good experiences with program managers in past companies. They understood the value they could add in successfully shipping products. We were still pains-in-the-ass, but in a helpful way. Secondly, the nature of the Android project lent itself to dedicated program management by meeting three important criteria: 1) lots of diverse contributors—Android devs, Google app devs, open source devs, 2) lots of diverse stakeholders—OEMs, carriers, SOC providers, and 3) hard timelines of the annual sales cycles for electronics. So Android was a good place to be a program manager."

The problem was huge: how to create, solidify, and ship an entire operating system, applications, and a device as soon as possible. Meanwhile, the team was still coming together and many of the fundamental pieces of the platform hadn't even been figured out, much less written. But they still needed to come up with a realistic schedule and start executing to it. And they needed the product to come out soon enough that it would actually be relevant. "Program management definitely played an important part. We were a year behind, and had we slipped into the next year might have been a historic footnote rather than a viable alternative. But we couldn't just ship anything—it had to be solid."

"Day one, Hiroshi handed me an electronic Gantt chart of hundreds of tasks, stretching out way past our delivery date. He accompanied it with an 'Aagh, help!' I think. In retrospect, it was a classic project management challenge, but it was all new to me. I talked with all the developers, about 30 at the time. It helped to come from being a developer with a startup background.

"I started off helping the software engineers organize their work into a series of milestones that led up to the 1.0 launch. That was a wild time, since we had to figure out how to stabilize the code base while the business and product plans were still up in the air. In those early days, I was pretty excited about Agile development,[10] but there was deep-seated skepticism within Android. Bad experiences of poorly run Agile groups at other companies had soured a lot of the leadership. But with an evolving product definition, the project actually lent itself to time-boxed development. No one knew when we'd be done since it wasn't clear yet what 'done' meant.

"I created a few initial milestones, 'm1,' 'm2,' etc., and flipped the question around: 'What could we get done by each milestone?' I cautiously asked the developers for rough estimates in 'Ideal Engineering Days' (IEDs) but avoided traditional Agile terminology as much as possible. IEDs largely worked for those first few milestones, and we figured out how to burn down feature work and see progress towards some goals. The biggest win was moving feature work tracking over from that Gantt chart into where bug work was already being tracked. Over the years, we migrated away from estimating in IEDs but a lot of the rhythm of the release—things like Zero Bug Bounce,[11] Feature Complete, etc.—stuck around. It's been improved immensely as we learned from our mistakes, and progressively got larger and more sophisticated."

DESSERT TIME

Android's tradition of using desserts for release names found its roots in Ryan's project management techniques. "I recall a lot of early debates about what '1.0' meant. Dianne, Swetland, and others felt really passionate about that definition. To move the conversation on, I suggested we use code names and figure out which one would be 1.0 later on. Dianne agreed on the condition they were alphabetical, so Astro Boy[12] and Bender[13] were obviously going

---

[10.] A popular process for software development that lends itself to projects whose requirements are constantly evolving.

[11.] *Zero Bug Bounce (ZBB)* is a goal near the end of the release where the team tries to fix at least all of the current known bugs (the 'bounce' acknowledging that there are always more bugs lurking out there, waiting to be found and filed). In all of my years on Android, I have yet to see the team get anywhere near zero. I redefined the acronym to Ze Bug Bounce. We definitely bounced . . . just not off of zero bugs.

[12.] Astro Boy, an android with human emotions, was a Japanese character first seen in manga form in the 1950s.

[13.] Bender is a robot character from the animated comedy series *Futurama*.

to be our first Android code names! We were set for C3PO to be the third, and that looked like it would end up being 1.0 . . . which turned out to be problematic.[14] Dealing with licensing issues would just slow us down, and we realized that could happen for a lot of future releases also. We needed something else, and I was (still am) pretty obsessed with cupcakes. I loved the idea too that we could celebrate our release with Sprinkles,[15] so the dessert thing kicked off for realz!"

Michael Morrissey remembered Ryan's contributions to getting the releases out there "by just being a constant velvet hammer, who understood enough of the technology side, but was focused on keeping the schedule moving ahead."

PEISUN WU AND PROJECT MANAGEMENT

A peer of Ryan's on Hiroshi's TPM team was Peisun Wu, who joined in September of 2007. Although she had been working at Google as an engineering manager, she joined Android as a TPM because she had done that job before and that's what they needed at the time as they moved toward shipping 1.0.

Peisun's introduction to computer programming matched that of many engineers': video games. When she was in third grade, her parents decided that she played enough games and that they wouldn't buy any more for her. "Heck," she thought. "If I can't buy a game, maybe I could try to figure out how to make my own." She spent much of the next year at the library, reading programming books and playing around with the computer at the library, until she'd saved enough money from household chores to get her own computer at home.

[14.] The reason we use dessert names is that desserts can't be trademarked. Of course, we have used trademarked names for a couple of the releases (K and O), but those involved agreements between companies. I don't think that anyone wanted to get into negotiating trademark agreements for every Android release back in the early days. Besides, there are a lot more dessert names to choose from than robots. Wouldn't it have been unfortunate to have stopped developing more Android releases just because we ran out of names we could use?

[15.] Sprinkles is a cupcake bakery in Palo Alto, near the Google campus. Steve Horowitz remembered, "I wanted to bring cupcakes for the whole team to the meeting. I called around to a bunch of places and nobody could get enough in time, but it turned out that Sprinkles had literally just opened at Stanford Mall that day and I was able to get dozens and dozens for the whole team."

Years later, with a degree in cognitive science, she worked at a couple of startups, dealing with ways to manage unstructured data. The second of these companies, Applied Semantics, was acquired by Google in 2003 for their advertising technology, which eventually became Google's AdSense product.

At Google, Peisun worked on the search appliance,[16] then Google Checkout, and finally joined the Android team in 2007, around the time that the public SDK was first released.

Peisun worked with several different groups on Android in her time there, starting with the media team. She managed relationships with external companies and their technologies, including PacketVideo (which provided the software that powered Android's video capabilities) and Esmertec.

Esmertec provided media applications that Android would ship with the device, including a music app as well as an Instant Messaging (IM) client. There were a lot of details to getting that app to work correctly with the underlying messaging platform on Android, as well as with the late changes in UI design, and Peisun joined the team for trips to Beijing and Zurich to work with the Chengdu, China–based engineering team of Esmertec to get those details right.

On one of her trips to Zurich, she noticed that one of the Esmertec engineers had brought a suitcase entirely filled with hot sauce. Chengdu, in the Sichuan province, is known for its spicy food, and Zurich is . . . not. The suitcase full of spice was seen as an important workaround for the current situation of living in Zurich for those two weeks.

Besides her work on media and messaging, Peisun also helped Dan Borstein with Dalvik launch schedules, helped get some of the early fonts for the device, and helped out with the hardware team in testing devices for FCC approval. This kind of multi-project work wasn't unusual on the team at the time: "Back then it wasn't like, 'This person's on this team—it was just like whatever help needed was required. Whoever was available just jumped in."

---

16. The Google Search Appliance project came up earlier when talking about the system team's Nick Pelly, who worked with Peisun on GSA prior to joining Android.

28

DEALS

Partnerships were critical for Android, and still are. One of the keys to Android's growth was that it wasn't just *Google* shipping Android phones; it was *everyone*.[1]

In the early days, several people were working on different aspects of partnerships and business deals. Andy Rubin had ideas about whom to work with and how to make this strategy succeed. After all, he co-founded and ran a successful mobile device company (Danger). But there was also Android co-founder Nick Sears, recently from T-Mobile, who was instrumental in signing T-Mobile as the Android launch partner for the G1. Hiroshi Lockheimer was crucial in partnership relationships as well, in project-managing the development of Android on partner devices. Rich Miner, another Android co-founder, had come from Orange Telecom, where he had worked with carriers and had run a venture fund that invested in mobile and platform companies (including Danger). In addition to managing the engineering teams working on the Android browser and speech recognition, Rich was part of the business team that helped make the deal for the Motorola Droid, along with Hiroshi and Tom Moss.

TOM MOSS AND THE BUSINESS DEALS

Tom Moss worked on many of the key business deals in early Android, but he didn't come into Google on the business side. "I actually started on Android as a lawyer. I am the worst of everything. We destroy the world."

---

[1] Okay, so maybe not everyone. There's a mobile device company in Cupertino that is not currently an Android partner.

Tom started in May of 2007 in Google's legal department. One of his specialties, prior to Google, had been open source technology. As soon as he started, he was told that he'd be working on an open source project called Android, which was launching an SDK that Fall.

"One of my first deals was Qualcomm, doing the license for the 7200 AMSS chipset code, to create Linux drivers that we could release. It was super complicated at the time because Qualcomm was scared to death of open source."

Tom originally helped out from the legal side but ended up doing deals directly. "I started supporting Andy on deals, and Rich Miner and some of the others as a lawyer. More and more, Andy would just leave me alone: 'Here's the deal we need. Go do the deal.' Andy was busy, so he wouldn't want to sit through all of the negotiations and everything."

He also worked on a strategy of how to connect all the different stakeholders: app developers, handset manufacturers, carriers, and platform software teams. One of the tricks with open source software is motivation; why would any of these partners care about the Android platform except Google? "How do you get everybody incentivized and invested into this ecosystem in a way that would maintain compatibility?"

Of course, app developers would care deeply about compatibility. Being able to run the same application across different implementations of Android would be a far cry better than what developers faced on platforms like Symbian and Java ME, where apps would frequently need to be rewritten to work across different devices. But the dynamics for manufacturers were different, and they were used to a world where they were responsible only for their own devices and implementations.

Fortunately, Google had popular apps that manufacturers wanted on their devices, including Maps, YouTube, and the web browser. So Tom hammered out a system where access to those apps was an incentive for partners to maintain compatibility by shipping Android as-is, rather than shipping a forked version of it.[2]

[2.] Shipping an un-forked version of the platform eventually became an incentive all on its own, after Android became widespread. Manufacturers benefit from apps running the same on their devices as they do everywhere else, without requiring developers to change those apps just for their unique implementation.

MOVING AROUND

Since Tom's job had become more about making deals than legal work, he moved into a group called New Business Development (NBD) that specialized in helping various Google teams on the business side. He continued working solely for Android, but still didn't report into Android directly.

In the meantime, Andy needed a team in Japan to help with development issues there (including internationalization and keyboard support). Tom volunteered to help. The move made sense for him since many of the deals he worked on were in Asia anyway. He transferred to the Google Tokyo office and hired a team of engineers, missing the G1 launch that happened in California just two weeks after he moved.

Meanwhile, Andy wanted to have more direct visibility into Tom's work for Android, so Tom transferred to the Android team. This meant, for silly reasons related to Android being part of a large company, that Tom had to be reclassified as an engineer. "I was, I believe, the first business person at Google to move to the engineering ladder.[3] So I was an engineer on paper. To be clear, I never wrote any code."

LAUNCHING PARTNER DEVICES

Meanwhile, from the Tokyo office, Tom was busy helping partners in that part of the world. "I did Japan. We launched Australia, I think Singapore.

"Google had an interesting role back then. To launch a phone, it's just a carrier buying a phone from an OEM, a handset manufacturer. But we were integral to a lot of these deals in terms of putting our brand or marketing either on the box, or the phone, or just on marketing campaigns. We set up these deals to create the momentum for Android. We would negotiate with the carrier. We would negotiate with the handset manufacturer.

"I'll give an example. I would go negotiate the deals to get the right content on the phone, the right apps or services, negotiate with the carrier, which was Docomo, negotiate with HTC. And then we worked on the marketing campaign with them. Monma-san [an engineer on Tom's team] and I proofread the translations of the user manual in both Japanese and English and made comments and fixed the really silly mistakes they had, like 'The

---

[3.] Maybe this is a secret strategy for passing the Google engineering interview: come in as a lawyer and transfer. You didn't hear it from me.

battery was consumable,' like you could eat the battery. We did everything. We did every part of everything that was necessary to launch a product."

Jeff Hamilton noted that this approach to global partnerships was how Android got to the scale that it has. "There are like two billion[4] devices out there. One company can't build that many devices and support them all. Especially the variety of things: different devices that people want, different price points, configurations, all that kind of stuff. It's a huge variety. By doing the open source thing and having one stack that supported that and having partners set up the factories that build out the things required—for networks in Turkey or whatever, the different requirements—one company can't take all of that on. There are different requirements in different regions. We scaled that by having different companies pick that up and take that on."

[4.] Actually over three billion, as of May 2021.

29

PRODUCT VS. PLATFORM

That's why it's called ANDroid not ORdroid. Because if we are deciding between two alternatives, we always pick both.

—TEAM SAYING (ANONYMOUS)

One of the ongoing debates on the team in those early times (and for years afterward) was: were they building a product or a platform? That is, were they trying to build one or more phones (products), or an operating system that would be usable across many different phones, from various manufacturers, now and in the future (a platform)?

It is clear now, especially given the breadth of the Android ecosystem, that Android is a platform. Yes, it runs on Google's phones, including generations of Nexus phones and the more recent Pixel phones. It also runs on many more phones across the world, most of which have never been seen by anyone on the Android team, but all of which run Google apps and the Google Play Store as part of the Android ecosystem. But at the time, it wasn't clear what the priorities should be. Since 1.0 was clearly targeting the G1 phone, the distinction between the two was muddied. Further complicating the debate was the fact that building a specific product is always going to be easier (and faster) than building a more flexible platform for the long term. So if Android's main priority was just getting something to market, focusing on a product was the right call.

Meanwhile, the iPhone took a very product-focused approach. As Bob Borchers (then Senior Director of Product Marketing for iPhone) said, "At that point, we weren't really thinking of iOS as a platform." In fact, the App Store wasn't even part of the plan for that first device; the iPhone was just an Apple device with Apple apps. This approach enabled Apple to focus on getting the details for that specific product exactly right.

Apple has had many follow-on phones since then, and now has the App Store and a large developer ecosystem. But they always know exactly what products they are building for and can tune the OS and the platform they ship appropriately. Google has also shipped many phones . . . but that number is insignificant compared to the quantity and variety of devices shipped by other manufacturers. So it is far more important for Android to be portable to all of those devices than it is for it to be perfect for Google devices but difficult for OEMs to deal with.

The product-versus-platform debates on the team were represented by the different companies that people came from: Danger, Be/PalmSource, and WebTV/Microsoft. The people from Danger preferred simpler solutions, which gave them more of a product focus. The people from Be/PalmSource and WebTV/Microsoft had more of a platform mindset and preferred that approach for Android as well.

Romain Guy said, "The folks that came from Palm worked on Palm OS 6, with compatibility for Palm OS 5. They saw firsthand what would happen to an OS that was not built for the future, that didn't have any concept of resolution, GPU, stuff like that."

Brian Swetland saw both sides, having worked at both Be and Danger. "You need both. It was a lesson I took away from Be. Be would get in a rut on that at times—so focused on being the platform. If you don't do real apps and you just build a pure platform, then you're not closing the loop. You don't build what people need."

Brian said that the debate on the Android team continues. "I don't think it ever became clear, to this day. This used to drive Andy batshit. We would have the all-hands meeting, and I or Dave Bort would ask what we were building. We were definitely building a platform and there were products in that platform. But were we building The Google Phone, a vertical thing, our product? Or were we building something we were expecting the OEMs to build phones on under their brand? Or something in between? Over the years, we did a bit of everything.

"The Nexus devices, and now the Pixel devices, feel much more vertical. But there's this whole wide ecosystem where people do all kinds of crazy things. Then you have Amazon and Fire where they're taking the platform as a starting point to build their own platform that's derived from it but not the same."

Mike Cleron said that Dianne "had the clearest vision of 'This is not just launch G1, live to fight another day.' She was laying foundations for things that were over the horizon, certainly for me, probably for most people. Dianne in 2006–2007 saw things that we wouldn't need until 2013, and somehow engineered those into some of the foundational concepts of Android."

The debate was also happening in the Google boardroom. Executive reviews at the time showed Google's top execs fell at different ends of the spectrum: some prioritized Android building a phone, some favored the platform approach, and some fell somewhere in the middle.

Dianne summed up the debates: "Platform or Product: That was always the Danger versus Palm OS people. Andy's answer was, of course, 'Both.' Which was the right answer."

PART III

THE ANDROID TEAM

From the moment that the Android team arrived at Google, they had their
own way of doing things. Team leadership took pains to keep it like that.

30

ANDROID != GOOGLE[1]

Nobody in those early years ever doubted that anybody else was not in
for the cause. We were all on the same train.

—BRIAN JONES

From the beginning, Android had a culture that was very distinct from
the rest of Google. Even though the tiny Android startup was absorbed
into the much larger company, Andy went out of his way to keep the team
separate.

Jason Parks said, "Andy and the leadership team realized for this to succeed we needed to be separate from the larger Google culture and come up
with our own culture to make this happen. I don't know how he sold it to
Eric, Larry, and Sergey, but he got it done. We were isolated and operated like
a small startup, with funding from Google."

Mike Cleron said that Andy keeping the team intentionally apart from
the rest of the company "gave the team breathing room without having to
constantly report in to big-G Google to do things."

Not everyone on the team agreed with this approach. Mike Fleming said,
"Android was walled off from Google. That was really a top-down decision. I
remember feeling that that wasn't a good idea and feeling opposed to that
idea. I really wanted us to connect and build bridges and participate in
Google culture. That really didn't happen."

The siloing of Android manifested itself in many ways, including keeping the project secret within the company and not participating in larger
discussions and company meetings, which the team felt would have bogged
things down.

---

[1] For the non-programmers in the crowd, "!=" is how you write "is not equal to" in code. Programmers end up injecting a lot of software jargon in our regular speech, maybe because we
assume that everyone we talk to speaks the same language. It's a self-fulfilling prophecy as
people who don't understand just stop listening.

All of these dynamics helped keep the team focused on the single goal of shipping every release. But much like the physical separation of Australia from the rest of the world's continents resulted in bizarre subspecies, Android developed a culture that was different, and a bit more reckless, than that of its larger, steadier, corporate parent.

Brian Jones commented on the Android culture and the singularity of mission that it endowed on the team. "We were a little startup within Google. We were shielded from the rest of the big company. We were this little enclave, and we had a lot of autonomy. Once you were in, everybody knew that you were on board towards that mission.

"We can have colorful, passionate arguments about what an implementation detail is, or what technical approach is needed to get there. But nobody in those early years ever doubted that anybody else was not in for the cause. We were all on the same train."

WEB VS. MOBILE

One of the things that kept Android separate from the rest of Google was that it was a fundamentally different product from what everyone else at Google worked on. Google, at the time, developed primarily web applications. This resulted in two important implications with respect to Android: unhappiness within Google that Android was not web-based, and incomprehension of the timeframe realities of mobile software.

First, there was a core distrust of what Android was doing because Google was fundamentally about web technologies. So much was possible using the web at that time; why wasn't Android based around web technologies instead? The fact that other mobile platforms at the time (including Palm's WebOS and even the iPhone, where Apple's original plan for external developers was web apps) were using web technologies bolstered this argument. Yet Android stubbornly refused to go in that direction.[2] It offered the ability to integrate web content in native applications (through

---

[2] While the web held a lot of promise at that time, it lacked some of the capabilities, performance, and ability to run under very tight constraints that were considered critical in mobile at that time. Note that although Apple attempted to go in this direction, they also ended up with native applications for their App Store. Palm tried really hard with WebOS, but that didn't succeed either. The promise of web technology as a general solution for mobile devices has yet to be realized many years later.

WebView, as well as offering a complete browser app), but applications were expected to be built with native (not web) technology, including a different language, different APIs, and overall different approach than web apps.

Second, Android was trying to ship a fundamentally different kind of product from the web app products that Google was used to writing. If you want to ship a new version of Search, you could do it this afternoon. And if there's a bug in that version, you could fix it and update the app later tonight. Web products tend to have regular releases every few weeks, and teams launch and iterate constantly. But Android had very different constraints that made that approach and that mindset unworkable.

Brian Jones explained: "In Android, there's a hardware component, there's a manufacturing component, there's a carrier component, there are partnerships. You can launch and iterate a search algorithm. You can't launch and iterate a piece of hardware. You have to set a date and work backwards."

Brian Swetland agreed: "The reality is, when you're trying to ship consumer electronics, and somebody's committing a factory line, or they're lining up a big marketing campaign to hit their sales targets, you can't miss or you really mess up things for your partners. You get a little crazy when you're trying to hit those deadlines, because the consequences if you miss the window . . . you might not be able to ship that product three months later. You might *never* be able to ship that product, because now you have to build a whole different product."

Swetland compared this approach to that of Google teams outside of Android: "It's all web stuff: you ship it, and if it doesn't work, you roll it back. It's not quite as easy when you're burning images at the factory."[3]

Chiu-Ki Chan, who had transferred onto the Android team from elsewhere in Google, talked about this hardware-driven dynamic: "Android was the first team that taught me that Christmas ends in October. If you want your device to hit the market for Christmas, everything has to be done by October. It was such crazy deadlines because boards[4] had to be finalized. It

---

[3.] By "burning images" Brian was referring to installing software on devices. San Mehat had a different take on burning things in Chapter 7 ("The Systems Team").

[4.] Selling phones for the holiday season meant that all of the hardware, including circuit boards, had to be finalized much earlier.

was the first time that I had real deadlines that could not be missed. Christmas doesn't wait for anyone and boards can only be printed so fast, so you cannot miss the October deadline."

This date-driven mentality ended up creating the hard-working, deadline-driven culture that defined Android in those early days.

31

THE WILD WEST

Android felt very much like the Wild West.

—EVAN MILLAR

Android also developed its own engineering culture, from a combination of its isolation from the rest of Google plus the fundamentally different products it was working on compared to the rest of the company. Evan Millar observed: "Android felt very much like the Wild West back then. There weren't very many rules. There weren't very many tools. There weren't really a lot of best practices or style guides or anything telling you the right way to do things. But the cool thing about it was that it meant you could kind of do whatever you wanted to do and try whatever you wanted to try. It was a very open-to-innovation, open-to-trying-things sort of culture that I really loved. I was really happy in Android for a long time.

"In retrospect, I can see the pros and cons of that approach. Obviously, there were a lot of people who had done this sort of thing before and knew what they were doing. Really smart people, really experienced people on Android. A lot of these people had been at Be and shipped an OS there. Some of them were at Apple and worked on similar things there. So it's not that we didn't have deep expertise and experience, because we did. But it just felt like the Wild West. It felt like nobody really knew what they were doing, and we were just feeling our way through it. We didn't know if it was going to totally flop, or if it was going to work. And when it worked, I think people were as surprised as they were excited."

There were also subtler differences between the Android and Google cultures. Google has long had a notion of "20 percent time," which allows employees to spend up to 20 percent of their time working on some project that could benefit Google.[1] It's a grand tradition that has resulted in some

---

[1] Taking Fridays off doesn't qualify for 20 percent time status.

fantastic products, including Gmail. Android engineers tended to be too busy doing their main work to ponder what else to take on, so 20 percent time wasn't as common on the Android team.

ANDROID VS. GOOGLE

> Adam Bliss, who worked on the first version of Maps, once remarked that he enjoyed working for Android, but sometimes he missed working for Google.
>
> **—ANDY MCFADDEN**

Many people at Google didn't actually know about Android at all for the first couple of years after Android was acquired, because the project was very secretive. But when people did know about it, it wasn't seen as a successful project in those early days.

Dan Egnor joined Android's services team from Google's search team in August of 2007, two months before the SDK launch. "When I decided to join Android, some people were like, 'Why would you do that? The iPhone is obviously dominating. It's such an amazing product, why would you go up against that?' In some cases they'd seen the early prototypes, and were like, 'Y'all are like months behind, why bother? Apple just obviously wins.'"

San Mehat also came to Android from another group in Google. "When we bought Android, most people were like, 'What the fuck are we doing?'"

Dave Burke was leading the Mobile team in London at the time, working on Google apps for non-Android platforms. He remembered the internal feeling toward Android: "It was just a random project on the side. There was no way it was going to succeed. People wouldn't be that negative, but they were like, 'That's crazy. How are you possibly going to influence the telecom industry?'"

Meanwhile, the Android team was so busy trying to get to 1.0 that they didn't have a lot of time to spend on collaborating with other teams at Google. Tom Moss remembered, "We burned a lot of bridges. But we kind of had to. We really did have to say, 'No, we have a mission and we have to stick to that mission. When we succeed, everything will be easier.'"

Bob Lee was one of the people to transfer from elsewhere in Google onto the Android team, "which was like a company in a company. Some people were kind of resentful of being acquired and wanted to keep the scrappiness.

In the beginning, we didn't have code reviews, it was a different interview process, people didn't write tests.... It was a bit of a culture shock for me."

Peisun Wu, who also came from another team in Google, agreed. It reminded her of companies she'd worked in prior to Google. "The typical roles of product manager: design docs, code reviews, etc., all went out the window when I got to Android. It wasn't as jarring for me because I had come from two startups, so it was kind of normal. It felt like I had moved to another startup again. It did not feel like Google at all. For other people who came from Google, it was kind of a rude awakening."

Ficus Kirkpatrick said, "From the other side, they looked on us as clowns. We didn't do modern testing software practice—we didn't do any testing at all . . . which was essentially true. It just became entrenched and religious."

Cédric Beust, who transferred to Android from Google's mobile team, said: "I had the distinct feeling that I was no longer part of Google when I was on Android. I entered a black hole."

Evan Millar moved from Android to a different team within Google in 2012. He remembered, "In a lot of ways, it was like joining another company."

32

FUN WITH HARDWARE

With everyone spending so much of their life at the office at that time, there were occasional attempts to modify and personalize the work environment.

NO GUNS

Romain Guy talked about his attempts to discourage interruptions, using firepower.

"We were working hard, and a lot of people were asking a lot of stuff from us [the framework team] all the time. At some point, I don't know why, I ordered a Nerf machine gun, because apparently that's what people do in open spaces in US companies.

"I had it hanging from the ceiling in my office, so when you opened the door, it was pointing at the door. There was a piece of paper on it that said 'No.'

"One day I worked from home. I came back the next day and found my Nerf gun mounted on a tripod, motorized and overclocked.

"Andy saw the gun, and while I wasn't there, he mounted it on the tripod and added the motor. And there was a trackball on my desk that could rotate the gun on the tripod and fire the gun faster than you could normally, because he had a more powerful motor."

ANY PORT IN A STORM

One day, Dan Morrill noticed a suspicious USB port in an outlet plate in the middle of a wall, with no indication of its purpose other than its cryptic label.

A mysterious USB port in the middle of a wall in building 44 (picture courtesy Joe Onorato)

Dan filed a work request to have the networking infrastructure team look into it, with the subject, "Why is there a USB port in the wall of B44-2?"

Google takes security, both physical and technological, very seriously. A bare, cryptically labeled USB port caused concern. Tickets were filed, security personnel were alerted, and an operation was started to remove it.

An electrical team took over the room on the other side of that outlet and a guard was posted outside. The electricians cut out the drywall behind the plate, which showed what was really going on.

Behind the wall plate was ... nothing. It was just a USB port embedded in the wall. It was a prank. Or, rather, it was engineers (specifically, Brian Jones, Joe Onorato, and Bruce Gay) with more hardware than plans. They carefully cut a hole in the drywall, and with a mixture of hot glue and inspiration, they inserted a USB port borrowed from an old workstation. Bruce added a label to make it look more official. They had no plans for anything more elaborate; they just thought it was funny sitting there, doing nothing. Google Security didn't share that feeling.

The electrician replaced the existing wall plate with a blank one, which provided the same functionality, but with less room for hijinks.

SWITCH STATEMENT

The temptation of the blank wall plate left behind from the USB port fix was too great; it cried out for something more. The team didn't want to freak out Google Security again. But they had to do something.

There's always tons of random hardware lying around in the Android department, especially around Brian Jones's desk. So Joe and Brian scrounged around for the parts that resulted in a switch to control the internet.

Flipping the switch[1] caused the light to turn green and the switch to buzz (the team found some haptic hardware to make the plate vibrate when it was switched off).

A green light indicated that the internet was on. Flipping the switch caused the light to turn red and the switch to buzz. (Photo courtesy Jeremy Milo.)

Security was fine with this one; they let it stay the rest of the time that Android occupied that building.

The internet still works, so presumably nobody has switched it off yet.

---

[1] When I first saw this switch in the hallway, I had two immediate thoughts: 1) That's hilarious! 2) I'd better not touch it. Because you never know.

33

FUN WITH ROBOTS

A ndy Rubin always had a thing for robots and machines of any sort. He continued that interest in all of his projects, including leaving Android in 2013 to work on robots in a different department at Google.

This penchant for robotics and gadgets of all types played itself out in early Android in different ways.

One robotics project Andy worked on was a barista; he built a robot to create latté art. It's not clear if he got it completely working, but there was an area in one of the upstairs micro-kitchens in building 45 that housed an odd-looking machine. The area was roped off for protection (of potential customers[1]).

Would you prefer nonfat or whole milk? Andy's barista robot makes a latté. (Picture courtesy Daniel Switkin.)

---

[1] Fadden: "That thing was a serious industrial model. I don't think I could have hurt that thing with a sledgehammer, but I'm pretty sure the reverse is not true."

Robots also decorated the hallways of the Android building. As Android grew and spread to other buildings, they scattered across the Google campus.

Robbie the Robot, from the film Forbidden Planet. *Robbie currently lives on the second floor of building 43, which the Android team occupied for several years.*

The robot from Lost in Space, *which currently resides behind the lobby of Google building 43*

The imposing Cylon warrior (from Battlestar Galactica*) stood guard in the framework team area in building 44. Over time he accumulated accessories such as a Canadian flag cape, a hockey stick, and a Noogler hat. (Picture courtesy Anand Agarawala.)*

34

WORK HARDER, NOT SMARTER

Putting in a shitload of hours was very valuable, culturally, in Android.

—FICUS KIRKPATRICK

The main thing that the Android team was known for, within Android but also across Google, was for working really, really hard. Ficus Kirkpatrick called it "The currency of Android."

"I don't think I'm that smart of an engineer, but I work my ass off. I'd make up for my lack of education by just working hard and putting in an unhealthy amount of hours. There were times in the first four to five years where it was essentially all I did when I was awake. And I didn't get as much sleep as I should. I know I wasn't alone on that.

"There was this month that I worked every day. The latest I got to work in the morning was 9:30 and the earliest I left was at 1:30 am. I remember getting home at 2:30 am and I just wanted to do something that was not work, to reclaim my life. I sat in bed playing this game, *Game Dev Story*. I could hardly keep awake, but I was, out of spite, like, 'I'm going to have fun playing this game!' And I realized that what I was actually doing for the last 20 minutes was simulating overseeing a software project.[1]

"For the most part, overwork was self-inflicted. We really wanted to do as much as we possibly could. I always compared it to some endurance athletic event; miserable in the moment, and you're glad when it's over, but you bond with the people. It's some low-level mental illness you keep signing up for again and again."

---

[1] Running a software project is the premise of that game. Those developers know their target audience.

Rebecca Zavin agreed: "There was that really fulfilling reward cycle of working intensely together with your comrades on something and delivering. That 'We're gonna stay late and get it done and we're all in this together!' focus. That is the startup thing."

Peisun Wu noted that the intensity was self-driven. Nobody was making them stay late or punishing them for going home at a normal time. "We all stuck around because we wanted to see something actually work."

Jason Parks: "We worked a lot of fucking hours. There would be weeks when the only time my wife saw me was when she came and had dinner with me. I would come home late, sleep for a couple of hours, and go back into the office. The only time she saw me was coming in for dinner."

Fadden remembered Brian Swetland's efforts and focus: "One day, Andy Rubin pops in and says, 'Hey Swetland, how's it going?' Without looking up, Swetland grumbles something to the effect that things would be going much better if he wasn't getting interrupted all the time and continues typing. Andy just stands there. Eventually Swetland looks up and realizes Larry Page is standing there too."

There were obviously negative impacts on the team from all of the long hours people were putting in. For example, Tracey Cole witnessed it affecting her ability to hire: "When I was first trying to build my admin team, nobody [from other teams at Google] would come here because they all heard that we worked too hard."

Tom Moss talked about the effect on the team's morale: "At the end of my tenure there, we had the lowest morale scores. But the magic is launching. Launching fixes all else. How many times were Swetland and other people like, 'I'm fucking going to quit!' Then we'd launch and we'd have a party and we'd all feel good, and we'd all sign up for it again.

"It was great. I loved it. We all loved it. We felt like we were the special forces of the Marines, working on this amazing project. It's us against the world and we get there by the grit of our teeth and camaraderie. Yeah, we were all depressed and overworking and not sleeping. But turnover was actually incredibly low, for as much as we complained and as much as we said, 'bad morale.'"

In 2010, Tom left Google to found a startup. He talked to Andy when he left.

"My daughter was born right around the G1 launch time. She was four months by the time we launched the G1. As I was leaving, [Andy] was like, 'How are you going to do this startup thing with a small child at home?'

"I'm like, 'Unless they invent a 25th hour in the day, I cannot work any harder than I've been working for you for these past four years.'

"It was one of those moments where you're like, 'Do you even realize?'"

San Mehat reflected on how hard the team worked: "I loved that team. They were really, really great. I don't think I could do it again. I think it would kill me."

Finally, 1.0 was done. An eerie silence descended.

Romain Guy remembered the period leading up to the actual 1.0 release. There were three weeks after they stopped working on the release before the device was available for people to purchase. "We had nothing to do. We didn't know if we were still in business. I remember being at home at 5 pm, which had never happened. I didn't know what to do. What do people do when they're home?"

Then 1.0 shipped, the device was in stores, and the machine started up again. The team got back to working hard and cranking more releases out. For one thing, there was constant pressure of delivering each release in time for partner hardware launches. Also, there was a team-wide desire to make Android successful. Although you could squint and see shades of things to come, that first product was not game-changing. It was a decent smartphone, but not enough to really capture the world's attention. So the team kept running, because they had a long way to go to make Android realize its potential.

35

BACON SUNDAYS

omens of autumn
float on a newly crisp breeze
perfumed with bacon

—MIKE CLERON

In late 2009, a year after 1.0 shipped, Android institutionalized extra working hours by starting the tradition of *Bacon Sundays*. Previously, people would simply be at work all the time. But eventually, people started spending weekend time *not* working. But Android still had the same do-or-die dynamic as it did before (albeit with more people to handle the load). Release deadlines were critical; they *had* to hit those dates. So toward the end of a release, management encouraged people to come to the office on Sunday morning with the promise of a big breakfast buffet spread (along with plenty of work). Participation wasn't required, and not everybody came in on those Sundays. But there was an understanding that there was a lot of work to do, and a team effort would help.

Hiroshi Lockheimer came up with the idea. "We were behind schedule for the Droid—we were probably behind our fourth schedule—and that was a Big Deal. There was a big launch, with a lot of marketing behind it, so we were like 'Shit, what do we do? Gotta come in on weekends and make it happen.'

"I wanted to make it fun. I love bacon. In retrospect, not everyone likes bacon, so bacon probably was not the best choice. I don't eat it that much anymore. Turns out it's not good for your health.

"We had launches coming up. We had devices that needed to ship. These OEMs needed our software by a certain date or else they were going to miss the holiday season. All Hell was going to break loose, and Andy was going to get upset.

"It was clear we needed more time. The only way I could think of to get more time was to work on weekends. So Sundays—not every Sunday—but in the summer it became kind of a . . . in retrospect, kind of a sad tradition."

By 10:00 in the morning (it's difficult to get most engineers in the office earlier than that, breakfast or no), there would be a full, catered spread with brunch goodies, including a large tray of bacon. People wandered into the cafeteria, ate their fill and caught up with co-workers, then headed to their desks to continue working on the product.

Mike Cleron, who managed the framework team at the time (and for many years afterward), was known for haiku that he would send out to the engineering team. He wrote some in celebration of Bacon Sundays:

> sunday brings strange scene
> androids battling killer bugs
> life, or bad sci-fi?

> lost in sleepless fog
> spirits willing though brains dim
> bacon, give us strength

Bacon Sundays went away by the time the team shipped KitKat, in the Fall of 2013. The team had grown, so there were simply more people available to help hit the deadlines. Also, the releases were not as frequent as they were in the early days, so there wasn't as much constant schedule panic. Finally, management recognized that enough was enough, and people wanted their weekend lives back.

So Bacon Sundays stopped. The team doesn't miss them.[1]

---

[1] Though I do miss the bacon.

36

POSTCARDS FROM BARCELONA

The GSM Mobile World Congress (MWC) is the premier business event in the mobile industry. Companies and individuals gather to hear about new developments in the field, to meet with partners, to pitch their ideas, and to see what the competition is up to.

This event was particularly interesting in the early days of Android, as the field was changing rapidly with the constant evolution in smartphone capabilities. The Android leadership team made the trek each year to show what Android was working on, and to see what was happening in the ecosystem and with various potential partner companies.

Every year, Andy went to MWC in Barcelona and would see capabilities that Android needed to incorporate to stay current, or to take the lead. He sent reports back to Mountain View, asking for these new features to be developed, which, inevitably, came at the very end of a release, causing the team to jump rapidly into feature development at a time when the product really needed to focus on quality and stability prior to launching.

These annual episodes were known as *Postcards from Barcelona*, where Andy would casually send in feature requests that were entirely too late to make a release . . . but which the team rushed to implement anyway, because it was Andy.

Hiroshi remembered these late feature requests. "It would be me sending these emails saying, 'I just had a meeting with Andy and he really wants these things fixed before we ship.' It always coincided with MWC. There are two reasons for that. One, that's when our maintenance release[1] schedule usually was, so we would do our release in the Fall, and we'd have our big follow-up maintenance release at that time. So it was towards the end of the release cycle, when we're trying to get launch approvals. Back then, Andy was the big approver. The other reason was because I was with him in Barcelona, I could show him: 'Andy, we gotta launch this thing. Take a look, are you ready?' And then always, almost on principle, he would point out at least one or two things, just because that was his style."

Andy's late requests were also a consequence of the release schedule and the inherent latency of software development cycles. "There's a lag from where we're done with the software to when it actually shows up in some consumer's hands. He didn't like that lag, so he didn't want to wait. When we said 'next release' he knew that meant like six months, nine months, a year from now, and he was like, 'I don't want to wait that long. Do it now before you launch.'

"So then I would like, tuck my tail, email the team saying, 'Sorry, but....'"

---

[1] Maintenance releases were minor versions, with smaller features, or bugfixes for problems that the team didn't have time to fix before the major release or for issues that had arisen as that major release gained adoption and real-world usage.

PART IV

LAUNCHES

From the moment the iPhone was announced through the first year after Android 1.0, everything was about the launches. Whether it was releasing the software in various SDK versions, iterating on the released platform from 1.0 forward, or launching a widening variety of devices, the team worked hard to hit deadline after deadline to get the platform out to an increasingly large audience.

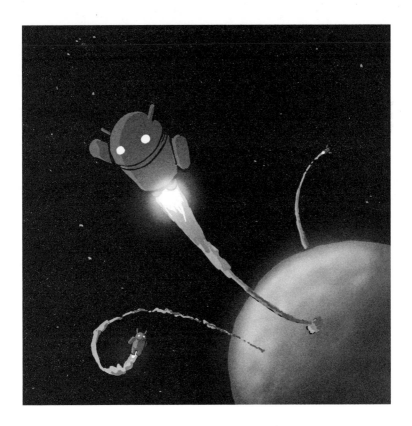

37

COMPETITION

Today, Apple is going to reinvent the phone.

—STEVE JOBS (IPHONE ANNOUNCEMENT, JANUARY 9, 2007)

The iPhone was announced in January of 2007 and released in June, six months later. The device relied on a touchscreen[1] for user interaction, and affected both consumers and the industry overall, changing what the world considered to be a smartphone and what Android needed to do to compete in the evolving smartphone marketplace.

There was a quote from an engineer on the Android team at that time that has appeared in various places since: "As a consumer I was blown away. I wanted one immediately. But as a Google engineer, I thought 'We're going to have to start over.'"[2]

This quote implies that the iPhone caused Android to change everything and reboot its development plans.

But it's not quite correct.

It's true that Android's plans changed, but the team didn't have to start over. Rather, they needed to re-prioritize and change product schedules.

When the iPhone was announced, the Android team was very much heads-down in development. The device they were working on was called Sooner, so named because they wanted it to come out sooner than the real target device for Android, the Dream (which was based on the HTC Dream

---

[1] It's worth noting that the iPhone was not the first capacitive touchscreen; that distinction goes to the LG Prada, which was both announced and released slightly before the iPhone.

[2] The quote is by Chris DeSalvo, an engineer on the Android team at that time, from the book by Fred Vogelstein (*Dogfight: How Apple and Google Went to War and Started a Revolution*, Sarah Crichton Books, 2013). The quote was excerpted and published in *The Atlantic* and elsewhere.

hardware). Sooner had no touchscreen. Instead, it relied on a hardware keyboard for UI navigation, which was a common user experience on phones . . . before touchscreens became must-have features.

The Dream device did have a touchscreen, and the Android platform was being designed to incorporate that capability. But Dream was slated to launch later while the team focused on shipping 1.0 with the Sooner device, well, sooner. Suddenly, touchscreen capability had to be prioritized and shifted from a future device to the first device. And that first device had to change accordingly.

The Sooner was dropped, and development pivoted to the Dream device (which was eventually launched in the US as the T-Mobile G1). Brian Swetland remarked on the team's pivot: "When the iPhone happened, the decision was: We're going to skip shipping Sooner and we're gonna ship Dream as soon as it's ready. Because it didn't make sense to ship a BlackBerry wedge after Steve[3] shipped the iPhone."

Dianne Hackborn liked the change in plans and saw it as an opportunity to finish the platform. "If it would have shipped, there wouldn't have been multiprocess. I was so stressed about that. I was glad that we dropped Sooner. The software schedule just didn't line up with the hardware schedule."

Meanwhile, the team also built out the platform capabilities to support touchscreen functionality in 1.0. Jason Parks said, "As soon as we flipped, Marco [Nelissen] got touch panels and hacked it up[4] and we had touch."[5]

Swetland talked about the rumors that Android completely restarted development because of touch. "I feel like we should be honored that they believe we could completely reset and rebuild the entire world in three months, and not that we spent years ahead of time building up adaptive UI and the tooling that let us rejigger the world and had all this work done ahead of time."

---

[3] As in Steve Jobs, CEO of Apple at the time.

[4] Pivots like this showed the advantage of the platform (versus "product") focus of the team's efforts. Cédric Beust said, "The reason why we were able to pivot so fast is that the code base already had a lot of flexibility built in for future and hypothetical hardware."

[5] Dream devices didn't come in for some time, especially in quantities that the entire team could use them. So they used hardware that would allow them to develop and test touch capabilities for the platform independent of the specific device that would launch with touchscreen support.

But there were some misgivings on the team about the change. Mike Fleming said, "I was upset that we hadn't shipped. I thought that we could've gotten out before the iPhone had we shipped the Sooner product."

In any case, the team was definitely talking about the iPhone after the initial announcement. A lot. *The Brady Bunch* is a classic American sitcom from the early 1970s. In one episode, Jan is tired of her older sister, Marsha, getting all of the attention. At one point, Jan exclaims, "Marsha, Marsha, Marsha!" Soon after the iPhone announcement, while the Android building was buzzing with discussions about the new device, Andy sent an email to the team that read, "iPhone, iPhone, iPhone!"

ANDROID GETS SOME ATTENTION

The iPhone drove a lot of people into our arms.

—CHRIS DIBONA

The phone rings off the hook after Steve's iPhone demo. Because Apple's not going to license you any of that shit—now what do you do?

—BRIAN SWETLAND

The iPhone announcement affected all of the mobile manufacturers, rippling through the entire mobile industry, causing fear and, ultimately and rather ironically, creating a major reason that Android was able to establish itself in the market.

When the iPhone was announced, users saw a new expression of the smartphone, with more capabilities and a touchscreen-driven user interface. But carriers and manufacturers saw a potential monopoly being formed, one that would exclude them.

The iPhone was going to have a single manufacturer: Apple. All of the device manufacturers not named "Apple" would be cut out of that market. Also, the iPhone would initially work with only a single carrier in each market (such as AT&T in the US), ensuring that no other carriers would benefit from iPhone users (and their precious data usage) on their network until that exclusive contract expired. Other manufacturers in the ecosystem, such as chip vendors, were also afraid of being excluded; if Apple didn't happen to choose their chips for iPhone hardware, then they too would be left out.

Suddenly, companies that had previously feared or disregarded Google were not only returning Google's calls; they were approaching Google all on their own. They needed a comparable smartphone product, and Android offered a way to have one much sooner than they could have had otherwise.

The iPhone launch "scared the industry," said Iliyan Malchev. "Nobody had anything remotely as good at the time. Frankly, neither did we; it took us time to converge. But there was no other game in town."

So the Android team continued developing the OS, and working with this growing group of partners, and eventually provided a platform that they could all use to build their own products for the evolving smartphone market.

38

MEANWHILE, IN CUPERTINO . . .

Bob Borchers was the Senior Director of iPhone Product Marketing[1] at Apple during the iPhone's development and when it launched.

Bob was in the original iPhone tutorial video on the Apple website when the iPhone was launched. What was remarkable about that video was not so much that it was an iPhone tutorial, or that it featured Bob, but that it was not starring Steve Jobs. Apple is famous in the industry for hiding most of the personalities in the company behind very closed doors. Only select

---

[1] One of the people I interviewed for this book said it would be really cool to know what Apple was thinking back then. It seemed like a pipe dream. I thought it unlikely that, if I showed up at the Apple campus, they'd usher me in and have a chat about what the corporate thinking was on whatever was happening on the Cupertino campus 12 years ago.

And then I realized: I happened to know someone that might help. I met Bob Borchers at a school event my kids were in, recognizing him as the guy in the original iPhone tutorial on the Apple website. I recognized him again, years later, when he was on my bus home from work one evening; Bob had recently joined Google.

Silicon Valley is a really small place. It's a ridiculously expensive and crowded place, but it's really small in terms of the people and companies that overlap in different and interesting ways.

people are anointed to be the face that represents the company. At that time, it was (of course) mostly Steve Jobs.

A friend who worked there explained it to me. Apple is a consumer brand. It is not, unlike companies like Google or Microsoft, about the technology, and therefore the engineers and engineering itself, but rather about consumer products that happen to be built with technology. Presenting a very slick, polished, and consistent face to the world is part of that consumer-branding approach.

Bob explained how he came to be in that video. "When Steve introduced NeXT, he did a video where he sat down for an hour and a half and introduced everybody to NextStep, the OS as well as the hardware, showed them all the great things, and helped people build their first program on NextStep. When we were thinking about how to introduce the iPhone to the world, we took that template and said, 'Let's do it again here.' Initially our job was to write a rough script, and for me to be the test presenter. As it turns out, that test run turned into months of wearing a black shirt on camera." When the team was ready to record the final version, Steve was too busy, so Bob got that job.

At the time, stories had been circulating at Apple about what was happening at Google. "There were rumors that Google was going to do something around a mobile operating system. It wasn't just, 'There was going to be this amazing piece of hardware,' it was, 'They're going to build a platform that others can use.'"

Bob was able to nail down the timeframe for some of those rumors because he had a meeting with Google at that time. "October of 2006. I remember, because the first meeting I had [at Google] with the team that we were negotiating with, the lead product manager showed up in a nun's costume. The first Apple, iPhone, Google, Maps coming-together moment was Halloween of 2006. I sat in a meeting room for 2 hours with a nun. A male nun at that."

But why was Apple concerned specifically with Google, especially since Google had zero track record with mobile devices? There were already plenty of other players in the mobile space, including RIM and Nokia and Microsoft. "Microsoft was already in the market with Windows Mobile. Our analysis was, Microsoft didn't know hardware, so that was a horrible experience. All of the other players didn't know software. We felt like software was going to be the thing that ate the mobile world.

"The big threat from Google was that Google knew software and services. In fact, probably knew them better than Apple did. So I think the fundamental concern was, here's Google, a company that's built software and services at scale before, and that could and would legitimately be a significant threat to a new platform like iOS.

"The other point was that Google was the only other company that had no existing business to put at risk when working with carriers."

Apple was very interested to see what the result was when the first Android device, the G1, launched. "I remember going, on the first day that they were available, to the store in San Francisco to buy one and bring it back to Cupertino to play with. The software experience was. . . . We saw potential." The actual G1 product didn't cause much fear in Cupertino.[2]

Apple wasn't as concerned about Android, or at least about the G1, after they saw the device, because they really saw themselves as competing on the product level, not the platform level: "We weren't really thinking of iOS as a platform. When we officially launched the first SDK and the App Store, which was like two or three years into it—that's when we started to think of it as a platform."

Meanwhile, Android beat Apple to the application marketplace, and Android 1.0 shipped with the Android Market app that allowed developers to distribute their own applications. The iPhone had originally shipped without any App Store at all, and no intention to provide one.

After the iPhone was available, there was mounting interest in having more apps. "There was so much developer desire and so many requests. The first step was to go build web apps. That was perfect, because nobody was actually installing any software on the phone, but you can have an app-like experience. Our hope was that web apps were going to be the thing."

But eventually, Apple was pressured by both consumers and developers to provide a way for developers to provide high-quality native apps for the iPhone. "We were utterly focused on the consumer experience, and consumers were telling us that they wanted higher quality applications, as developers were telling us they wanted to build higher quality applications." The App Store was launched, with a more curated model than Android, in keeping with Apple's approach to controlling the overall experience more tightly.

---

2. Apple headquarters are located in Cupertino, CA, in the heart of Silicon Valley.

Bob also commented on the effect that the iPhone had on carriers. The iPhone launched with an exclusive deal with AT&T in the US, and similar exclusive carrier deals in other countries. This forced other carriers like T-Mobile and Verizon to seek other options. "We early on established that we were going to launch exclusively with one carrier in each market. That meant that there would be two or three other carriers in every market who needed to fill up that vacuum some way, somehow. So there was a vacuum created for Android to fill."

Bob left Apple[3] in 2009, two years after the iPhone was released.[4]

---

[3] At the time, back in 2009, I asked Bob what it was like to not be at Apple anymore. He said, "Well . . . Steve no longer yells at me."

[4] At the time of my interview with Bob, he was the Vice President of Marketing for Platforms & Ecosystems at Google (including Android and Chrome). By the time I finished the book, he was back at Apple, as a VP of Product Marketing. In Silicon Valley, it's not just the devices that are mobile; the people are, too.

39

THE SDK LAUNCH

Brian Swetland and Iliyan Malchev record a clip for an intro video that posted[1] on November 5, 2007. (Picture courtesy Peisun Wu.)

By providing developers a new level of openness that enables them to work more collaboratively, Android will accelerate the pace at which new and compelling mobile services are made available to consumers.

—OPEN HANDSET ALLIANCE PRESS RELEASE, NOVEMBER 5, 2007

A ndroid launched an early version of the SDK long before it shipped 1.0, or the source code, or any physical hardware. Launching the SDK early gave developers plenty of time to learn about Android and build and test their applications. Early access to the platform also gave the team a chance for feedback from developers, pointing out problems that needed to be fixed before 1.0.

---

[1] "Introducing Android" is still available at *https://www.youtube.com/watch?v=6rYozIZOgDk.*

NOVEMBER 5, 2007: THE OPEN HANDSET ALLIANCE

On November 5, Google announced the formation of the Open Handset Alliance.[2] The OHA was an important step toward the ecosystem that the team envisioned. In stark opposition to the traditional model exemplified by Apple and Microsoft, where a single company controls the platform, the OHA promised to provide an open source platform that could be used by all companies. It was a collection of carriers, hardware manufacturers, and software companies, including:

- Mobile carriers, featuring companies like T-Mobile, Sprint Nextel, and Vodafone

- Handset manufacturers, including ASUS, Samsung, and LG

- Semiconductor companies (manufacturers of chips that are assembled into handsets), such as ARM and NVIDIA

- Software companies, including Google and ACCESS[3]

The announcement promised great things, but it was just a press release—lots of nice words, painting the picture of a bright future, with no actual product to show for it.

NOVEMBER 7–8: INDUSTRY RECEPTION

Existing players in the mobile space who weren't part of the OHA didn't appear to think much of the announcement.

On November 7, two days after the OHA announcement, John Forsyth, an executive at Symbian, the most prevalent mobile phone operating system in

---

[2] The OHA website still exists at *https://openhandsetalliance.com/*; you can browse information about the organization, including many more partner companies that signed on since that first press release, and various quaint pictures and videos that are from a different era of the Android platform. There is even a "What's New" section on the home page, with the most recent press release update on July 18, 2011 . . . which is an indicator of the relevance of that organization in today's Android ecosystem. But it was an important piece of Android's history and growth.

[3] I was amused to see ACCESS on the list. This company was mentioned earlier as the company that acquired PalmSource, Inc., after which several disenchanted ex-Be employees left to join Android.

---

the world at that time, said in an interview with BBC, "Search and a mobile phone platform are completely different things. It's costly, arduous, and at times a deeply unsexy job of supporting customers day by day in launching phones. That's something there's very little experience of in Google's environment. They are talking about having a phone by the end of next year. It's not one that is going to ignite developers."

The following day, Steve Ballmer (then CEO of Microsoft) said during a news conference, "Their efforts are just some words on paper right now, it's hard to do a very clear comparison [with Windows Mobile]. Right now they have a press release, we have many, many millions of customers, great software, many hardware devices."

There seemed to be a general sense of *vaporware*[4] in the air. Press releases are one thing, but shipping a phone platform is a different kettle of software fish.

NOVEMBER 11: SDK LAUNCH

On November 11, six days after the OHA announcement, the Android SDK was released, with a build that was lovingly labeled *m3*.[5]

When the original OHA announcement went out, the SDK was completely ready. But the decision was made to do the press release first and let it float out there a few days before dropping the code. This allowed time for industry sentiment and general misbelief to fester. Six days later, the team shipped the actual software, making the announcement very real indeed.

Now that the SDK was out there, application developers could download it, tinker with it, and start building apps against it, but it wasn't final by a long stretch. For example, that first release had an emulator that looked like the Sooner device (complete with a hardware keyboard taking up more space than the tiny screen, but that also had touch support the actual Sooner

---

[4] There is a long and sad tradition in tech of announcing a product way too early, when it may not even yet exist in anything but dream form, hence the term *vaporware*. Maybe they do it out of hope, or fear, but companies do sometimes present products way too early and end up having to retract those promises later, when reality catches up.

[5] *m3* stands for milestone 3. *m1* and *m2* were internal milestone releases. Later releases were follow-ons from m3 (bugfix releases), then m5 (when APIs were changed). The milestone naming was dropped by the time the final beta version shipped, which was just called .9.

device lacked). The emulator also had many functional apps already. Android really was a mostly complete system, albeit without a physical device to ship on and with APIs that were not yet final.

The emulator in the first SDK release resembled the original Sooner device, with a hardware keyboard, although unlike the Sooner, it also had a functional touchscreen.

The emulator available in the m3-r37 release of the SDK, in December of 2007.

In the third SDK version, *m3-r37a*, released just a month later, the emulator offered a more modern device with a larger touchscreen.

It's worth noting that all of these SDKs are still available[6] on the *https:// www.android.com/* website, including emulators that still run. Why you would want to spend time with these pre-release versions of Android is another

---

[6.] Or at least they are now, when I am *writing* this footnote, many years after these SDKs were released. Whether they are still available when you are *reading* this footnote is not clear. The future is like many software projects: it's difficult to predict exactly what it's going to be like, but we'll find out eventually.

question, but it's cool that you can; Android has always been about openness, and that apparently extends to obsolete versions of the operating system that never actually shipped with running hardware.

WHAT'S IN A NAME?

Naming products can be a difficult task, especially when lawyers get involved.[7] It's one thing to have an internal code name that the team uses. It can probably be anything, because the wider world may never know and there won't be any conflicts with other people's or companies' own products or names.[8] But when that internal product becomes external and public, things get complicated. You have to do trademark searches. When someone already has the rights to the name you wanted, you have to figure out what to do about it, which usually involves coming up with a new name.

In the weeks prior to launch, there was a fear that the name *Android* would not be available for use externally. Dianne said, "I remember us being really worried about the potential name change, because the word Android at that point was used everywhere—all over the SDK, everywhere. If we had to change it in our APIs it was going to be a mess."

So the team brainstormed some other options, including *Mezza*.[9] Dan Morrill explained the logic behind the name: "It was supposed to mean mezzanine,[10] like enabling middleware. Needless to say, nobody liked it and the correct decision was ultimately reached."

---

[7] There are other examples of this difficulty in Android history, such as the use of the word "Nexus" for Google's line of Android phones, which was challenged by the estate of the science fiction writer Philip K. Dick.

[8] Even internal names can sometimes be problematic. Apple once used the code name "Carl Sagan" for one of its computer systems in the early 90s and was sued by . . . Carl Sagan. The team changed the code name to BHA, which stood for "Butt-Head Astronomer."

[9] Another name being considered was Honeycomb, which would return in 2011 as the dessert name for the 3.0 release.

[10] Mezzanine is better than my guess when I first saw it, which was, "Meh." Mezzo is an Italian word I remember from far too many years practicing classical piano. I'd read it in the dynamics specified for a section of music, like *mf* for *mezzo forte*, which means "kinda loud." Mezzo isn't even a specific thing, it's just an adjective meaning half. And "mezza" itself isn't even a word. So, meh indeed.

THE ANDROID DEVELOPER CHALLENGE

One of the difficult things with launching a new software platform is actually getting anyone to use it. When the SDK was released, it had exactly zero users outside of the Android team in the entire world, and it would be many months until that number could possibly change, since Android devices would not be available to purchase until 1.0 was released. The team had to figure out how to get developers interested in investing their time and energy in this new and speculative platform with zero users.

So the team came up with the Android Developer Challenge. The first blog post about Android, on November 12, 2007, ended with a tantalizing hook: *"We're really looking forward to seeing all the amazing applications that developers will create on an open mobile phone platform. In fact, you may even want to enter your application into the Android Developer Challenge—a USD $10 million challenge sponsored by Google to support and recognize developers who build great applications for the Android platform."*

On January 3, 2008, the contest officially opened. The team accepted entries until April 14 and then sent them off to judges around the world to come up with the short list of the top 50 apps. Those 50 developers were awarded $25,000 each and asked to submit for a second round. From that second round, the top 10 apps were awarded $275,000 each, and the second 10 $100,000 each. If you do the math, that's five million dollars Google gave away in this single contest.

Whether the team got their money's worth is difficult to say, since these apps couldn't even be offered to users at that point. Nobody outside of Android could even get a device that would run these apps at that time; the finalists were announced in August of 2008, a full two months before the first G1 was available for sale. But the challenge definitely got developers interested, as 1,788 apps were entered into the contest for this platform with zero users and an unknown release date.

The exercise benefited Android not only in developer excitement about the platform; the experience of onboarding all of these developers and getting their feedback also helped the platform team get things in better shape for the eventual launch of 1.0. Dirk Dougherty explained: "We had to figure out how to write apps, and then explain that. And deal with all the feedback. We think we get a lot of feedback today, but this was a brand-new API surface, on a brand-new platform, and no one had really written apps with this kind of access to sensors and things like that before. So there were tons of new use cases that we hadn't thought of."

Even the process of judging the apps was … unique. Google wanted to use judges across the world that were known to the developer community. They wanted to make things easy for these remote judges, but Android wasn't "easy" at that point at all. To run an application, a judge had to install the SDK on their computer, run the tools, boot up the emulator, run a command to load the app into the emulator, and launch the app. With nearly 1,800 apps to judge, that wasn't going to scale.

So Google sent laptops to every judge, pre-installed with a tool that Dan Morrill's developer relations team had written that launched the emulator and had a UI to choose the app to test, which installed and ran it on the emulator. "We shipped out a laptop to every one of the judges around the world. It was crazy! Most of these laptops never came back. One came back in a box packed with all kinds of stuffed animals, for some reason."

The top 50 winners of the preliminary round are still listed on the Android developers blog;[11] the first one on the list is "AndroidScan" by the Android team's very own Jeff Sharkey.[12] No, he didn't cheat by entering the contest as a Google employee: Jeff was recruited by the platform team because the team saw his work in the contest. "I was invited to Mountain View to develop on confidential devices (the G1). I was so excited I didn't actually work on the app while in Mountain View. Instead, I wrote another app[13] that would do area-code-to-city caller ID lookup using a super optimized algorithm that didn't require a network connection." Jeff continued work on AndroidScan later, renaming it CompareEverywhere, and ended up being one of the 10 overall winners.

---

[11] If you're ever curious about details in Android history that aren't in the book, all of the old blogs are out there. They may not have the internal details, but they provide a lot of information about the state of the Android development world over the years. You can start here: *https://android-developers.googleblog.com*.

[12] Another entry further down the list is by Virgil Dobjanschi, who was also later hired onto the Android team. The Developer Challenge wasn't intended to be a recruiting tool, but it was a nice side benefit.

[13] Jeff's second app that he worked on while visiting the Google campus was RevealCaller, which is open sourced at *https://code.google.com/archive/p/android-cookbook/source/default/source?page=18*.

Once the contest was over, the team continued finishing up the product, shipping 1.0 in October of 2008. In May of 2009, they ran a second challenge, giving away another five million dollars. But in the meantime, Android had attracted actual users and Android Market was open for business. Now Android had a real user and developer base, not just contestants for a pre-release platform.

40

THE RUN UP TO 1.0

Nearly a year passed between the initial launch of the SDK in November of 2007 and the release of 1.0, which was launched with the G1 phone nearly a year later. So what was happening during that whole time?

First of all, it wasn't actually as long as you'd think.

Some software products can ship quickly, depending on the situation. If you are simply updating some code on a web page, you can release it immediately. And if there's a bug in that release, you can ship again as soon as you've fixed it. But if you are shipping a product that is not as easy to distribute to your users as simply updating a website, you'll want to do some amount of testing and stabilization before releasing it. You don't want to make your users go through some arduous update just to discover a horrible bug and make them update again. Now you're looking at some number of weeks[1] at least. Shipping hardware, like the G1, in addition to the software it depends on, involves even more time.

The Android SDK was just software, and the team could have kept updating it with bug fixes (as they did continuously during the beta period prior to 1.0) until they declared it "done." But that release needed to work well on the G1, which involved different constraints entirely. Phones go through

---

[1] Or longer, depending on the size of the product and the context in which the software is used. Software for a nuclear power plant, for example, should probably undergo more thorough testing than, say, a dating app.

rigorous compliance testing by carriers, which meant that the team needed to be done far sooner than they would have for just another release of the SDK. Romain talked about it: "Pencils down was a month before the launch in stores. But before that was like three months of carrier testing." So for G1 availability in mid-October, the team had to be effectively finished with platform development (apart from fixing critical bugs that came up during this final testing period) in June of 2008—only seven months after the initial SDK launch.

Many things needed to be fixed during those seven months, including smoothing out the rough edges of the public API, critical performance work, and bugs, bugs, bugs.

THE COST OF COMPATIBILITY

The public APIs needed to be polished before the release. The SDK was beta; developers were encouraged to write apps for it, but the APIs (method names, classes, and so on) were not final. Once 1.0 was launched, however, that was it; those APIs were set in stone and couldn't change. Changing APIs between releases meant that applications using those APIs would mysteriously crash on user devices.

This compatibility dynamic is especially true on a platform like Android, where there is no way to force developers to update their apps, or to get users to install those updates. Suppose a developer wrote and uploaded an app to the Play Store 10 years ago. Somewhere, someone is using that application happily. Then that user upgrades their phone to a newer release. If that newer release changes any of the APIs that that old application uses, it might not work correctly, or it might even crash, which is obviously not something that Google wants. So the old APIs stick around and are supported for way . . . too . . . long.

The trick, then, for developers on the Android team, is to be very sure about any new API, because the team will have to live with it forever. Of course, there will always be mistakes or things you would have done differently in hindsight.[2]

---

[2] Developing APIs is the process of building future regret. Even if it looks good now, you would probably do it differently in a few years given changing requirements and future developments. But you do the best you can and move on, because shipping anything is better than not shipping perfection.

Ficus Kirkpatrick observed, "You can try to design something perfect. Then while you're busy polishing it in the lab, somebody's going to come out with something and make you irrelevant."

The team worked to make the APIs something that they were happy with and willing to live with for, basically, ever. Some of the pre-1.0 changes, like method or class names, were minor. But some APIs were completely removed, because they just weren't something that the platform wanted to support for all eternity.

Romain Guy said, "A lot of the time during 2008 I spent cleaning up the APIs and removing as much as possible from the framework before we shipped." For example, he removed PageTurner, a class that implemented a cool paper-tearing effect. It was originally written for an earlier version of the Calculator application to show a fun animation when clearing the display. But the design of Calculator had changed, and it no longer used that animation. It was such a specific kind of effect that it was too niche to live in the public API, so that class was deleted.

The paper-tearing effect for the calculator app was cool, but not generally useful. It was removed from the platform APIs before 1.0.

Jeff Sharkey, who was an external developer at that time, commented on the API churn during this phase of the project: "Portions of the Android SDK were pretty turbulent through the various preview releases before the 1.0

release. UI components were being added, removed, and reskinned[3] at every snapshot. Entire features were gutted."

This is not to say that bad APIs didn't sneak their way in and stick around past 1.0 (see the earlier footnote comment about "building future regret"). One example is ZoomButton, a utility class for interpreting a long-press as multiple click events, sent to another piece of logic that handled zooming. ZoomButton didn't actually do any zooming itself. In fact, it didn't really do anything except reinterpret one type of input (long-press) as another (multiple clicks). But unfortunately, it stuck around past 1.0 and only got deprecated[4] years later, in the Oreo release.

PERFORMANCE

Another critical area of work during this phase was performance. Even though hardware at that time had come a long way since earlier mobile device generations, making it possible for smartphones to exist, the CPUs were still incredibly limited. Also, everything that happens on a phone uses battery and shortens the time until the user needs to recharge their device. So it was important for the platform and application engineers to do everything possible to make things run faster, smoother, and more efficiently. For example, Romain Guy, along with others on the UI toolkit team, spent much of this time optimizing animations and drawing logic to avoid doing unnecessary work.

BUGS, BUGS, BUGS

The hardware for the G1 was finally starting to become available for wider internal use around the time of the SDK launch, so the team could finally

---

3. Reskinning refers to changing the look of the UI in more of a visual than functional way. For example, the buttons and the other UI elements might get a new color or look, but still be the same size and do the same thing. It's the device equivalent of giving the house a fresh coat of paint; there might be broken doors, leaky faucets, and a trashed kitchen on the inside, but it looks new and fresh on the outside.

4. Deprecation is as close as Android comes to removing APIs. It's a means of marking an API as "you shouldn't use this" without actually removing it. Developers that use it will see warnings in their code when they build their applications, but applications that use it despite those warnings will continue to work.

---

start testing their code on real hardware. Once the devices were available in quantity, everyone could also dogfood the G1 as their daily phone, which generated many bugs that needed to be fixed before 1.0.

Romain said, "What happened during that time? Tons of debugging."

EASTER EGGS

One of the things that didn't make it into 1.0 was an Easter egg[5] listing the names of everyone who worked on the release, reminiscent of the classic Macintosh team signatures that decorated the inside of that computer case. Romain Guy implemented the feature, but it never shipped.

"You can register an intent for what's called a 'secret code' in the Dialer. When you dial like *#*#, a number, *#*#, it's basically a system command. Sometimes your ISP might ask you to type something like that to ask you to do something.

"Launcher registered one of those codes. If you entered it, launcher would be woken up and would find, in one of its icons I had hidden in the metadata, the list of the people on the team who had worked on Android 1.0. It would bring up a UI to just scroll the list of names. The code to do that was written inside a comment, in the Java sources. So the code was kind of hidden.

"We turned it into a feature. We started gathering even more people, including contractors. We added more and more. It was canned because someone was afraid that we would have forgotten about someone.

"So it was a cool little Easter egg that got productized to death."

Recent releases of Android have Easter eggs, most of them implemented by Dan Sandler on the system UI team. This Android tradition started several releases after 1.0, maybe when the team had time to breathe and think about something non-critical. Or maybe just when someone with Dan's level of art skills, humor, and coding speed could make it happen. Long-pressing on the build information in the system settings will bring up . . . something. Sometimes it's just a pretty visual, sometimes it's a simple game or application. But it's never a list of people working on the product because that would be too complicated.

---

5. Easter eggs are hidden features in applications that are placed there for the joy of the users who discover them and the delight of the developers who hid them.

APPS

The team also spent some time in the run up to 1.0, especially toward the end when only critical bug fixes were allowed, writing applications. Mike Cleron said, "That's where most of my app-writing career happened. Kicking the tires on the framework."

Mike and Romain, both passionate landscape photographers, worked on photography applications. Writing real-world apps not only provides more functionality for users, it also helps platform developers understand the platform from an app developer's point of view, which feeds into better APIs and functionality in future versions. And, of course, it also helps find bugs that can then be fixed.

41

1.0 LAUNCH

Software releases in tech have a long tradition of being celebrated by t-shirts given to the team. This 1.0 launch t-shirt was the first of many such t-shirts for Android releases. (Picture courtesy Chiu-Ki Chan.)

The launch of Android 1.0 happened in four phases in the Fall of 2008.

SEPTEMBER 23: ANDROID SDK

The first piece of the launch was the SDK itself, when 1.0 was released on September 23, 2008. On one hand, 1.0 was just another update in a long series of updates since the initial m3 release 10 months before, up through the 0.9 release a mere five weeks earlier, on August 18.

But 1.0 was more than another iteration; it was, well, *1.0*. It represented the team's final thoughts on what the official, supported API would be for Android from here on out, because there was no more changing of APIs without breaking applications that had been built against them.

In typical fashion, Google simply released this developer product without big fanfare. There was no press event; just some bits uploaded to a server, along with Release Notes about the fixes that were in this version. Even the introductory sentence of the Release Notes is understated. If you didn't know what you were looking at, you'd think it was just another update (which, to some extent, it was):

Android 1.0 SDK, Release 1

This SDK release is the first to include the Android 1.0 platform and application API. Applications developed on this SDK will be compatible with mobile devices running the Android 1.0 platform, when such devices are available.

The Release Notes for the major bombshell of the 1.0 release were . . . understated.

But these release notes do contain a key feature-omission apology: *"We regret to inform developers that Android 1.0 will not include support for dot-matrix printers."*

SEPTEMBER 23: T-MOBILE G1 ANNOUNCEMENT

Google didn't gather the media for the developer-targeted SDK launch, but they did get up on stage at a press conference in New York City with T-Mobile to announce the consumer phone that would run 1.0. The same day as the 1.0 SDK shipped, representatives talked about the new device, and T-Mobile issued a press release entitled, "T-Mobile Unveils the T-Mobile G1—the First Phone Powered by Android."

The G1 device would have a touchscreen, a slide-to-open QWERTY keyboard, and a trackball. It would run Google Maps, search, and it would offer apps from Android Market. It would come with a three-megapixel camera and would run on T-Mobile's new 3G network. It would sell for $179 on contract, or $399 unlocked, starting in the US and expanding to other countries in the following weeks.

And it would be available in a month. Customers could pre-order the G1, but would have to wait until October 22 to get one.

OCTOBER 21: OPEN SOURCE

One day before the G1 became available, the source code for 1.0 was posted. Once again, there was no big, staged event for this developer-focused release. In fact, this time there wasn't even a press release, just a short three-paragraph blurb on the Android Developers Blog[1] with the title, "Android is now Open Source."

It wasn't much. But it was *everything*.

Android had planned on having an open source platform since before it existed. It had pitched the idea to investors, to Google, to team members, to carrier and manufacturer partners, and to developers worldwide. And now, 11 months after the first public SDK and one month after 1.0, it made good on all of those promises and published all of the code for everyone to see and use.

OCTOBER 22: T-MOBILE G1 AVAILABLE

On October 22, one day after Android was open sourced, the G1 was finally available for people outside of Google to try and to buy.

The T-Mobile G1

When the G1 went on sale at the T-Mobile store on Market Street in San Francisco, Romain Guy was there, taking a picture of the first buyer. Nowadays, it's hard to imagine caring who is buying what phone where, but at the

---

[1] *https://android-developers.googleblog.com/2008/10/android-is-now-open-source.html*

time, this first purchase was the culmination of years of hard work by the development team; it was exciting to see their efforts make it into the real world and to see people line up to purchase them. Someone else who was at the store that day was Bob Borchers, the Senior Director of Product Marketing for the iPhone. He was purchasing one for his team to play around with back at Apple.

Michael Morrissey visited the G1 display in the T-Mobile store with his kids that first week that it was for sale. (Picture courtesy Michael Morrissey.)

The G1 was the first in a long line of devices that were developed as a collaboration between manufacturer (HTC), carrier (T-Mobile), and Google. The original idea behind these Google-collaboration devices was that they would showcase the new capabilities of the latest release. At the same time, these phones also allowed the team to prove out new functionality to ensure that what was being built actually worked on real hardware. In the case of the G1, this hardware allowed the team to prove that the Android platform worked, could provide full capabilities for a functional consumer device, and could provide building blocks for more platform functionality and more devices to come.

42

G1 RECEPTION

The G1 didn't overtake the iPhone in sales, didn't become a worldwide best-seller, and didn't become the phone that everyone had to have.

The reviews shared the opinion that it was . . . interesting. The hardware wasn't awful, although the screen was quite small. It didn't support video recording. And there were not many must-have applications beyond the pre-installed Google apps.

On the Android team, too, the reception was mixed. As Fadden said, "The G1 was right on the edge of good but was a bit lumpy and awkward."

Dan Egnor agreed: "It was kind of this enthusiast device. Some people were excited about it, but in many ways, it was kind of a crappy device. It showed a lot of potential. But for somebody to adopt it? It wasn't exactly flying off the shelves."

Dave Burke talked about the G1: "The impression was: 'Wow, this thing is sophisticated, it can do a lot. If anything . . . it can do almost too much.' It had a keyboard and it had a trackpad and a rollerball and touch. It had everything. All these sensors. You got a feeling initially that Android was trying to do everything. I remember thinking at the time, What's going to survive? Is the keyboard and the touchscreen going to survive? Is that trackball really going to be the thing? There was recognition that this thing was super-powerful, but total uncertainty that it might have been a one-off and flopped. It wasn't clear to people."

Dianne said, "The G1 was definitely an everything-and-the-kitchen-sink device . . . which as a general consumer product, is not the best thing in the world. But it was good for the platform since we had to support all of that stuff." So while it might not have created the best consumer experience for a phone,[1]

---

[1] Descriptions of the G1's features remind me of the car that Homer designed in *The Simpsons* episode, "Oh Brother, Where Art Thou?" It had every feature imaginable, which is not necessarily what people want. Except Homer.

it paved the way for a myriad of follow-on devices that were able to take advantage of the myriad of capabilities that the platform provided.

Holiday sales are the biggest time of year for new devices. Dan Egnor remembered that first holiday with the G1: "Michael Morrissey [manager of the services team] had bad memories of Christmas day spikes [from Danger], and nobody on the team being available while things were melting down. So he was like, 'We're gonna have an on-call coverage that day. We're gonna have a War Room. Who's gonna be around? Big sacrifice, working Christmas Day.... 'I was like, I'll do this, sure.' And then nothing happened. We had more activations than a typical day, but there wasn't even a particularly large spike."

So the G1 wasn't an immediate overnight triumph. But there was promise.

It was decent enough for people to take the phone seriously. And it was purchased in real, if not overwhelming, numbers. T-Mobile reported[2] that it had reached sales of over a million units in the US six months later. This was, coincidentally, the number of devices needed in that timeframe to convince the Google networking team to not take back its dedicated VIP resource[3] from the Android services team, which would have caused serious problems for all of the Google apps on Android.

The G1 also provided a decent enough experience for people to take Android seriously as a platform. Android had finally been released out into the world. People were able to use the device and the platform to do what they needed to do, and that was good enough for now. Consumers could take Android seriously as a phone, and potential partners could take Android seriously as a platform. It allowed manufacturers to see that Android was real and that they could use it to build their own devices, which would eventually be more interesting and more powerful than that initial G1.

Hiroshi said, "The G1 made Android. Commercially, G1 wasn't a huge success. The G1 was good but wasn't a huge volume driver and didn't really get that much attention outside of the tech industry. But launching it made it real for the OEMs: 'OK these people can actually ship. It's a real thing. It's not vaporware.' By the time G1 launched, we were already in discussions with all the major OEMs, who eventually became our partners."

---

[2] *https://www.cnet.com/news/t-mobile-has-sold-1-million-g1-android-phones/*

[3] See Chapter 20 ("Android Services") for more details on this back-room deal.

43

JUST DESSERTS

The 1.0 release went out, the G1 launched, and everyone breathed a quiet sigh of relief on completing a difficult job. And then they went back to work.

It was clear to the team that Android was far from complete; there was so much more to do in terms of features and quality to make Android more competitive. And there were more devices to come.

For the next year, the team worked furiously on smaller bug-fix releases as well as larger "dessert" releases, culminating in the Eclair release that shipped with the Droid device at the end of 2009. In one year alone, the team shipped four major releases 1.1 (Petit Four), 1.5 (Cupcake), 1.6 (Donut), and 2.0 (Eclair).

Tom Moss noted that this frantic pace was intentional: "Two reasons: Andy's a perfectionist, and he wanted the product to get better. It really upsets him personally when the product is not good enough. But it was also an intentional strategy to stop OEMs from trying to fork by saying, 'By the time you get your fork up, we'll have the new version of Android out, and you're going to have to start over again.'

"He intentionally pushed us to have multiple releases per year in order to disincentivize or disable people from forking."

1.0 R2: NOVEMBER 2008

The first bug-fix release was notable because, well, it was the first. Version 1.0 was released in September of 2008. That release was the one installed on the G1 phones that were then sold in October. In November, r2 was released, which added some functionality and apps, in addition to various bug fixes.

1.1 PETIT FOUR: FEBRUARY 2009

Version 1.1 was the first named release: *Petit Four* (a small cake, French for "little oven"). It was a relatively small release, with bug fixes and a few API additions. It also provided localization for other languages (1.0 had support for English only), which turned out to be an important feature for this very international platform.

From this point on, whenever there was a bump in the "dot" version number (the number after the first dot, in this case 1.1 versus the original release of 1.0), it meant that there were API changes in the release. API changes meant that applications built against the previous version of the SDK would run on the newer version (Android always tries to maintain forward compatibility), but applications built against the new version might not run on the old version (because use of new APIs that don't exist on the older version would cause an error on the older system).

The 1.1 release was the first one in which Android Market enabled applications for sale. Prior to 1.1, the mechanism for charging users for applications wasn't yet working, so Market allowed only free apps.

Petit Four was also the first time a dessert name was used for an Android release, although it was clearly not following the convention of starting with successive letters in the alphabet; that tradition would start with the next release, Cupcake.

1.5 CUPCAKE: APRIL 2009

Cupcake was the first release that established the tradition of consecutive-letter-desserts. It started with "C" because it was the third major release and "Cupcake" was chosen as the C dessert name because Ryan PC Gibson (the person running the releases at the time) was obsessed with cupcakes.[1]

---

[1] See Chapter 27 ("Managing All the Things") for more about the dessert-name convention.

Cupcake brought some notable features for developers and users. App Widgets[2] first appeared. Video recording was now available. Developers could develop and distribute their own keyboard applications. Also, there was a new sensor and logic to detect rotation, so users could rotate their phone for landscape versus portrait mode display. Prior to that change, users needed to slide out the keyboard on the G1, which automatically put the display into landscape mode.

The Cupcake release was also coincident with a new device: the HTC Magic. The Magic was the first touch-only device; the hardware keyboard of the G1 was replaced by the now-familiar onscreen software keyboard.

The release notes for Cupcake did have one piece of bad news for developers and users: *"We regret to inform developers that Android 1.5 will not include support for the Zilog Z80 processor[3] architecture."*

1.6 DONUT: SEPTEMBER 2009

The Donut release rounded out various pieces of the platform for general use. The telephony stack now supported CDMA, the system used by Verizon (this would come in handy with, for example, the Motorola Droid, which launched on the Verizon network). The framework team finished adding support for arbitrary screen sizes and densities, which was important in enabling a broader ecosystem of all kinds of different form factors.[4] Donut also included a speech-to-text engine. It was not nearly as powerful as the systems used in phones today but was an indicator of where things could go.

The Donut release notes also carried some unfortunate news: *"We regret to inform developers that Android 1.6 will not include support for RFC 2549."*[5]

---

[2] App Widgets are simplified apps that run directly on the home screen. For example, there is a Calendar widget that displays a live Calendar view, and a Gmail widget that displays a message list.

[3] The Zilog Z80 was an 8-bit processor developed in the mid 1970s, last seen in home computers and video game arcade consoles in the 1980s.

[4] Dianne said, "There was a Dell device that was going to ship that needed that support, which is why we finished it here (instead of in Eclair for Droid)."

[5] RFC 2549 is a proposal entitled "Internet Protocol over Avian Carriers," or network data through homing pigeons.

Hiroshi enjoying a "donut burger." Peisun Wu introduced the team to this concept to celebrate the Donut release in September of 2009. (Picture courtesy Brian Swetland.)

2.0 ECLAIR: OCTOBER 2009

One thing that's interesting to note about the Eclair release is how soon it shipped after the Donut release—just one month separated them.[6] Not only was the team working very hard at the time on multiple, frequent releases in parallel, but in fact the Eclair release was actually finished *before* the Donut release shipped.

Various features were added in Eclair, including Live Wallpapers and turn-by-turn navigation.[7] But perhaps the most notable thing about Eclair was that it was implemented in conjunction with the new Droid and Passion (Nexus One) devices, which launched soon after Eclair was released. The Passion device was the one that the team really had its heart set on, but the Droid was the first device that was successful with a large consumer market.

---

[6] The timing of Donut, in addition to the specific feature set of that release, was set by a Dell device that was going to ship earlier than Eclair.

[7] Chapter 15 ("System UI and Launcher") discusses Live Wallpapers, and Chapter 21 ("Location, Location, Location") covers turn-by-turn navigation.

44

THE EARLY DEVICES

A pile of Sooners (picture courtesy Brian Jones)

One of the things that defines the Android ecosystem nowadays is an almost infinite variety of devices. Not only are there many different models of phones made by many different manufacturers, but there are also tablets. And cameras. And TVs. And autos. And watches. And IoT devices. And entertainment screens on airplanes.[1]

BEFORE 1.0: SOONER, DREAM (HTC G1), AND MORE

The very early plans included four phones. As Swetland recalled, "The four devices that were under discussion in June 2006 were Sooner (HTC wedge), Later (LG wedge), Dream (HTC G1), and Grail (a Motorola device that would slide one way for qwerty and the other way for keypad). Grail (or some variant

---

[1] It's fun to see whether the TV on the back of an airplane seat is running Android. Sometimes you can swipe up from the bottom of the screen to see a familiar navigation bar. Then you can swipe away the video app and be left at the home screen of Android. Which doesn't buy you much, since the airline doesn't have any other app installed besides the entertainment one you just killed.

Okay, maybe it's not that fun. But on a 12-hour flight when you're tired of all of the movie options, it's something to do.

of it) would keep popping up and going away over the years." But the plan eventually settled into just Sooner and Dream, whose respective demise and development is discussed in earlier chapters.

SAPPHIRE (HTC MAGIC)

Android's second flagship device, code-named Sapphire, was based on the HTC Magic. It came out in the Spring of 2009 with the Android 1.5 Cupcake release. The actual hardware specs were similar to those in the original G1, although the Magic had more memory. But the biggest change was the keyboard: Android was finally comfortable with going fully touchscreen and dropped the hardware keyboard that was on the earlier G1 device. The Magic also supported multi-touch[2] for the first time on Android.

MOTOROLA DROID

The Droid phone was so important to early Android that it has its very own chapter (Chapter 45, "Droid Did"). You can go read that now if you'd like. I'll wait.

PASSION AND NEXUS

In parallel with the Droid phone, the team was working on another device code-named Passion. It was released in early 2010 as the Nexus One.

The Nexus One was released in January 2010, soon after the Motorola Droid.

---

[2] Multi-touch uses touch input from more than one finger at a time, which is useful for gestures like pinch-zooming or rotating a map.

Passion was one of the "Google Experience" phones. The Google Experience process has gone through many names and types of collaboration over the years. At the time of Nexus One, the collaboration with HTC was given the brand "With Google." The slogan was invented in engineering. Marketing had come up with the slogan, "It's got Google." But Rebecca, on the systems team, complained to Andy Rubin: "It's not even grammatical! What about 'With Google' instead?" Andy said "Okay!" The co-branding slogan was born.

Passion had a large (for that time) screen and hand-fitting curves. But the unique thing about Passion wasn't the hardware or software; it was the sales model that Android attempted. In the US, the way that everyone bought their phone back then (and now, for the most part) was through a contract with their carrier. Rather than buying a device on its own and then paying a carrier to be on their network, you went to a T-Mobile store (for example) and bought one of the phones they offered. Phones were sold at a substantial discount, along with a contractual lock-in for some period of time. That's just how the phone market worked.

But Android leadership had this idea that people should have options. What if they chose their phone independent of the carrier, paying a carrier just to be connected to their network? They would be free of contractual obligations, and users would have more choice because people wouldn't have to pick from just those devices that happened to be on the carrier store's shelves.

Google didn't have store fronts, so they offered the Nexus One for sale online. And they waited. But it turns out that people didn't really understand this model of buying phones and weren't in a rush to figure it out. Moreover, if there were problems with a phone they bought off the website, there wasn't a customer service number to call, and there also wasn't a store that they could return it to or get help from.

Android eventually gave up on this idea, and the Nexus One was offered by carriers. It never sold as much as Google had hoped and was far outsold by the Motorola Droid.

The Nexus One was the first of many phones in the Nexus series. Nexus phones were devices that the Android team would work on in conjunction with manufacturers to create an overall Android phone experience. The team couldn't control what other manufacturers would produce and sell, either in the hardware or the software and apps that might be layered on top of Android. By shipping their own phones, Android could ensure that those devices had exactly the hardware they wanted (within the range of what hardware partners could offer, at least) and exactly the software they wanted.

The other, and perhaps main, reason for the Nexus program was to produce a "reference device." Nexus phones showed the world (and partners) what Android was capable of in that release. But the team also ensured that the platform reliably supported new capabilities, which might have been harder if the hardware were being developed separately from the software. For many years and releases, a new Nexus phone launched in conjunction with each software release, showing off the latest hardware advancements along with new capabilities of Android.

Throughout Android's history, one of the most important dynamics about Nexus, and other devices that Google helped launch, was that they were made by different manufacturers. This was very intentional, as a way to get the entire partner community invested in Android. Early devices from Google included phones by HTC, Motorola, LG, and Samsung.

Charles Mendis said, "A lot of credit to Andy and biz dev. We didn't just partner with one; we'd switch between them. We managed to get some of the biggest players in the hardware space invested in Android, where it became *their* platform, and now all this phone hardware is done by them. We made them feel like everybody else owned Android, too; Android wasn't owned by Google.[3] I think that really helped the success of it."

BRIAN JONES AND DEVICE DISTRIBUTION

I was the [equipment] hook-up guy.

—BRIAN JONES

In every tech company, there's the person you have to know to get the best equipment to get your job done. That person is the glue between all of the people on the inside and all of the things that those people need.

[3.] That is, the Android project was clearly owned by Google and the team owned that code. But by releasing it to open source, they created a system where manufacturers could download it, change it, and then own their own implementation, independent of Google. It is this shared ownership across the entire ecosystem of Android devices to which Charles is referring.

On the Android team, that person was Brian Jones (known to everyone as "bjones").

Brian has always been a tinkerer. In early elementary school, he wanted to know how telephones worked, so his teacher created a class activity and brought in her own telephone from home. "I took it apart all the way down to the wax-enclosed transformers. There was no hope of me putting this back together. It was waxy. It made a big mess in the cafeteria. I had never actually done this before. I got in a lot of trouble because she expected to be able to take her telephone home and use it that night, and that was not going to happen."

Brian's route to the Android team was atypical, starting with his college degree in Classics. When he moved to the Bay Area and needed employment, he got a job as a receptionist for building 44, where the Android team worked. He got to know many of the people on the team, including Andy's admin, Tracey Cole. Brian's advice: "Befriend the admins. They're the second—if not first—most important people you can possibly gain the trust of in life."

In the Spring of 2007, Tracey went out on leave. Andy needed someone to do her job while she was out. "Tracey was like, 'I don't want to have to go find a temp. Brian is already somebody we trust. He's the only one I want to leave this to.' So I was Andy's admin for three to four months."

Brian's etching machine, set up in a small kitchen area. Brian programmed it to open, close, and rotate the device inside in coordination with the laser. (Picture courtesy Daniel Switkin.)

When Tracey returned, Brian took on a new role on the team: he became the dogfood manager, in charge of Android device distribution. When phones came in from the manufacturer, Brian would laser-etch them with unique IDs. "That was my job, to etch every phone as quickly as I possibly could, for hundreds of people who needed to get them. If there were ever leaks, we could trace them back. But it was also good for fleet management."

Laser etching wasn't limited to test devices. "Mugs. Glasses. We tried ham. Turkey. We lit several fires. I learned a lot about lasers in that time of my life."

Brian enjoyed the random hardware he needed to do the job. "There were lasers. There were UV printers. I remember getting sunburned from looking at the custom-backed G1, watching those things get printed, because every back would change. It would warp a little bit differently, and if they warped too much, you had to change the printer setup. I got sunburned. Inside. In a windowless section of the building."

Brian Jones's test device, a pre-release G1, which he used to calibrate the machine before etching a new set of devices.

One of the reasons that Brian ran device distribution was that his priority was always helping the product. He didn't play corporate games. "It landed on my shoulders to be the guy who decided who got what. One of the things I think I'm good at is not being swayed by people's titles or salesmanship or personalities. If somebody comes and says, 'I need this thing,' my first question is, 'Why do you need it and what's the impact if you don't get it?'

"If you're an executive, some of the impact is: we can't make product decisions. But gauging how those executives actually factor in is important. In the early days, if you were a VP or SVP in Sales or Ads, that had nothing to do with Android, I didn't care who you were. That didn't have anything to do with my product line. You were treated no differently than somebody off the street.

"I don't have a problem telling people to f-off, regardless of who you are. If somebody on the team that I knew worked on it, like Mike Cleron, says, 'Our team is short, we need some devices, what can you do for us?' Whatever you want. You guys make the product happen, you're going to get whatever you want, no red tape. I know that you are important, you're a core component to this, and you're not puffing up your request."

Eventually, Brian became a focal point for everyone who needed anything from Android. When devices came in, there would be a constant line of people at his desk. There would also be a constant stream of people coming into the building, looking for him and his devices, and asking people in the building where they could find him. Bruce Gay, who sat next to Brian, hung a sign on his desk that said "Not Bjones." Just to make things clear.

Brian delivering the goods in December of 2007. These are either Sooners or very early G1s on their way to the eng team. (Picture courtesy Brian Swetland.)

45

DROID DID

"iCan't but Droid does"
muscular meme picks a fight
please compost bruised fruit

—MIKE CLERON

The marketplace success of the Motorola Droid was the first sign that maybe Android would do all right. Android had been slowly gaining in adoption and acceptance, but the Droid was the first hugely successful Android-based product, especially in the US. One element that distinguished the Droid from previous Android devices was that it was the first one with a real marketing campaign. Verizon spent $100 million on marketing and covered the airwaves with their commercials for "Droid Does."

Launched on October 17, 2009, and released in early November, the Droid became a commercial success, as consumers took Android phones more seriously. At the same time, partners also took Android more seriously, eventually resulting in other products (*many* other products) that pushed sales of Android-based devices even further.

Michael Morrissey remembered the impact of the launch: "We were small and scrappy and churning out all these OS updates and it didn't feel like we were getting a hit at all with consumers. And then the Droid had this big first day. And then the second day was very similar to the first, it was maybe like 65,000 [devices sold]. But then it was like, 'Oh God, what's going to happen now? Is that it? Were these just super-excited early adopters, and it's going to go away?' But the numbers continued to be pretty good. My recollection of numbers is bad, but it was like 30,000 a day for a long time. Once that kept going and the Droid was really, really big, it was like 'We're going somewhere now.'"

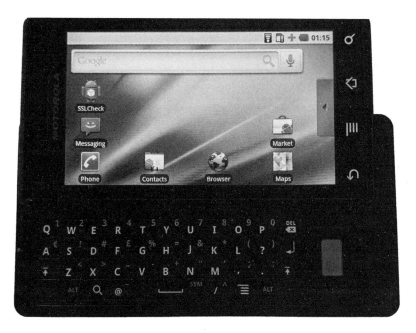

The Motorola Droid. Sliding the phone open revealed a hardware keyboard.

But Droid development looked quite different on the inside of the Android team. At first, it was a product that nobody wanted. At the same time that Motorola approached Google to work on this device together, HTC had also approached Google to work together on the Passion phone (which was eventually released as the Nexus One). The team was much more excited about the Passion device because it was going to be a Google-branded phone, with more ownership and control over the final product.

Meanwhile, the Droid languished without love internally. Andy Rubin didn't even want to do the deal to begin with, for various reasons including the carrier network details. Rich Miner recalled, "Andy didn't want to do CDMA [the Verizon cell phone network technology] because all of our first phones on T-Mo were GSM. We [Rich and Hiroshi] had to get that thing far enough along basically against Andy's desire so that it had enough momentum that it was clear that we shouldn't stop it."

Wei Huang remembers the tension between the Droid and the Nexus One: "Andy was more into Nexus One because it's the product he imagined. It was a better device, I think."

Meanwhile, the Nexus One would have more co-branding support than the Droid. Verizon wanted the Droid to be a Verizon device, and the main brands associated with it were Verizon (the carrier) and Motorola (the manufacturer). The Google brand was not on the Droid.

Not only was the Droid suffering from a branding and ownership standpoint, it was . . . ugly. Tom Moss said, "It was all sharp edges. You could cut yourself on the corners."

But marketing can help, and the marketing campaign for Droid did just that. The campaign capitalized on the unique aspects of the device, and made that potential weakness its strength, pitching it as a robotic device that did so much more than the competition. It apparently worked, and people bought Droids in much larger quantities in the US than had bought any other Android phones before. The days of Android being outsold hugely by the competition were over, as the market share of Android continued to grow, overtaking iPhone sales completely by the end of 2010.[1]

Cédric Beust commented on the Droid versus Nexus competition internally: "So we're all feeling a bit smug and saying, 'Yeah, we're doing Verizon, but it's more because we need to put money on the table. But really the thing that matters is the Nexus.' Google, or Android, was arrogant enough to think that just selling our phone on our website[2] was good enough. Looking back, it was so naive.

---

[1] Source: IDC Quarterly Mobile Phone Tracker, Q4 2019

[2] The Nexus One was initially offered only on a website, off-contract. See Chapter 44 ("The Early Devices") for more details.

"Then we were shown the first TV commercial,[3] which impressed a lot of us. It was a pretty freaking good commercial. And the Droid ended up being a huge success, our phone [the Nexus One] not doing well. I think it was a very humbling lesson for all of us. We started realizing the importance of product and marketing, and understanding that maybe it was time to pass the baton. We'd been driven by technical things. The technical foundation is here; now we need to let the real market take over. People like Verizon were going to take it to the next level."

Charles Mendis agreed. "Their marketing campaign was really interesting.

"Initially, Andy and Larry in particular wanted to sell this Droid as a much cheaper device. They wanted this to be the device for everyone. But Verizon was like, 'We don't have the iPhone. We can't sell this as a cheap device, from a brand and marketing point of view. We have to be seen as being as good as the other one.'"

Verizon came up with a marketing plan for the Droid and presented it to the team. Charles said, "I felt like a cheaper device would have been better. But Verizon did an amazing job. They hit it spot-on. And the sales and the reception showed that."

Another aspect that Charles felt contributed to the Droid's success was the priority placed on it internally. Initially, the Droid and the Nexus One were going to launch at the same time. But eventually the decision was made to get the Droid out first, then launch the Nexus One afterward. The Droid launched in November of 2009, and the Nexus One came out two months later, in January.

"Kicking Nexus One out to the next year was another big part of what made Droid successful. Before, there was a confusion in the team: should I work on the Nexus One bug or the Droid bug? The Nexus One is the company's device.

"Andy ended up making the difficult decision. Saying 'Nexus One is going to be after, the whole team should work on the Droid' really helped us land Droid as a device."

The Droid's hardware performance also helped. Charles Mendis said, "One of the biggest problems [on the G1] we had in Maps was the cache

---

[3] Search on YouTube for "Droid Does" or "iDon't."

would blow up. We'd get 'Out of Memory' exceptions, and the app would die while you were using it. We did a bunch of stuff to get around it, but there just wasn't enough RAM to work with. When the Droid came in, we could actually deliver the experience.

"In G1, we were forced to develop in such a tightly constrained thing that when the Droid came out, things actually worked well because we had targeted G1. I felt like the G1 was almost like a Beta product, forcing the team to be on very tight constraints. The experience [on the Droid] was pretty nice because we built for a much tighter environment."

Another aspect of the Droid hardware that was significant for Android was the screen. The Droid was the first device with a screen size (480 × 854) that differed from that of the original G1 (320 × 480). Also, the Droid had a higher pixel density than the earlier devices (265 versus 180 pixels per inch). This meant that developers could, for the first time, see the advantage of building their apps in a way that scaled to different screen form factors automatically.

The Droid was the *hockey stick*[4] moment for Android, where the adoption curve of Android hit a swiftly increasing slope. Hiroshi recalled: "I remember reading an article that came out maybe a day or two after the Droid had launched, where the reporter had interviewed some app developer who had published on iPhone, iOS and had already published on Market. They were saying, 'Wow, we're noticing the Droid already.' Like two days in, the developer saying, 'Our installs are going way up on Android.' It was also a moment, not only a consumer moment, but also for developers, where they were like, 'Shit, this platform might have legs. There are people who are buying these things.'"

The Droid launched in November. A couple of months later, Dave Sparks remembered a staff meeting he attended. "It was right after the launch, like

---

[4.] I hadn't heard the phrase "hockey stick" before I got to Google (except in reference to, well, a hockey stick), but I've heard it a lot since then. It's a visual indicator in a graph that the slope increases sharply, much like the hockey stick changes its slope between the heel and the shaft.

Of course, this only works if you hold the stick in the right orientation. Upside-down, a hockey stick graph could indicate that sales have plummeted sharply. But I don't think that's what the marketing folks meant in these meetings.

January, and we were just starting to see the hockey stick. Eric Schmidt called a meeting of Andy's staff. I remember Dianne was there and Mike Cleron, basically all the big wigs. Hiroshi, obviously.

"Eric looked around the room and said, 'Don't fuck this up.'"

46

SAMSUNG AND MORE

There's general agreement that the launch of Droid is when Android's growth really started. But even so, Android device sales lagged far behind iOS at the time, and other phone manufacturers still had significant market share at the time.

But in 2010, things really started to change, as other manufacturers came out with their own Android phones. Then it wasn't just people buying the single Verizon phone, or Android fans buying G1s or Nexus phones—it was people all over the world buying all kinds of different Android phones.

Hiroshi talked about the OEM effect on the ecosystem. "The OEMs need to build devices. So by the time the next year came on, we started getting the Galaxy series, and then it really became sort of this mainstream product. It's the traditional partnership thing, where there's a lag. A turbo lag. There's a little bit of lag in the beginning while things are spooling up. That's what G1 and Droid were, just the spool-up period for the industry. And then all the partners, OEMs, kicked in, their products started launching, and that's when the hockey-stick started."

One of those OEMs was Samsung.

It's impossible to deny the positive impact that Samsung has had on Android; they are the largest manufacturer of Android-based devices, and their Samsung *Galaxy* devices are *the* brand name in Android phones. Even the "exploding phone" problem with the Note 7 batteries,[1] an issue that

---

[1] The Note 7 had battery defects that caused many phones to overheat or even explode, causing fear and anxiety on flights. Wikipedia's page on the Note 7 says, "Due to the battery defects, the device is considered a hazmat product, and is prohibited from being taken on-board at many airlines and bus stations."

would have decimated smaller companies, didn't keep people from rushing to buy new devices when they were available.

Tom Moss signed up Samsung as an Android partner while he was living in Japan. Samsung was not the first to market with Android; they took some time to join the ecosystem. But when they did, they were all in.

"My job wasn't just to cut deals. My job was to help foster an ecosystem. Part of that effort was to make sure that there was a balance in the force. At the time, HTC had this huge advantage over everyone else. The second phone, the third phone was HTC. They were charging a really high price to carriers for Android phones, which was bad because that would translate to a higher price for consumers.

"The point was to try and create this equal. We really needed an active ecosystem of OEMs competing with each other. So a big part of my job was not just signing an OEM—it was helping them to actually do something with it. With Samsung, for example, I had selected them to be our first launch phone for China." That phone didn't end up launching, but Samsung phones eventually launched elsewhere.

Tom talked about the changes the company made when they adopted Android, including committing a large marketing budget for these new Android-based devices. "Samsung believed. Back when OEMs weren't spending anything, they were spending co-marketing to create the Galaxy brand.

"In Japan, I know they licensed Darth Vader from Lucasfilm, they had Ken Watanabe[2] as their spokesman. They hired thousands of engineers, designers . . . everything. JK Shin[3] bet the farm on Android for smartphones. They were the first to really spend on the last mile. They were the first to think about having Samsung sales reps in stores to help promote it, having little areas in the store. They did brilliant execution.

"The technology and the phones caught up later to where the business and sales went. But really, it was led by this strategy of marketing and sales that allowed them to leapfrog, and then their devices got better and better and better."

Once the technology was there, they took on the smartphone market leader: Apple.

---

[2] Japanese actor, known in the US for his role in *The Last Samurai*, among other films.

[3] JK Shin was the President and CEO of Samsung's mobile division at that time.

"They did that brilliant marketing campaign of pitting them against the iPhone directly. They were kind of making fun of the iPhone, and people are like 'Who's this idiot company putting itself against the iPhone?' But they changed the conversation from Android vs. iOS to iPhone versus Samsung Galaxy.

"Even on airplanes, you would hear, 'Please turn off your iPhones and Samsung Galaxies' instead of your Androids."

47

THE HOCKEY STICK

As Samsung and other manufacturers started selling their own Android-based devices worldwide, the uptick in sales that started with the Droid increased dramatically and continuously.

When the Droid launched, in late 2009, Android was comfortably at the bottom of the heap of smartphone platforms. By the end of 2010, just over one year later, Android devices were outselling all of them except Nokia's Symbian OS, and they passed Symbian as well in the following year.

At the same time, people were increasingly choosing smartphones over *feature phones*,[1] the traditional low-end (and larger) portion of the mobile market, and many people chose Android smartphones.

---

[1] *Feature phone* is the designation of non-smartphones; most of the phones of that day (apart from the Danger and BlackBerry phones) were considered feature phones. They didn't have much capability beyond phone calls and basic texting support, the screens weren't very big, and they didn't have the ability to install and run arbitrary apps. It's not clear to me how they got the name feature phones, since features are pretty much what they lack. Seems like a clever phrase from a marketing department somewhere.

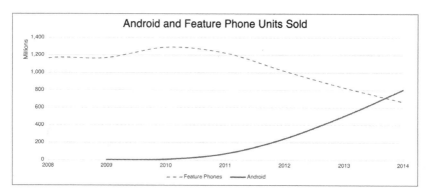

Android took a couple of years to catch on after it launched in late 2008 into a crowded market of smartphone makers.[2]

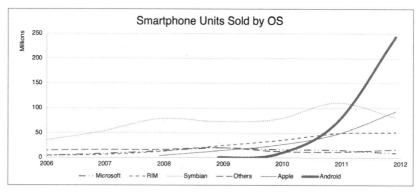

Smartphones eventually affected the feature phone market, as people increasingly chose these more capable devices over the more limited low-end phones.[3]

If you broaden the view to consider all computing devices, including personal computers, the numbers get even more interesting. Fulfilling one of the points that the early Android startup team made in their pitch deck,[4]

---

[2] Source: IDC Quarterly Mobile Phone Tracker, Q4 2019

[3] Source: IDC Quarterly Mobile Phone Tracker, Q4 2019

[4] See the discussion of PC versus phone sales in Chapter 4 ("The Pitch"). At that time, they were talking about all mobile phones, but by 2011, the same argument was true for just smartphones, and for Android in particular.

sales of Android devices have outstripped PCs since 2011 and have beaten them by more than four times since 2015.[5]

This comparison seems, at first, perplexing; PCs (desktops and laptops of all makes and models) have been a requirement of modern life for decades. But many people in the world consider a PC as a luxury item, not a necessity; the first computing device they purchase is a smartphone. Smartphones, unlike PCs, have become *essential*; they satisfy that sweet spot of filling a need that people have (for communication, navigation, entertainment, business, or whatever) while being affordable enough that people who could not previously justify purchasing a computer could buy in to the smartphone world. They are also personal in a way that the "personal computer" never was; PCs tend to be shared equipment in a household, whereas most smartphones are used by only one person, which makes the potential market for these devices much larger than the market for PCs ever could be.

These trends continued in the years since. By May of 2021, there were more than three billion active Android devices[6] throughout the world.[7]

[5.] Sources: IDC Quarterly Mobile Phone Tracker, Q4 2019 and IDC Quarterly Personal Computing Device Tracker, Q1 2020

[6.] This number includes more than just phones. When Android was first launched, it was all about phones, but now the OS is used on everything from watches to tablets to in-flight entertainment screens.

[7.] Unless they forgot it at home, which is always a serious bummer. You realize, during your commute, that your phone—the keeper of all of your data, events, people, conversations, and, admit it, memory—is not with you. It's like forgetting a friend, except that friends usually don't have all of your data.

PART V

WHY IT WORKED

I think in a nutshell that's why Android worked: Everyone's in it together. We never would have reached the scale and the success that Android reached without that approach of partnership.

—FICUS KIRKPATRICK

Y ou read a lot of pages[1] to get here. Congratulations! Here I pull it all together to answer the question: How did Android succeed? Given all the factors that could have led to its failure, and did just that for so many other companies and platforms trying to compete in the smartphone space in that same time period, why Android? As with any successful project, there were many contributing factors, but it all started with the team.

---

[1] Wait, you didn't skip, did you? You might want to go back and read it now. I don't want to spoil the ending for you.

48

THE TEAM

The thing we were always really proud of—Apple looming in the background—we were fast. The speed of this team was nothing I've ever seen anywhere. Before or after.

—JOE ONORATO

The Android team consisted, from the beginning, of people with the right skills and drive to build what was needed. Creating an entire platform, along with the applications, services, and infrastructure that Android needed, was a huge effort, and demanded strenuous effort by people who could dive in quickly to make things work.

It wasn't a large team . . . but it was the right team.

THE RIGHT EXPERIENCE

Most of the team came in with exactly the right experience, which allowed them to hit the ground running. Having worked on related platform and mobile projects at companies like Be, Danger, PalmSource, WebTV, and Microsoft, gave them the technical grounding in exactly the right domains to know how to approach similar problems that Android presented.

THE RIGHT ATTITUDE

The Android team grew as it approached 1.0, but only to a size of about 100 people by the time of that first release. This meant that everyone had more than enough work to do to ship the product. But people did what they needed to do to move the work forward, including individuals owning large areas of functionality as well as working across multiple areas, wherever help was needed. Coupled with the startup environment that pushed everyone to work insanely hard in those early years, the team was able to write Android from scratch and deliver a robust platform and device in time to become relevant in the nascent smartphone industry.

THE RIGHT SIZE

The small size of the team meant that everyone had to work incredibly hard to finish the project, but it also meant that they were much more efficient.

Ficus talked with Brian Swetland after he started leading the Play Store team, years after 1.0: "He asked how big my team was. I told him 300 people. His eyes popped out, 'With 300 people you could do a new Android!'

"I said 'No. With 300 people, you couldn't—you need 20 people.' That larger team is riding on the code and practices built by the individuals that had consensus by default. In the early days, with all of the communication and coordination. . . . If you start with a big team, you spend all of your time debating."

THE RIGHT LEADERSHIP

Great teams benefit from great leadership to help everyone gel and drive forward together. One aspect of that leadership was sheltering Android and running it like a startup inside the big mothership of Google. Another aspect was having decisions being made by a single person, not by a group of people.

San Mehat said, "Much like Apple, it really helped to have that visionary asshole type. The one person. Not a committee. Not five people. One person that was like, 'This is the way I want it, and that's the way it's going to be and I don't care.'

"Having a single person at the top making these decisions resulted in the team and the product continuing to move toward the goal. It was making a decision, even if it's not the right one, but just a decision to move the ball forward. You can't steer if you're not moving."

49

DECISIONS, DECISIONS

A good team makes good decisions. Solid technology and business decisions helped propel Android toward a successful launch and ensuing growth as it was able to realize its potential with manufacturers, developers, and users.

THE TECH—FEATURES THAT FOUND FANS

Most of Android's technology was just fundamental tech that any smartphone required: a device with data and wireless capabilities, plus standard applications like a browser, email, maps, and messaging applications. These features weren't factors in Android's growth; they were more like checkbox items that had to be there for the platform to even be relevant.

But other pieces of technology were unique to Android, which helped create a loyal fan base of both developers and users. They were features built into the platform from the start that distinguished Android from the other smartphone platforms.

NOTIFICATIONS The system of notifications on Android helped bring the whole system together, as applications cooperated with the underlying system to propagate information to the user about things that they wanted to know about.

MULTITASKING Allowing users to easily and quickly switch between applications with UI elements like the Back and Recents buttons foresaw the new dynamic of mobile computing where people constantly use several apps to get things done.

SECURITY From the beginning, the team realized that mobile apps were fundamentally different from desktop apps, and built a system that isolated applications from each other. Security has only become more important over the years, but Android provided the fundamentals from the start, all the way down to the lowest layers of the kernel and the hardware.

SIZE MATTERS The team enabled applications to scale to different screen sizes and densities, which proved critical in enabling all kinds of devices and sizes, where applications would work just as well.

THE TOOLS—CREATING AN APP ECOSYSTEM

In the days before the iPhone and Android, third-party applications for mobile devices did exist. But apps weren't really the reason why people bought their phones, and they didn't dominate users' time on their devices. Instead, the phones came with built-in applications that handled most of their needs: they could talk on the phone, check email, message, and maybe browse the web (in a limited way).

But once people started using smartphones, they could do so much more, and wanted so much more than device companies could provide in their own apps. So while the Google-provided Gmail, Maps, browser, and messaging apps were all very important on the early Android system, it was even more important for Android to open the door to *external* developers. Android allowed developers to write and provide their own applications, helping to create a rich ecosystem for users to be able to do much more than they ever could with just the apps that Google provided.

Enabling this app ecosystem was critical to the platform; any platform trying to enter the market now that doesn't offer a rich selection of apps simply doesn't have a chance. The team provided developers with a rich toolbox of capabilities that enabled these applications, and the entire application ecosystem, to exist.

LANGUAGE The choice of the Java programming language enabled new Android developers to bring existing skills over to this new platform.

APIS Android was written from the beginning to be a platform for all developers, not just for the Android team. Offering public APIs for these developers to access core system functionality was critical for enabling powerful applications.

THE SDK APIs alone would have made application development possible ... but difficult. With the addition of documentation, an IDE, and a myriad of specialized tools for programmers, Android application development became possible for a large audience of developers anxious to create their own applications.

ANDROID MARKET Creating a centralized destination for developers to sell their applications, and for users to find a large and growing set of apps, jump-started the huge ecosystem of apps that everyone uses today.

THE BUSINESS—CREATING A DEVICE ECOSYSTEM

From the beginning, Android was intended to be an open platform that other companies could use to build their own products, not just a system for building a Google phone. A few key decisions and initiatives allowed this aspect of Android to achieve wide industry adoption.

OPEN SOURCE Prior to Android, the only options that device manufacturers had were either building a platform themselves, licensing one for a significant cost, or cobbling something together from existing, but incomplete, solutions. Android provided a powerful, free, and open option for manufacturers that desperately needed it.

OPEN HANDSET ALLIANCE Bringing together the group of partner companies to form the OHA provided a single vision of what Android needed to be for the entire ecosystem. In the beginning, there were not even any Android users, much less devices, so having all of these competing interests and companies come together to support the shared vision was important in establishing the future that they were all hoping would come to pass.

COMPATIBILITY One of the key elements to make Android work across a diverse ecosystem was compatibility of implementations, ensuring that developers could write apps that worked everywhere, instead of having to rewrite them for the plethora of available devices. To solve this problem, the Android team provided the Compatibility Test Suite (CTS) for manufacturers to ensure that they are providing a compatible implementation on every new device.

PARTNERSHIPS   Establishing relationships with a diverse set of partners and bringing them all into the Android community was crucial. It's one thing to offer a platform. But manufacturers need help getting that platform working well on their devices in order to establish the momentum that Android needed to succeed. The Android team worked closely with partners to get the platform working well on new devices, building up a pipeline of devices for the market, establishing a large market of Android phones from manufacturers across the world.

THE ACQUISITION—BUILDING ON A SOLID FOUNDATION

When Android was a fledgling startup, they had a choice: to continue to be independent, with venture funding they had secured, or to join Google. They opted to join Google, deciding that they had a better chance of achieving their vision for Android within that larger company than they could have on their own.

The fact that Android was developed inside of Google was undoubtedly an important factor in its growth. For one thing, Google had deep pockets, which made funding easier, including purchasing technology when it made more sense than building it from scratch. But Android's achievements were due to more than just having access to Google's money and resources. After all, many other large and successful companies did not fare as well with their mobile efforts during the same time period.

One of the aspects that worked for Android at Google was autonomy. Keeping themselves separate from the rest of the company gave the team that startup dynamic that they felt Android needed in those early days to ship the first product. At the same time, being a part of Google gave Android more leverage with partner companies than it would have had as an actual startup company.

Meanwhile, Google had exactly the right kind of existing technical infrastructure that Android needed as it grew. Not only did the services team have the right experience to connect the Google apps to backend servers, but the team also had the advantage of relying on an infrastructure that could scale to their needs. A company that could handle the extreme download requirements of YouTube was able to deal with OTA updates for the small but growing base of Android users.

50

TIMING[1]

It was the right product at the right time.

—CARY CLARK

We were just in the right place at the right time.

—MIKE CLERON

Part of it was being in the right place at the right time.

—DIRK DOUGHERTY

It was right thing at the right place at the right time.

—MIKE FLEMING

The right product at the right time.

—RYAN PC GIBSON

We were at the right place at the right time.

—ROMAIN GUY

It has nothing to do with the architecture. It's about being in the right place at the right time.

—DIANNE HACKBORN

It was at the right place at the right time.

—ED HEYL

---

[1] All of these quotes came from different individual conversations. I asked everyone I interviewed why they thought it all eventually worked. People cited many different reasons, but there was apparently some group consensus on this particular factor.

The right thing at the right time.

—STEVE HOROWITZ

All of us need to acknowledge that some amount of this was being in the right place at the right time.

—FICUS KIRKPATRICK

It was the right place at the right time.

—HIROSHI LOCKHEIMER

Android was there at the right time.

—EVAN MILLAR

Right place, right time.

—RICH MINER

The right time to put together a smartphone operating system.

—NICK PELLY

Opportunity: It's being at the right location at the right time. There was a lot of that.

—DAVID TURNER

The biggest thing has to do with time. We were at the right place at the right time.

—JEFF YAKSICK

Timing is everything. It's true for comedy, it's true for life overall, and it's certainly true for Android's success. For Android, it was the difference between being an interesting mobile platform (of which there were several at the time) and becoming an operating system that now runs on over three billion devices worldwide.

There are many aspects to the timing of Android: How fast the team could ship 1.0 and deliver update releases, when hardware was available and fast enough for this new device form factor, and on and on. But the most important element of timing can be summarized in one word: *competition*.

COMPETITION AND COLLABORATION

After the iPhone was announced, manufacturers were desperate for a touch-screen offering of their own to compete in the evolving smartphone market. Given the closed ecosystem of the iPhone, these other companies were on their own to create a compelling system, but nobody was in a good place to do that. Meanwhile, Android had been working on a platform that was intended to support different kinds of devices and requirements including, for example, a touchscreen.

The timing was right for those other companies to collaborate with Android and use that open source platform to create their own smartphone devices.

MOBILE HARDWARE

Timing also had a positive impact on hardware capability at that time. CPUs, GPUs, memory, and display technology all converged to enable more powerful smartphones. This increase in hardware capabilities enabled not only new kinds of phones, but also an entirely new niche of computing hardware that could break away from the bonds of the existing, entrenched platform players of the old PC world.

HIRING

Timing also had an impact on building the original team. Android was staffing up at a time when a core group of OS people from companies like Palm-Source, Danger, and Microsoft were available and anxious to take on a new project together. The fact that all of these people joined around the same time meant that Android was jump-started by a group of people who not only had relevant experience, but also had worked together already and didn't have to spend time building team dynamics. They just got down to work.

EXECUTION

The final part of timing was that the team was able to move fast enough to capitalize on the opening they were given. For one thing, the team had been able to build up the core Android platform to a reasonable place by the time the iPhone was announced, so it was nearly ready for manufacturers that needed a competing solution quickly. Also, the team was able to pivot in reaction to the new reality of touchscreens, getting 1.0 and the G1 to market before other viable solutions could.

Without the unique combination of hardware capabilities that enabled smartphones, and the singular impact that the iPhone had on an industry thrashing about for a way to compete with that new device, Android may not have found a foothold, and would have just been another of the many failures littering the curbside of mobile device history. Instead, it was able to become a viable alternative at the right time for manufacturers across the world to ship their own smartphones, enabling the Android ecosystem that we know today.

51

~~SUCCESS!~~
WE'RE STILL HERE!

We've hit 2 billion actives, and I guess that's a form of "We've done it."
But man, the competition: it never ends. It's relentless. Every day we're competing.

It just never feels done. That's why I'm still here.

—HIROSHI LOCKHEIMER

The original premise of this book was to try to answer the question, "Why did Android succeed?"

But "success" is not really the right word, or even the right concept. In any project, success is never guaranteed, no matter how great things look at any given moment. This is even more true in tech, where changes in hardware, software, fashion, consumer interest, or any of a million other things can send a seemingly successful product into the sinkhole of obsolescence almost overnight. Things change so quickly in this field that there is never a sense of "We made it!," but rather a slightly nervous, "We're still here!," or maybe even a doubtful, "We're still here?," while looking over your shoulder to see who's behind you and how fast they're catching up.

For Android, the platform gained enough traction with manufacturers, carriers, developers, and users to be allowed to continue to exist and improve over the last several years. And in high tech, that's about as good as it gets.

APPENDICES

APPENDIX

An internal organ that can be removed without harming the system,

and without the system really noticing at all.

It is only there to cause potential mortal danger when it must be removed.

Other than that, it can be safely ignored.

A

JARGON

This was never intended to be a technical book for engineers who love all the geeky details. Instead, it's supposed to be a book for everyone who is interested in the meteoric rise of a business and technology, and of the people behind that effort.

But when these people write code and create highly technical things that lead to that result, it's difficult to not get lost in the techy weeds every now and then. So when I'm explaining, for example, that Ficus Kirkpatrick enjoyed working on drivers at the lower levels of the system, or that Brian Swetland worked on the kernel at Danger and Android, or that the engineers at Be and PalmSource were creating a platform and APIs for software developers, it's necessary to use terms that might lose or confuse the non-engineers in the audience.

In an attempt to keep the techy noise to a minimum, I'm cramming many of the explanations of that stuff into this appendix. Hopefully this brief section will help explain the salient terms and, more important, how the different pieces of the system relate to each other.

FIRST, A SYSTEM OVERVIEW

It is typical in my industry, when discussing platform software, to end up at the whiteboard drawing what we call a "layer cake diagram," which shows the relationship of the various components of the system to each other. This diagram typically shows the components going down toward the hardware. At the top of the diagram, we see the pieces that users interact with, and at the bottom we see the components that talk directly to the hardware. All the pieces in between are layers of software written by the engineers to get from the higher-level user actions (for example, clicking a button) to the hardware (for example, displaying the button in a pressed state, launching an application, firing the nukes, whatever).

Here's a (very simplified) diagram for the Android operating system:

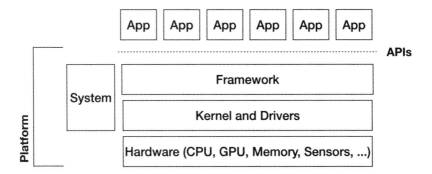

There's actually nothing specific to Android here; this is a very typical view of most operating systems. Android obviously has elements that are unique to that OS, which are explained elsewhere. But in general, the Android platform is similar to most other operating systems.

Let's walk through the diagram from the top to the bottom to talk about what these pieces are and how they work together.

Apps

The *apps* on Android are the main entry points for users. Users launch apps from their icons, they interact with the buttons, lists, and other pieces inside of apps, they click on links in apps that launch other apps, and so on. This is basically the world in which users live, interacting with the apps directly, while accessing all of the platform functionality only indirectly, through what these apps expose.

Note that the system-provided functionality of the home screen, the navigation bar, the status bar, and the lock screen are all considered apps. Even though they are provided by the platform (either Android itself, or in some cases by a manufacturer like Samsung, which provides its own system apps), they're still just apps.

APIs

Application programming interfaces (APIs) are the pieces of functionality in the platform that applications interact with. The platform APIs are the functions, variables, and other code pieces that are public-facing in the platform. For example, if an application needs to compute a square root, they might call a square root API function provided by the platform. Or if the application wants to display a button to the user, they might use a button API to handle its functionality and visuals.

The APIs are the tip of the iceberg for the platform. Although there are thousands of APIs in Android, they are really just the entry point to the platform functionality, most of which is embedded in the code that implements these APIs. So, for example, an application may create a button by calling a couple of API functions to do that, but under the hood the platform is doing a lot of work to satisfy all of the details that a button entails (including how to display it, how to handle click events on the screen, and how to draw the text for the button's label).

Framework

The *framework* is the large layer of system software that handles all the functionality exposed through the public APIs. That is, the framework is responsible for both the APIs as well as the implementation of those APIs. In the previous example, this is where the button functionality lives, among other bits. The framework encompasses, really, everything that the entire platform is capable of, like location services, data storage, telephony, graphics, UI, and, well, everything. The UI toolkit for Android is a subset of framework functionality that is specific to user interface APIs and implementation.

System

The system piece in the diagram above denotes software that is running that is not directly accessible by applications, but that is responsible for the device's overall functionality. For example, on Android, the *window manager* is responsible for displaying applications in their own windows and navigating between those windows as different applications are launched. There is also a service running that handles low-memory situations by killing applications that have not been used recently so that more recently used applications can have the memory they need. All of those things are running indirectly, on the user's behalf.

The system calls public APIs for various pieces of necessary framework functionality, but the system may also call functions in the framework directly (which is why it is shown in the diagram beside, rather than on top of, the APIs layer).

Kernel

The *kernel*, with its device drivers, is the lowest level of software running on the device. It handles the fundamental capabilities of the device that the overall system needs. For example, each application runs in a *process*; the management of the many processes running on the device (isolating them from each other and scheduling time for them to run on the CPU) is the kernel's responsibility. The kernel is also responsible for loading and executing the drivers on the system. All of the software we've talked about so far is generic to any device, but drivers are specific to particular pieces of hardware. For example, to receive clicks on a button, a piece of hardware in the device is able to turn touches on the screen into information about where those touches occurred. A driver in the kernel does this, routing the information from hardware-specific data into events that are then sent into the framework for processing. Similarly, there are drivers for storage, sensors, display, camera, and any other hardware that a device may have. The kernel loads these drivers when the device boots and communicates to these pieces of hardware through the drivers when necessary.

Platform

Finally, I use the term *platform* to encompass everything here except the applications. It's a very generic term, and I use it broadly to refer to everything that Android provides for application developers and for users. The platform software for Android is all of the stuff that provides facilities for developers writing applications as well as everything that the device needs overall to display the basic UI and functionality to users. So when I talk about the platform team on Android, it's basically everyone that works on all of the stuff above other than the applications: the engineers working on the kernel, the framework, the system software, and the APIs.

OTHER GEEKY TERMS

In addition to everything that fit conveniently in the previous diagram, a few other technical terms used in the book are also worth explaining. I'm sure I'll miss a few. If only there were some kind of "search engine" capability on the internet so that readers could easily look up terms that I inadvertently forgot to include. . . .

Changelist

Changelist (CL) refers to the code change required to fix a bug, implement a new feature, update the docs—whatever. A CL can be as little as a one-line fix or as much as thousands of lines of code to implement a large swath of new APIs and capabilities. Peer developers far prefer the former because one-liners are easy to review and approve. Woe be unto the developer that leans on their team to review a 10,000-line CL when everyone is under the gun already to deliver their own fixes and features.

Changelist is apparently a term used primarily by Google engineering. Other software systems use terms like *patch* or *PR* (pull request) to mean the same thing.

Emulator

An *emulator* is a software program that mimics a hardware device. Developers use emulators (in particular, they use the Android emulator) to make it easier to run and test their programs on the host computer they are using to write their applications. Instead of requiring a physical device to test an app (and perhaps to suffer delays downloading the program to the device every time it is recompiled), they can simply run a virtual device on their powerful desktop computer instead.

There is a difference between an *emulator* and a *simulator*; an emulator actually mimics everything happening on a real device, down to the CPU and the instructions running on it. A simulator is usually a simpler (and, often, faster) program because it does not bother emulating everything on a device, but rather just enough to make it work essentially like a device. A simulator is good enough for testing basic functionality of a program but might miss out on enough important details (such as how the hardware sensors work), so a developer is better off using an emulator or a real device to validate the actual functionality in the real world. Android had a simulator in the very early days, but eventually stopped maintaining it and switched to having only an emulator.

IDE

An *IDE (integrated development environment)* is a suite of tools that programmers use for writing, building, running, debugging, and testing their applications. This includes things like a text editor—which is usually knowledgeable about the language(s) that programmers use, with shortcuts for formatting and highlighting code written in that language, plus other features like code completion and linking—as well as a compiler for building the application. For example, Android Studio (the IDE provided to developers by the Android team) includes a large and growing suite of tools, including various editors (for Java, XML, and C/C++), the compiler for building the code into an Android application, a debugger for stepping through the program as it runs on a device, and various other specific utilities for analyzing performance, monitoring memory usage, and building UI assets.

Java ME/J2ME

Java ME (or J2ME,[1] during the early days of Android development) is short for Java Platform, Micro Edition, a software platform for early mobile devices. Java ME used the Java programming language and provided functionality that application developers needed to write apps for those devices.

J2ME promised something in the mobile space that developers desperately wanted: a common platform that would allow them to write applications for many different devices, as opposed to having to re-tune their apps for vastly different hardware.

However, unlike the desktop or server versions of Java, Java ME came in a large variety of versions, called *profiles*, which meant that the capabilities of any particular implementation of Java ME on a device did not necessarily match that of another device, so Java ME developers had to deal with device variety issues after all.

OEM

An *OEM (original equipment manufacturer)* is a company that makes the actual hardware.

Object-Oriented Programming: Classes, Fields, and Methods

The software used to write the Android platform, and to write Android applications, uses an approach called *object-oriented programming (OOP)*.

---

[1] J2ME = Java 2 Platform, Micro Edition. The naming switch between Java and Java 2 was also confusing on the inside of the company (Sun Microsystems) that was responsible for those names.

Most popular/modern languages use a similar approach, including Java, C++, Kotlin, and more. In an OOP system, there are functional blocks called *classes* that present an API for doing a particular set of things. For example, Android has a String class for performing operations on text strings.

Each class may contain a set of *fields* or *properties*, which hold values. For example, a String object might hold the value of a text string, such as "I want a sandwich."

Each class may also contain a set of *methods* or *functions* that perform operations on that class (and potentially on other classes as well). For example, Android's String class has a method named toUpperCase(), which does exactly what it says. So our sandwich string from before, if called with toUpperCase(), would return a value of "I WANT A SANDWICH."

Classes, with their various methods and fields, can be bundled together to create a *library*. The classes, fields, and methods in that library represent the API of that library, which applications (or other libraries) can call from their code to perform the operations that the library's API offers.

SDK

An *SDK (software development kit)* contains the pieces a programmer needs to write programs for a given platform. This includes the APIs they can call to perform functionality on the platform as well as the libraries that implement those APIs. Using an SDK, a programmer can write their application. Then using tools (usually supplied with the SDK), they can build the application (compile it into a form that is understandable by devices running the platform). Finally, they can run and debug their program on a device (or emulator) that is compatible with their compiled application.

Toolkit

Toolkit overlaps in meaning, and usage, with framework, library, and APIs. In general, toolkit is used to mean a framework that is specific to user interface (UI) components. On Android, the toolkit is synonymous with the *UI toolkit*, or the APIs and implementation for the user interface technology of Android. It is considered a part of the overall Android framework, specifically the subset of the framework that deals with most of the visual aspects of the framework.

View

All UI platforms have the concept of some kind of UI element, for things like buttons, or checkboxes, or sliders, or text, or containers of all of these objects. But the way that they refer to those things differs between platforms, so it's confusing to tell what platform developers are talking about because they use different terms. Java's Swing toolkit called them *components*, some platforms call them *elements* or *widgets*. On Android, UI elements are referred to as *Views*, named for the class that all of these elements inherit from (View). The container of Views (including other containers) is a view called ViewGroup. Finally, a *View hierarchy* is, well, it's what it sounds like; a hierarchy of Views and ViewGroups, descending from the top-level parent ViewGroup, with its set of children, and down into any ViewGroups contained therein with their child Views, and so on.

B

RELATED CONTENT

In the course of writing this book, I read many books, articles, docs, websites, and anything else that I could find that related to Android, other mobile technology, or just tech history in general. Here are some of the more useful and memorable resources I enjoyed.

STUFF ABOUT ANDROID

"The (updated) history of Android," *Ars Technica*, by Ron Amadeo (*https://arstechnica.com/gadgets/2016/10/building-android-a-40000-word-history-of-googles-mobile-os/*): This multi-part series of articles covers every release of Android from 1.0, detailing the user-visible changes in apps, devices, and the UI. One of the best parts is all the screenshots, because you can't even get them anymore (even if you have one of the old devices, chances are it doesn't talk to the same services anymore).

"An Android Retrospective," a presentation by Romain Guy and Chet Haase (*https://youtu.be/xOccHEgIvwY*): My friend Romain and I gave this presentation several times at different developer events, where we talked about some of the internal details of how things were developed and what it looked like from the inside of the team.

Android Developers Backstage, podcast by Chet Haase, Romain Guy, and Tor Norbye (*https://adbackstage.libsyn.com/*): This is a podcast that I host with my friends and Android colleagues Romain and Tor. I mention it because, while it is mostly a podcast by and for developers, there are some episodes along the way that are more about the history of Android. In particular, we spoke with Ficus Kirkpatrick (episode 56), Mathias Agopian (episode 74), Dave Burke (episode 107), and Dan Bornstein (episode 156) about some of the old days that I talk about in the book. My favorite part of writing this book was the conversations I had along the way with the people on the team; these episodes offer a glimpse into what some of those conversations were like.

Modern Operating Systems, 4th edition, by Andrew S. Tanenbaum and Herbert Bos (Pearson, 2014): For anyone who felt that the level of technical depth about Android OS internals was lacking, I recommend picking up this textbook on OS design and digging into Chapter 10.8 on Android. That chapter was written by Dianne Hackborn and covers things like Binder and Linux Extensions in a satisfying level of detail that I felt was out of scope for a book that was already bordering on too technical and too long.

MOBILE TECHNOLOGY CASE STUDIES

Several excellent books cover the history of some of the phone platforms and mobile companies that didn't fare as well during this time period. I particularly enjoyed these two:

Losing the Signal: The Untold Story Behind the Extraordinary Rise and Spectacular Fall of BlackBerry by Jacquie McNish and Sean Silcoff (Flatiron Books, 2015).

Operation Elop: The Final Years of Nokia's Mobile Phones by Merina Salminen and Pekka Nykänen: The original Finnish book *Operaatio Elop* was never published in English, but a crowd-sourced effort resulted in an English translation in PDF and other formats, which are available online at *https://asokan.org/operation-elop/*.

SILICON VALLEY TECH HISTORY

There are also many great books and documentaries about tech history, including these which I really enjoyed:

Revolution in The Valley: The Insanely Great Story of How the Mac Was Made by Andy Hertzfeld (O'Reilly Media, 2004): This is a wonderful book for understanding how one of the canonical pieces of Silicon Valley history came to be. It's also a great look into the people and the team behind that project.

Steve Jobs by Walter Isaacson (Simon & Schuster, 2011): I enjoyed this book not only for its interesting portrayal of Mr. Jobs, but also (even more) for the history of Silicon Valley and high tech that it told along the way.

General Magic (documentary) directed by Sarah Kerruish and Matt Maude: The movie gives a close look into the culture and vision of a company that might have been one of the early successes in mobile computing, except that they were at least 10 years too early.

INDEX